ADDITIONAL PRAISE FOR *SUSTAIN YOUR GAME*

"If you want to sustain excellence in any area of your life, you need to work toward mastering the basics every single day. This book is filled with practical examples to help you consistently evolve into the best version of yourself."

—SASAN GOODARZI, chief executive officer, Intuit

"This book shares a practical approach to overcoming three common ailments in today's business world: stress, stagnation, and burnout. Alan provides provocative stories, stats, and principles that will immediately influence your sustainable performance, fulfillment, and engagement."

—CLAUDE SILVER, chief heart officer, Vaynermedia

"*Sustain Your Game* provides invaluable tips and tools to help develop resilience, refocus energy while avoiding stress, distraction, and other outside forces. It's packed with immediately actionable steps and practical insights to boost your performance! Alan presents the most relevant and useful scientific research from different experts, writers, and clinicians, while adding from his own personal experience working with some of the highest performers in the world!"

—DANIELLE CANTOR JEWELER, executive VP and partner, F.A.M.E.

"Achieving optimal performance is incredibly challenging. And sustaining it? Even harder. This book provides the practical tools to do just that. Alan's game plan is a must for anyone looking to excel over the long haul."

—SHAKA SMART, head men's basketball coach, Marquette University

"In order to win the outside game of performance, we must first win the inside game to lead ourselves. *Sustain Your Game* is the playbook to do just that. It will teach you the fundamentals to persevere and endure any climate, while staying disciplined to achieve the success and significance we all seek."

—PAUL EPSTEIN, former NFL and NBA executive,
author of *The Power of Playing Offense*

"Alan is not only an incredible performance coach, keynote speaker, and author, but more important, he is an incredible person. He truly cares about helping others become the best versions of themselves and that is reflected in this book. *Sustain Your Game* will leave you with tangible tools and strategies to not only take your game to the next level but keep it there as well."

—LAUREN JOHNSON, former mental conditioning
coordinator, New York Yankees

PRAISE FOR *RAISE YOUR GAME*
BY ALAN STEIN JR.

"Alan played a huge role in my development on and off the court and his guidance helped me get to where I am today. *This book is a must read.*"

—KEVIN DURANT

"*Raise Your Game* is a look inside the locker room to see how the best raise *their* game. Alan Stein has worked with the elite and has blazed trails in basketball. In this book, he takes from over two decades of sweat equity and shares the secrets of success with you."

—BRENDA FRESE, head women's basketball coach,
University of Maryland

"Alan shares what it takes to take your game to the next level. *Raise Your Game* provides tools, concepts and strategies you can utilize today to enhance your influence and make an immediate impact on your team, culture and organization."

—JON GORDON, bestselling author of
Training Camp and *The Carpenter*

"*Raise Your Game* shares the principles required to be an impactful leader and an influential teammate. This book looks at what the highest performers in sports and business do consistently to create winning cultures and championship teams. The stories, lessons and practical takeaways will help players, coaches, executives and entrepreneurs unlock new levels of performance."

—RIC ELIAS, CEO of Red Ventures

"Whether building a start-up as an entrepreneur, or developing innovations as an 'intrapreneur' at a Fortune 500, the fundamentals of success are the same. It comes down to habits, preparation and mindset. *Raise Your Game* shares the building blocks used by the world's top athletes, executives, coaches and entrepreneurs to reach unparalleled success and perform at the highest level. I am recommending *Raise Your Game* as a must-read for all of the entrepreneurs and executives I work with."

—MARK FRENCH, serial entrepreneur
(sports / entertainment / media / technology)

PRAISE FOR ALAN STEIN JR.

"Simply put, Alan Stein is the best in the business. I worked alongside Alan for years and his ability to motivate and inspire is second to none. His passion inspires everyone he connects with to push their limits. Alan gets results. Period."

—JAY BILAS, ESPN

"In every interaction, from a one-on-one discussion or a pre-program team call, to delivering to an audience of thousands, Alan makes everyone feel important. His program customization is exceptional, allowing Alan to ALWAYS deliver a relevant, targeted, and aligned presentation to his audiences. His takeaways are meaningful, memorable, and actionable. All around, a JOY to work with!"

—KATRINA MITCHELL, founder, Franchise Speakers

"We have had Alan speak at four of our events in the past eighteen months and have experienced an unparalleled 26 percent growth in sales during that span. He has been a key part of our high performance culture."

—JEFF SCHLOSSNAGLE, VP of sales, Omnicell

"For the past two quarters we have produced 35 percent year-over-year growth, a rate nearly twice our historic trend. It is no accident that these results began to take hold almost a year to the date following Alan speaking to our leadership and sales teams."

—DAVID DEWOLF, president and CEO, 3Pillar Global

"Alan's innate ability to speak passionately and with substance make him one of the best corporate speakers I've had the pleasure of experiencing. He recently received a standing ovation after his keynote performance in Cancun, Mexico at our annual company convention (where he addresses hundreds of fitness executives, managers and directors). His talk was one of the highlights of our event. We will undoubtedly have him back to speak again."

—KIRK GALIANI, founder and co-executive chairman, US Fitness

"Alan has a unique ability to enthrall any audience with his passion, energy and authenticity. His experience with world-class athletes provides an unparalleled perspective on teamwork and leadership. Alan is extremely impactful when sharing the tools needed to level-up any organization in today's hyper-competitive and dynamic marketplace."

—MICHAEL COHEN, COO, Whistle Sports

SUSTAIN YOUR GAME

HIGH PERFORMANCE KEYS TO MANAGE STRESS, AVOID STAGNATION, AND BEAT BURNOUT

ALAN STEIN JR.
WITH JON STERNFELD

hachette
BOOKS
New York

Hachette Go, an imprint of Hachette Books
Hachette Book Group
1290 Avenue of the Americas
New York, NY 10104
HachetteGo.com
Facebook.com/HachetteGo
Instagram.com/HachetteGo

First Edition: April 2022

Hachette Books is a division of Hachette Book Group, Inc.
The Hachette Go and Hachette Books name and logos are trademarks of Hachette Book Group, Inc.

The publisher is not responsible for websites (or their content) that are not owned by the publisher.

Print book interior design by Jeff Williams.

Library of Congress Cataloging-in-Publication Data

Names: Stein, Alan, Jr., author. | Sternfeld, Jon, author.
Title: Sustain your game : high performance keys to manage stress, avoid
   stagnation, and beat burnout / Alan Stein Jr. with Jon Sternfeld.
Description: New York, NY : Hachette Go, 2022.
Identifiers: LCCN 2021040157 | ISBN 9780306926259 (hardcover) | ISBN
   9780306926235 (ebook)
Subjects: LCSH: Motivation (Psychology) | Stress management. | Burn out
   (Psychology) | Success in business.
Classification: LCC BF503 .S744 2022 | DDC 153.8—dc23/eng/20211104

LC record available at https://lccn.loc.gov/2021040157

ISBNs: 9780306926259 (hardcover); 9780306926235 (ebook)

Printed in the United States of America

LSC-C

Printing 1, 2022

Luke, Jack, and Lyla . . . I love you, I believe in you,
and I am so proud to be your father.
You inspire me more than you will ever know
to sustain my game.

CONTENTS

FOREWORD

I consider myself incredibly fortunate. I get to make my living working for a wonderful company (ESPN), with people I really enjoy, covering my two favorite sports. Don't get me wrong: I respect and appreciate all sports, but I love college football and basketball.

So needless to say, I am beyond grateful.

As I reflect on my journey, it's been quite a ride! I started an internship with the CBS affiliate in Tuscaloosa while still a student at the University of Alabama. At the conclusion of a nine-week internship, they hired me as a reporter, giving me valuable on-air experience. After graduation, I worked on my craft during stints in Columbus, Georgia, and Flint, Michigan, before finally making it to ESPN in 1995.

Actually, I started on ESPN2, which was relatively new at the time. I was host of a show called *SportsSmash*. Show probably isn't the right word. It was an update segment within shows, but it helped me establish myself at ESPN. After getting in plenty of reps (and there is no substitute for live reps), I got the opportunity of a lifetime and was put in the rotation to host *SportsCenter*.

This was a sports journalist's dream, as I got to work alongside legendary sportscasters like Keith Olbermann, Chris Berman, and Dan Patrick. Stuart Scott and Scott Van Pelt were also rising stars who became transcendent hosts and set the standard for professional excellence.

After *SportsCenter*, I spent the next few years improving my craft on a variety of shows—from NASCAR to the NBA—before landing the lead studio host role for college football and college basketball. More than fifteen years of fifteen-hour days at the command center of college football Saturdays thoroughly prepared me for my current role as the host of *College GameDay*, which, in my judgment, is the best job in television.

What did those experiences teach me?

When you are first starting out and trying to climb the ladder, looking for that next step can feel daunting and overwhelming. It's easy to get consumed by what's next and constantly search for what else is out there.

But you should never compromise the job you have pursuing the job you want. Your #1 priority should be to do the absolute best job you can in the moment, wherever you are.

You should work to be genuine and authentic, never veer from your core values, and always stay true to who you are. Know what you do well and find ways to double down on your strengths.

Doing so is a surefire way to set yourself apart, open doors, and create new opportunities.

For me, I've always stayed focused on being reliable, being consistent, and being prepared. Before every show, I repeat these words to myself: *poise, presence, personality, preparation*. Those are things I control.

My current role on *GameDay* requires a variety of skills. Skills I've worked hard to develop over time, and skills I continue refining to this day.

I have to be informed and prepared and have the ability to think and react quickly. I have to know my stuff and be able to improvise and go off the cuff. We don't use a teleprompter on *College GameDay*. We didn't use one for the college football and basketball studio shows. I thoroughly prepare what I want to say. It's just not completely scripted. You have to be able to react to what your analyst says or something that happens in the crowd.

I have to maintain high levels of energy and enthusiasm. I have to prioritize my self-care and make sure my mental, physical, and emotional buckets are full.

I also have to quickly move on after a mistake. When you do live television, things are going to go wrong. You are going to make mistakes. It's inevitable. The key is staying composed, staying humble, and staying confident. That's where poise and presence in my "four Ps" come in.

I can't get distracted or consumed with negativity or criticism. I must continue to believe in myself, put in the work, and run my own race. Everything else will take care of itself.

I've been in this business for over thirty years and I've observed firsthand how to sustain high performance from brilliant colleagues like Jay Bilas and Kirk Herbstreit; from Hall of Fame coaches like Nick Saban, Mike Krzyzewski, and John Calipari; and from pop culture icons like Matthew McConaughey and Keegan-Michael Key.

In a similar fashion, I've had a chance to spend time with Alan on the *GameDay* sets for Duke basketball and Penn State football and really respect and appreciate his perspective on how to not only Raise Your Game but how to sustain it as well.

Regardless of your experience or vocation, I'm confident you'll benefit from Alan's stories and strategies on managing stress, avoiding stagnation, and beating burnout.

I congratulate you on investing in this book and wish you well in your pursuit of sustaining excellence, optimizing performance, and living a truly fulfilled life.

RECE DAVIS
Host of *ESPN College GameDay*

INTRODUCTION

Though it's been years since I've worked directly with athletes, I still consider myself a coach. And though my primary area of focus is no longer in sports, I still teach the principles, lessons, and strategies that apply to the court and the field. Sports are elemental. They're about performing in pressure moments, managing your emotions through adversity, communicating with others toward a collective goal, and staying disciplined when others don't. I think of these as **fundamentals**, and no matter your domain, your ability to do them will distinguish you from everyone else—even those who may have more opportunity, natural talent, or intelligence. I've never believed that what you have is most important, but rather *what you do* with what you have. That's what matters most.

The highest performers in all walks of life have taken full ownership of themselves, their work, and their choices. They got to where they are—and have stayed there—because they have chosen to establish, refine, and repeat the habits that serve them best. These men and women understand that you can't be selective when it comes to excellence: how we do *anything* is how we do *everything*.

I've worked with the likes of NBA stars Kevin Durant and Victor Oladipo when they were young and watched superstars like Kobe Bryant and Steph Curry in their private routines. I've sat across from Mark Cuban and Jesse Itzler as they talked about how they built their empires and interviewed Jay Bilas and Jay Williams about how mental toughness creates success. In sports or business or anything else, the best aren't the best by accident, genetics, or good fortune. They are at the top because of their commitment to the fundamentals. True superstars never get bored with the basics, and they never underestimate their importance. My primary job is to inspire, guide, and coach people on the fundamental building blocks of high performance (both individually and organization-ally). I think of my role as one who works to inspire, motivate, and instruct people in the ways of the basics.

"Nobody wins all the time," mental performance coach Brian Levenson told me. Levenson works in both business and athletics, recognizing the natural bridge that exists between the two. "And I think it's one of the values in sports. The value of learning that losing is possible."

I agree 100 percent. Losing, failure, and obstacles are real and there's not a sport in the world that doesn't have those ideas baked in. A game literally doesn't make sense without them. Pro athletes, even successful ones, lose. Sometimes constantly. Athletes are also well versed in making mistakes—dropping passes, missing shots, and stepping out of bounds. There's a reason our everyday language has absorbed the terms from sports to mean errors: *fumble, strikeout, choke.*

For athletes, the failure and the requisite feedback are constant. If they don't absorb and make use of that feedback, they won't be playing very long. Because of this, sports are a wonderful way to study improvement, success, and adaptation. Jerry Seinfeld, one of the all-time great comedians, once said, "If you could take your experiences and ask to trade them in, the last ones I would trade would be the failures. Those are the most valuable ones." He's not the best in spite of those failures. He's the best *because* of them. And he's the best because he knows this.

This work is my calling. I am passionate about serving, impact-ing, influencing, and connecting with people. Experience has taught me that success is a choice, and I want to inspire and em-power people and organizations to make that choice. I've turned a successful basketball performance coaching career into a professional speaking business. Now, major companies from all over the world hire me to teach, train, and consult on effective leadership, performance, and teamwork.

My time as a coach with top high school players led me to opportunities with pros, so I've seen both sides of the coin—what it takes to get there and what it takes to remain there. My last book, *Raise Your Game*, was all about bringing your A game to your job, your relationships, and your life. But that is really only half the battle. Keeping it up is even harder. The commitment to raising your game—in any area of life—is no easy feat. But the commitment to *sustaining* your game is even more challenging. An athlete has to execute—on the play, for the season, and for a career. In business, publishing, or whatever your field, succeeding along these three timelines is equally important: the moment (short term), the stretch (medium term), and the long haul (long term).

Sustain Your Game is about succeeding in all three, looking at the particular challenges of all three timelines:

- **In the moment, we have to battle stress.**
- **In the stretch, we have to fight stagnation.**
- **In the long haul, we have to beat burnout.**

This book is for high performers who want to learn practical strategies and actionable tools for how to sustain their game across all three timelines. It will distill advice and lessons from successful athletes, entrepreneurs, social scientists, journalists, CEOs, motivational speakers, business coaches, and consultants, as well as my own personal stories.

Succeeding along each of the three timelines requires discipline. And discipline is doing what you said you would do long after the mood you said it in has faded. Most people refer to me as a motivational speaker, but that's not really what I do. I'm there to stimulate change. I'm there to encourage, empower, and guide the audience to think, feel, and act differently. To change their perspective and to change their behavior. I believe in motivation, but I never confuse it with discipline. I meditate every day whether I'm motivated or not. I make my bed whether I'm motivated or not. I don't always want to get up early, work out, travel for work, but I do it with or without the motivation. I do it because I'm disciplined.

Discipline has a negative connotation and is often associated with punishment. But I think of discipline as the opposite: **it is the foundation of freedom**. Do what's hard now so things get easier later. Mental coach and entrepreneur Todd Herman told me that "most people want the noun without the verb," which is a great way to put it: they want the result without doing what it takes to get there. It's a common misconception that you need to be motivated before you act, when oftentimes we have it backward: acting first will end up motivating you.

My goal is not perfection; it's progress. Am I closer to where I want to be than I was yesterday? That's my measurement.

When I was young, I got advice that I have carried with me to this day: Find something you love to do, find something you're good at, and find where those two intersect. That's your strength zone, and the more you can stay there, the more you can engage with that space, the more fulfilled you will be. As you grow, continue to be self-aware and reflect on what has changed because that point of intersection is going to move.

Sustain Your Game will give you the tools to perform your best in your arena, wherever that may be. It will help you manage stress, wherever it shows up; fend off stagnation, however it presents itself; and beat burnout, whenever it rears its head.

I am not speaking from a place of mastery. Like everyone else, I am under construction, a work in progress. Coming off a successful first book, I understand the challenge of continuing to perform at a high level and navigating the obstacles along the way. In essence, this book is a manifestation of the very thing I am writing about, a perfect marriage of author and subject, form and content. I am sustaining my game by helping others sustain theirs.

Thank you for joining me on the ride.

How This Book Is Organized

The goal of my first book, *Raise Your Game*, was to help readers achieve high performance in whatever they do. The goal of *Sustain Your Game* is to get them thinking about the next step: remaining there. The book is organized along a timeline of short term to medium term to long term because we are always battling all three: stress in the now, stagnation in the present, and burnout in the long term. I think of stress as a "too much" problem, stagnation as a "too little" problem, and burnout as a combination: "too much of too little." Since I believe that an easily decipherable structure is the best way to retain knowledge, I've designed this book into three parallel sections:

Part I—PERFORM is about managing stress in the day-to-day (short term)

Part II—PIVOT is about avoiding stagnation in your current situation (medium term)

Part III—PREVAIL is about beating burnout and making a lasting impact (long term)

PART I

PERFORM—Managing Stress

I can't think of a single person in my life who isn't at least partly stressed. And I'm not the only one.

Stress is a reality for three out of four Americans, and one of the main culprits is the workplace. Whether the stress comes from our boss, our colleagues, our own expectations, or just the rigors of the job, the feeling tends to be the same: we have too much on our plate and we can't handle it. If you feel this way, take heart: you are not alone.

We are all working longer hours, and work is seeping into a larger portion of our lives: holidays, weekends, vacations, first thing in the morning, last thing at night. "An office used to be a thing you went to for a certain number of hours a day," noted a 2020 *Atlantic* article about work stress. "Now, work is an entire plane of existence."

An office was once a place, and now it's a state of mind. Worse, we're spending more and more time there because we carry it with us. We can't pack up and leave work behind for the day as easily as our grandparents once left their offices. We now pack up our office itself, bring it home, into our beds and our relationships, to our kids' soccer games, to family dinner, and to nights out with friends.

Those in the workplace with a college degree "spend 10 percent more time working now than they did in 1980," which was not a lax period for the workforce. The total effect of all these work hours has been brutal on the individual. And it's not just what we think of as high-stress jobs like ER doctors and police officers. It's everyone's job. Two out of three American workers suffer sleep problems due to work-related stress. And this disrupted sleep ends up spiking the very stress that causes it, setting us up in a cycle that's tough to break.

Of course, the workplace is only one arena where stress rears its ugly head. In the twenty-first century, stress seems to have spread to all corners of our lives. Who knew that having a Wi-Fi–connected smartphone in our pocket with the ability to know every fact in the world and access to everyone we ever met could have a downside?

Just kidding.

All this stress is unnatural, as in not what nature intended. Our minds and bodies can't handle it. "We're simply not designed to flee from predators for 10 hours a day with no breaks," a recent *Experience Life* article explained. "But that is essentially what we do." We once needed our stress reflexes to avoid predators out on the savannah and we evolved to survive those types of situations. Now, though those moments are unlikely, our body still reacts as if bison are lurking around the corner. (Evolution is slow!) Stress once arose out of a biological need; it was a threat response that meant life or death. Though the modern world has gotten rid of many of these bodily threats, we are still walking around with brains that act as though they're still everywhere.

"Stress is defined as a reaction to environmental changes or forces that exceed an individual's resources," psychologist and author Melanie Greenberg writes. That's important: **Stress is a response**, the *feeling* of the world imposing itself on us. Notice I said "feeling." That's because—news flash—the world is not actually imposing itself on us. The world is just going about doing its spinning. So stress is not about a hard reality that you are experiencing, but rather your perception of that reality.

Once we accept that to be true, that stress is a response, then our next step is to embrace the obvious flip side: *there are things we can do about it*.

That idea is empowering. I used to get stressed out by all kinds of things: being stuck in traffic, before a game or big presentation, in the lead-up to a tough conversation. I was constantly on edge and rarely felt at ease. But I've worked hard to lower my stress response. I've conditioned myself to effectively manage that response. No longer am I being driven by that uncomfortable feeling that I can't handle what's coming. I've developed the tools to take control.

* * *

Everyone in your life and office is expecting you to be your best self, and stress is the daily enemy that gets in your way. But what are you doing to combat it? Well, first ask yourself this: What are you doing to *invite* it?

Stress is a choice. I know what you're thinking: Who the hell is this guy anyway? Telling me I'm *choosing* to have to do five things before I can leave the office, and my boss is now asking for *x* and my wife needs me to do *y*, while my kids beg for *z*?

Trust me: Stress has to pass through our brains first. The event is not the stress. **Our reaction to the event is the stress.** The events themselves are inherently neutral. They simply take on the meaning, feeling, and emotion we assign to them. If you take nothing else from this section, remember that. Your mind is the ingredient that makes stress what it is. Stress doesn't exist independently outside of us.

In my first book, *Raise Your Game*, I emphasized a phrase that I try to live by: **control the controllables**—whether it's on the basketball court or in the office. The key is to work on your own effort and attitude, which is all you can really do anyway. Your day is going to be filled with things beyond your control, but your response is 100 percent your choice. You may not always have control of your situation or circumstances (in fact, you rarely do), but you *always* have control of how you respond. Choose responses that empower you, move you forward, and improve your situation. It's that simple. And that hard. So stress comes from inside of us, and with this knowledge and understanding we can take action against it.

CHAPTER ONE

Focus

When Diane Van Deren was in her twenties, the epilepsy that she experienced as a child came back with a vengeance. Though she tried various treatments and interventions, she found only one thing stopped the seizures: running. She would leave her sneakers by the front door and whenever she felt an aura (the sense that a seizure was coming on), she'd lace up her shoes and take off for a long-distance run through the national park near her house.

At thirty-seven Diane had brain surgery to remove "a golf ball–size portion of her brain," which left her entirely seizure-free. However, it came with a strange side effect: she no longer has any short-term memory. It causes struggles in her daily life, and it makes it difficult for her to follow trails, but there's an upside. In distance running, where obstacles are both physiological and psychological, having no short-term memory is *a gift*. It's better than big lungs or strong calves. Because she is always focused on the present moment, Diane is never dragged down by thoughts about where she is, how far she's come, or where she's going. She can run farther and longer than anyone else.

Diane can't "keep track of where she is on a course, she doesn't focus on the challenge ahead of her," writes Alex Hutchinson in *Endure*. "She has no choice but to focus on the immediate task of forward motion, taking one more step, and then another." Though

I can't assume Diane's regular life is very easy, I imagine her lack of memory is an asset in the long-distance running world, where she has excelled. She has a superpower that very few have: she is always focused on the present moment.

Be where your feet are. It's so simple yet increasingly difficult in our modern world. We must learn from the past and plan for the future, but true presence, living in the here and now, is the first step to reducing stress in your life. This is becoming increasingly more challenging given the constant bombardment of distractions we face nearly every moment of every day.

Focus is the first chapter here because if I had to pick one fundamental strategy to help manage stress, it's **live in the present moment**. Even if the present moment is stressful, (a) you'll be able to handle it better when you focus on it, and (b) there's only so much stress one present moment can offer. Stop getting upset over events from your past and getting anxious about a future that hasn't happened yet (and may not happen at all). That's time travel and it actually increases stress.

Stay where you can have an impact: right now.

Eye on the Ball

In an article about NBA legend Kobe Bryant, psychologist Benjamin Hardy singled out one thing as Kobe's strongest trait. It wasn't his shooting, jumping ability, or agility on the floor. It was his *short memory.* Kobe's superhuman focus, his ability to wipe the mental slate clean, truly stood out for Hardy, who has made studying such things his life's work. Like Diane Van Deren, Kobe was not weighed down by what was and, because of that, what might be. On the basketball court, where possessions often last less than twenty seconds, that gave him an edge.

Some call it having a whiteboard memory, one you can quickly erase. "The less you hold on to mistakes or painful experiences, the better you're able to adapt to what the situation requires and perform in order to achieve your goals," Hardy writes. "What happened in the past doesn't impact the next thing you do, or stop you from being entirely present at this moment." A basketball player has to be able to block out the failures, the missed shots, and the blown plays or the game will get away from him.* The action is simply too quick, and even the best players are going to regularly make mistakes and miss shots. That's just the game. Coach Mike Jones, whom I worked with at DeMatha Catholic High School, a powerhouse that has produced a long line of NBA stars, used to lean into this strategy as well. One of his favorite things to yell, especially after a turnover or missed shot, was, "Next play!" It was a shorthand that his players understood. It meant: *move on.*

Coach Jones made dealing with what's in front of you a consistent approach. In the locker room after one practice, Coach Jones handed out a printed copy of the game schedule to the players. The very next game was against the last place team in the conference, an easy win as far as the players were concerned. But three games after that was a showdown with Gonzaga, DeMatha's rival, which would be broadcast on ESPN. Jones asked the team, "What is the most important game left on our schedule?"

Most quickly shouted, "Gonzaga!"

"No," he calmly corrected them. "The *next game* is always the most important game on our schedule. It's the one right in front of us."

The thing in front is always the most important. If that's your colleague's presentation or your child's baseball game, then that's where your focus should be. Attempting to solve A while staring at B and thinking about C is a guarantee that you'll do all three poorly. It's the perfect recipe for unnecessary stress.

Processing our past and planning our future are crucial, but neither mean a thing if you are not **handling the moment**. Strike

---

* Note: I use "him" in this book to refer to an individual person, but I never mean it in a gendered way. Everything in this book applies to everyone equally.

a balance between what you need to know and what can wait. If your attention is tipping too far into the past or future, then you are failing the moment. And the moment will fail you.

Athlete's Mind

One of my favorite demonstrations of the "next play" philosophy was from New England Patriots head coach and *eight*-time Super Bowl champ Bill Belichick. A journalist once asked Belichick, "With all that you have accomplished in your career, what are some of the things left that you still want to accomplish?"

His answer? "I'd like to go out and have a good practice today. That would be at the top of the list right now." Belichick has a reputation for being prickly with reporters, but he isn't being coy here. He was answering the question literally but honestly: his mind was focused on the thing in front of him, the one he had a chance to control. It wasn't even the upcoming game. It was that day's *practice*. That's why he has been such a consistently high performer for decades.

Athletes and coaches are a particularly useful group to look at in terms of focus because it is a necessity in their line of work. Even a good season will be filled with a mix of wins and losses, sometimes on back-to-back days. If any one game matters too much, the stress would overload them. Picture the conveyor belt at the factory, with workers moving at the steady speed, never too slow or too fast. That's the ideal athletic mind.

University of South Carolina basketball coach Dawn Staley knows the effects that dwelling on the past can have on performance. This is especially true for younger minds, and even more so with those with high standards, like Division I basketball players. In response, Coach Staley has implemented a "24-hour rule" with her team. She tells her players: "You got 24 hours to bask in your victory or you got 24 hours to agonize over your defeat. And then we put one foot in front of the other and we keep moving."

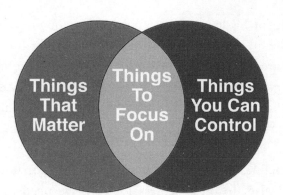

Original diagram idea by Peter Rea; designed by Jeremy Stein

Staley was influenced by her own experience as a UVA player. In the 1991 national championship game, Staley missed a game-deciding layup, a devastating moment that she watched and re-watched and perseverated about over and over. When she became a coach, and she saw her players' competitive drive was causing losses to overwhelm them, she instituted the 24-hour rule. She knows from experience how detrimental living in the past can be. Time moves one way. You can either operate in harmony with this idea, or in conflict. Those are your choices.

Be Where You Are

Author and spiritual teacher Eckhart Tolle, born in Germany, educated in London, is a slight and unassuming man. In his late twenties, and suffering from depression, Tolle was struck by a revelation. In his lowest moment, a thought came into his mind: "I can't live with myself any longer." But after he said it, he stopped. Tolle realized something: *What does that even mean? How can I separate from myself?*

Tolle realized that if one self couldn't live with the other, then that meant there must be two selves! Well then, which was the real him? *(Will the real Slim Tolle please stand up?*)*

---

* My coauthor and I had a lively debate about leaving this in. Guess who won?

Tolle spent his life trying to answer that question and, in discovering the answer, has taught millions of others how to handle their own stress, dissatisfaction, and depression. His solution to the two selves problem is that there is always the you who is living and the you who is watching that you. And that observing you, the one who runs our internal dialogue, is the source of our stress and anxiety.

Tolle defines stress as the **desire to be somewhere and some***when* **else**. In order to lessen stress, we need to get out of the past ("memory") and the future ("anticipation") and stay in the now. Your body can only be in one place, so your mind and spirit need to be there, too. When all three are unified, you are fully *present*. "When you're really in the body there's not much thinking anymore," Tolle has said. When you're in the present, the two selves become one.

When we're worried about something that has happened or anxious about something that will happen, our stress has so much to feed on. It can be never-ending. So how do we stop it? **Acceptance**. "The pain that you create now is always some form of nonacceptance," Tolle writes, "some form of unconscious resistance to what is." Be where you are because you have no other choice.

This is what you're doing, so do it.

When our energy is hovering away from the here and now, we're unsettled. That's why people who take things as they come are called *grounded*; they stay where they're standing.

Fear comes from the past, anxiety from the future. The here and now is controllable.

Tolle teaches that we should "always say 'yes' to the present moment: What could be more futile, more insane, than to create inner resistance to what already is?" It's not like you can successfully say no to the present moment, but when you try to do so, you're opening your arms wide to all types of stress.

Sitting in Traffic

The key strategies to managing stress are really not complicated. They may be difficult, but that's because of our own habits and assumptions. Understanding the fundamentals is quite easy. I am a creature of the basics: that was true for me in basketball, and it remains true in speaking and in my personal life.

If you can control it, change it. It you can't control it, let it go.

Sitting in traffic is the epitome of this idea. If you're like most people, it's safe to say that your blood simmers when you're stuck behind other cars with nowhere to go. This makes almost everyone crazy, and it's strange because there's not a single thing we can do about it. A German study even found that sitting in traffic "more than *triples* your chances of suffering a heart attack over the following hour." Now, if stress is the feeling that your resources are overloading, this doesn't make any sense. You don't have to do anything when you sit in traffic. There are no choices to compare, or decisions to make: there is not a single thing you can do about the situation. You are literally sitting still, surrounded by others sitting still.

In *The Art of Taking It Easy*, Dr. Brian King uses traffic to stand in for all the things in our lives that we can't control but that still stress us out. "The traffic was real," King explains, "but it was your own beliefs, values and expectations that made the situation into one that you found stressful." He refers to all things worth worrying about as "bears" and all the rest of the little annoyances as "traffic."

As I mentioned earlier, we're not being hunted by lions anymore, but our bodies still tend to act like we are. So managing stress is about knowing which are the bears and which is the traffic. I'm sure you know the answer. "The vast majority of the stress we experience is self-induced," King argues, meaning we regularly react to things like traffic as though they are bears. If we're to take an honest look at what we're facing, it's mostly traffic. And if you accept that, you'll be better equipped when the bears do show up.

Shrink Your Window

As a professional speaker who has to give each audience my full self, I live on my ability to focus. When thoughts of what was or what will be start to accumulate in my head, and the stress begins, *I shrink my window*. Onstage, I only have my audience and my content in mind. I block everything else out. It's taken years of practice to reach this point, but it allows me to truly stay focused.

I do between sixty and seventy paid speaking gigs a year, and I can't afford to lose focus. Many of these people are seeing me for the first and only time. So my career depends on giving each speech as though it's the most significant one of my life. I need to behave like this is an important moment for me if I want it to translate as an important moment for them. My enthusiasm isn't automatic, but it's necessary. My focus is my lifeline. I know my material, make sure I have a connection with the audience, and keep eye contact with as many as possible. Every once in a while, mistakes happen. Maybe I stumble on words or forget to make a certain point. But as long as I'm in the present moment, I can resolve it easily and stay in the flow. And the audience rarely even notices.

Two-time gold medalist and US women's soccer midfielder Lindsay Tarpley Snow told me that she focuses best by slicing up her larger goals into smaller ones, and then making sure everything is aligned. That way she can be in the moment while also keeping an eye on the big picture. "In order to make sure I can handle and manage things day to day I look at those short-term goals, things I want to accomplish," she told me. "I make lists and know priority-wise what needs to be accomplished first and then I work my way down. For me that really helps me from feeling overwhelmed." It's the perfect middle ground between being so in the moment that we lose sight of our direction and being such a planner that we miss what's in front of us. "It's amazing how much you can accomplish by looking at it day to day, [using] short-term vision," she told me, "which ultimately leads into your long-term goals."

Settled Mind

Mental skills have become such an accepted part of sports that more than half of NBA teams have a coach specifically dedicated to this facet of the game. Paddy Steinfort, who works with Olympians and other professionals, helped Indiana Pacers guard T. J. McConnell with his pregame jitters. Steinfort taught McConnell a simple but powerful way to be where he is. His advice? During the National Anthem and lineup announcements, McConnell should just focus on reading the signs and banners hanging from the stadium rafters.

Seems simple, right? Almost silly? Well, it worked. "It kind of got me into this Zen," McConnell said. It allowed him to reorient himself and get out of his head. *This is where I am and this is what I'm doing.* Is there a space in your home or workplace that you can turn into your "banners in the rafters?" Something that brings you back to where you are? For a week, when you get stressed or unable to focus, try putting your eyes there for thirty seconds and breathing. See if it brings you back.

Steinfort had similar advice for Rockies outfielder Kevin Pillar, who was having anxiety at the plate. Steinfort taught Pillar that when he stepped into the batter's box, he should focus on the way his back foot stepped into the dirt of the batter's box. Wherever his mind went, he should return to that visual and tactile cue to feel present. Feel that, focus on that, and everything else will snap into place.

Focus is a habit, and it takes work. You have to remind yourself to take each thing as it comes, to address what's in front of you. This is how the best athletes on the planet manage a kind of pressure most of us can't even conceive of.

Dr. Hendrie Weisinger and Dr. J. P. Pawliw-Fry are the authors of *Performance Under Pressure*, a book all about stress in the moment. Pressure is essentially a form of stress in which the outcome of an event, and the importance you bring to it, risks throwing you off your game. In order to manage this, high performers learn to *downplay* the importance of the pressure moment.

Athletes tend to do this automatically: they never act like any game is more important than any other. In pregame or postgame interviews, they rely on mostly stock answers about taking it "one game at a time." Sportswriters may get annoyed, but the players are not trying to be dull or repetitive. In order to execute at a high level, **that's all they allow themselves to think**. They are locked in, focused on what matters. It doesn't behoove them to think in terms of larger context or outside distractions, so they don't do it. If you had to play a hundred games a season, each watched by millions and dissected into pieces, you'd train yourself to think and talk this way, too. **Think about ways that you can take this mindset into your own workplace.** What aspects of your job throw you off your focus? How can you get it back? How can you shrink your window?

Peak

Weisinger and Pawliw-Fry studied twelve thousand people over ten years and found that no one is immune to the effects of pressure. It's simply not possible. Those who succeed in high-stress situations—like performing artists and athletes—have just trained themselves to be less affected by it. In pressure situations, they are better than others at performing *as they normally would*. Elite athletes like Serena Williams, LeBron James, and Tom Brady feel pressure just as we all do. But they have learned how to manage the feeling of pressure and their response to it.

Michael Jordan had twenty-five game winners in his career, twenty-four of which came with less than ten seconds on the clock. The only other player in the conversation as the GOAT, LeBron James, leads in a similar statistic. LeBron also leads all NBA players in game tying or go-ahead shots in the final possession. These players' almost supernatural ability to sink difficult shots with all eyes on them comes from the way they have adapted to the pressure. Watch videos of Jordan's and LeBron's game winners and you can see it in their approach coming out after the timeout, in their face as they catch the ball, in their movements as they release: *they are assured*. As much as they can, they are going to treat it like just another shot. That's why it goes in.

Adam Vinatieri is one of the all-time great NFL kickers, a position with little glory and tons of pressure. "We're on an island," he told an interviewer. "Everyone is watching us. It's not like some play where only the coaches who can see the film can tell who screwed up. The difference between kickers is, can you do it when the lights are on?" *With the lights on.* Exactly—that's all that really matters in their world. And it's why focus has to be their bread and butter.

The Big Mo

Besides helping us manage stress, a commitment to focus also helps to generate momentum. When you are constantly zeroing in on the one, present thing, you are continually getting things done. This creates a cycling momentum that helps us stay positive about the long haul.

For instance, the book you are reading may not be done for another twelve months, but I am winding down the first chapter, which gives me something to celebrate. A small victory. If I only thought about completing the book, and never focused on literally what was in front of me, I would have nothing to celebrate and no momentum. I try not to think of myself as writing a book: I am writing fifteen linked chapters that will function as a whole. And I do that by writing one paragraph, one sentence, and one word at a time.

You don't have to wait for those victories—promotion, end of the year, finished project. You can create them yourself. When we take note of something we've done that we feel good about, we actively trigger a release of dopamine in our brains, "a chemical that elevates your mood and gives you a feeling of greater confidence. That will get you to the 'unflappable' stage much faster than trying to deal with all aspects of a situation at once." Chop up your current work into little victories, give yourself a way to briefly acknowledge them, and see if that doesn't help rev you up for the next thing.

Focus is about changing your perspective to the immediate: **You, The Here, The Now.**

1. Focus on **you**—the what
2. Focus on **here**—the where
3. Focus on **now**—the when

Steady Mind, Steady Hands

Performing well in a pressure situation is not about ignoring or blocking out the pressure. **It's about not letting the pressure dictate what you do and how you do it.** Science writer Taylor Clark studied high-pressure jobs like hostage negotiators, air traffic controllers, and surgeons for his book *Nerve*. What he found was that high-pressure achievers don't block out pressure. They just don't allow themselves to be dictated by it.

As proof, Clark points to one of the highest pressure moments of the twentieth century: Neil Armstrong on July 20, 1969. Flying the lunar module before landing, "the *Eagle*'s instruments showed that [Armstrong's] heart was thumping out of his chest," yet he spoke in a calm, relaxed voice to the world that was listening. He betrayed no evidence of the stress we biologically know he was feeling. It's not that Armstrong didn't feel the stress. He just didn't *react* to it.

We all feel stress relative to our current situation. Studies have shown that actors on opening night feel *as stressed as car accident victims*. Meanwhile, competitive ballroom dancers feel as stressed as skydivers jumping out of a plane with a parachute.* It's not really the content of your action; it's the emotions you bring to it. That's why controlling our reactions is so important.

Focus allows us to outperform the competition because it gives us the ability to notice what others don't. Think about quarterbacks at the line of scrimmage. Every NFL quarterback gets the same amount of time before the football is snapped into their hands to start the play: forty seconds. But not all forty-second periods are treated equally. Those who are focused get the most out of that time. Michael Vick once described the seconds before the snap as a chaotic checklist of things he's paying attention to. But once the snap comes, "everything just stops. My mind slows down. I go deaf. Everyone is moving in slow motion, when they're really moving 100 miles an hour. It's only 3 seconds but it feels like a minute and then you make a throw. And next thing you know the sound comes back in and everything is back to normal."

Vick's forty seconds is not the same as yours and mine is, as he can "extract more information" out of those forty seconds. Think of Neo dodging bullets in *The Matrix* by seeing them in slow motion. He doesn't have the power to literally slow them down; they just feel slower to him because of how his mind is trained.

All In

I used to roll my eyes when someone would suggest meditation to me. Sitting alone in the quiet with nothing but my breath and thoughts? *Hard pass. I have too much to do!* But that all changed for me in the summer of 2017. Entrepreneur Jesse Itzler invited me to his home in Connecticut to speak at a retreat he was hosting called the Live Life for a Living retreat. Jesse had invited an eclectic group of remarkable human beings to spend a few days together connecting and learning ways to optimize performance and cultivate fulfillment.

---

* Not their first time, but their second time.

On the first night, Bob Roth, an affable grey-haired gentle-man with a wide smile, led a session on meditation. Bob is one of the most experienced and sought-after meditation teachers in the country, having taught it to thousands of students over a forty-year career. His book *Transcendental Meditation* has been translated into over twenty languages, and he directs the Center for Leadership Performance in New York.

Though my natural resistance was up, Roth explained that a meditation practice should feel natural and effortless, nothing that would require any change in lifestyle. It is not something to believe in, he explained, it's something you do, like breathing. Meditation is not about controlling your thoughts, but rather about being aware of them and learning to let them flow.

After our session, Roth recommended to newcomers an app called Headspace. The next morning, I downloaded it and did my first ten-minute session. For three years straight, a short but impact-ful guided meditation is the second thing I do every single morning of my life (after making my bed). In fact, as I type this sentence, I've only missed ONE day in four years.* Daily meditation has drasti-cally improved my mindfulness, my awareness, and my focus. It's heightened my ability to be calm and grounded.

None of that happened overnight. It came from the cumulative effect of prioritizing and valuing my meditation practice. My mind-fulness and poise are sharper than they've ever been. I no longer get rattled, frazzled, or knocked off center. And it didn't require that I believe in anything except the value of stillness.

The science has been around for a while, and the culture is starting to catch up: mindfulness sessions are everywhere—the gym, the office, prisons, hospitals, and classrooms. People are finally com-ing around to the power of sitting, breathing, and just *being*. We are all so overscheduled and busy that we are naturally resistant to

---

* A story for another time.

not doing anything for ten minutes. But those ten minutes can be life-changing if we meditate regularly and with deep focus. Those who meditate don't have more control over what happens to them, but they do have "much better control over how they respond." Remember: *control the controllables.*

Accepting Growth

Years ago I worked as a performance coach at the NBPA Top 100 Camp. The camp, run by former NBA players, was designed to teach the top high school prospects everything they needed to be a pro, on and off the court. Mental skills coach Graham Betchart addressed the athletes on his concept of *playing present* in one of the most powerful talks I've ever seen. Hailed as "one of the NBA's premier resources," Betchart has worked with many NBA stars, including Ben Simmons and Karl-Anthony Towns, teams like the Utah Jazz, as well as banks and corporations. He is a distinctive and electric figure with a shaved head and an impressively bushy woodsman beard. Betchart wasn't mystical or spiritual, but he got underneath things in a way that sports guys rarely do. Great players, he explained, let go of the play that just happened and never worry about what might happen; they simply focus on what is.

Betchart still calls himself a *coach*, a subtle reminder that focus requires practice, intention, and repetition. It's as much a skill as dribbling. "Mental strength is like physical strength," he told me, in that you have to keep working at it. You don't work on your body and say: *Okay, now I'm in shape, I can stop.* If we step away, we lose ground and stall progress.

Betchart works with some of the most superb athletes in the world, those who know about physical sacrifice and hard work. However, some do not realize that the same discipline applies to the mental game. He teaches them to be where their feet are so those feet can do what they are trained to do. The goal, he told me, is to be less outcome based. There's a point where the result is out of your control and *you need to be okay with that*. This acceptance opens the door to so much else while also lowering your stress.

Bang Bang

Stu Singer is a performance consultant for the Washington Wizards, the WNBA's Washington Mystics, and various Division I basketball teams. When I interviewed him, he told me about how he prioritizes **refocusing**. Anyone can focus off the bat, he reasoned. The differentiator is to come back after you've been pulled away.

"Can we find that space just after we react to say *hold on . . .* and refocus." He teaches his players that the situation does not dictate how you feel. *You* do. "Stress and anxiety live in the replay and the prequel," Singer told me. Like Betchart, he also emphasizes being where your feet are. And Singer doesn't mean this as a metaphor; he means it as a physical sensation. He reminds players to feel each foot hit the floor. *Bang Bang*.

Feeling your feet is a strategy that "forces the brain to change its place of attention." If you're concentrating on the feeling of your feet on the floor, it is harder for your mind to wander to past failures and future outcomes. You can be instantaneously brought back to where you are—you can refocus on what you need to. Try it where you are sitting right now. Feel the soles of your feet against the floor, *Bang Bang*. If you find your mind wandering, try it again until it becomes a normal practice.

Invisible Tiger

In *Hyperfocus*, productivity expert Chris Bailey explains that focus actually requires meta-awareness, which means **being aware of our awareness**. "The more you notice what's occupying your attentional space," he writes, "the faster you can get back on track when your mind begins to wander, which it does a remarkable

47 percent of the time." For those who work a traditional desk or computer job, Bailey notes, "on average, we work just *forty seconds* before we're either interrupted or distracted." Forty seconds! What can you get done in forty seconds? Very little.

Bailey says we should root out distractions in our workspace, especially the smartphone, which he calls "a productivity black hole that sits in your pocket." Keep in mind that the average person checks his phone every six and a half minutes. Bailey challenges us to investigate why we do this. Meta-awareness is the process of noticing our habits and asking why. *Why do we keep going to our phones? What are we resisting?* Just by noticing how often you do it, you'll automatically start to do it less. You'll be conscious that you're doing it, which is a start.

Jeremy Dean's book *Making Habits, Breaking Habits* notes the average millennial checks his phone a staggering 153 times *a day.*★ Worse, phones are not just distractions when we're using them. They're distractions even when they're just there. The presence of a phone in a room—whether it's being used or not—affects the connection among those in a room. Our dependence on our phones has created a self-perpetuating cycle. We claim to look at our phone when we're bored, but researchers found that it's the constant looking at the phone that actually creates the very boredom we're looking to relieve. We are not solving our boredom by pulling out our phones; we are introducing it!

It's not just about the wasted time checking our phones or email; it's also about the extra time it takes to get refocused, as "it can take over a minute to 'recover' from the interruption and carry on with the task you were previously carrying out." Think about a work activity that often takes a few hours. Does it actually take a few hours? If you were to mark how much time you spent *not* doing it, what would you find?

★ The average American checks his phone eighty times a day.

To combat this, I've made significant changes around my phone use. Since the release of *Raise Your Game*, I've cut my screen time in half. How? I removed every app that wasn't essential (including social media, which I only use on my laptop and check once per day at most), and I turned off all notifications. I also leave my phone in another room or in my car during meals or when I'm with my children. Its absence makes it easier to forget about it entirely.

Flow

The term "flow state" was coined and first studied by esteemed psychologist Mihaly Csikszentmihalyi. Flow is the ability to "disappear" into an activity. It is a place where our nonessential thoughts vanish, time seems to stop, and a sense of pure joy floods through us. Those in the sports world know it as being "in the zone." Human beings are actually the happiest overall while being fully immersed in a task. And when are we the most stressed? When *we're thinking about it and not doing it*. Larry Bird once said his stress "was a persistent nausea that would not subside until he hit the pregame layup line." Why did it stop then? Because that was the beginning of action.

Csikszentmihalyi first studied creative people to understand the idea of flow, a state which he describes as when "[the creative person] doesn't have enough attention left over to monitor how his body feels, or his problems at home. He can't feel even that he's hungry or tired . . . existence is temporarily suspended." The flow state is desirable, but like sleep, we can't just snap into it. Flow requires the commitment and practice of focus, but also something else: time and energy, which is the subject of the next chapter.

Action Steps

- **Write:** Using a pen/pencil instead of a keyboard has been shown to help focus and performance. A study out of Princeton and UCLA found that "students who wrote out notes longhand retained more and had a better conceptual understanding of the material than students who typed notes on a keyboard." Writing it down sends a *signal to your brain that it is more important.*

- **Listen** intently when people talk—even when they can't see you (like on phone calls). When you spread your mind into two different places, it creates stress. Being elsewhere is not possible, and the effort is anxiety producing. *Be where you are.*

- **De-Alert:** Are you an ER doctor? Firefighter? If not, how often do you actually need to be "on call"? Rarely. Maybe never. Shut off your notifications or leave your phone elsewhere during times you need to dig in. Your phone adds stress and breaks focus.

- **Schedule:** Jeremy Dean recommends being a "scheduled checker" of your phone. (He suggests every forty-five minutes.) Choose times during the day to shut off your alerts and notifications. No one—not even your boss—gets a monopoly on your time.

CHAPTER TWO
Time and Energy Management

In many ways, time is the great equalizer. At the start of our lives everyone's hourglass gets flipped and the sand starts flowing. After that, three things become true:

1. We don't know how much sand is at the top.
2. We can't stop the sand from falling to the bottom.
3. Once the sand hits the bottom, it's gone forever.

Now, everyone understands these facts from around the age of six. But considering how central they are to our existence, do we live by these principles? We all say time is precious, but very few people truly act that way. Knowing that your time is finite and making the most of it are two very different things. The difference between what we know and what we do is called our **performance gap**, and it is central to my work.

The ancient Greeks had a word for when your will was too weak to act according to your best judgment: *akrasia*. We are all guilty of this, especially when it comes to how we manage our time and energy. A key element of tackling stress is to recognize the limits of time (which is not replenishable) and energy (which is). Time and energy are the currencies of performance, and we are in control of how they are used—and misused.*

One-Sixty-Eight

Even just the act of sitting down and taking an inventory of how you spend your time and energy is a valuable exercise. It helps you clarify *what you care about*. We may convince ourselves otherwise, but here's a hard truth: **we make time for the things we believe are worth our time**.

Laura Vanderkam is the author of books on time management, including *168 Hours: You Have More Time Than You Think*. She measures a good day by how many hours she spends on "things that relate to my life goals." I love that framework. It's not about what you accomplish according to some outside metric, but rather how much have you satisfied of what you care about. The litmus test should be: *Does what I'm doing right now contribute to my life goals?*

I am forty-five years old. I have a crystal-clear vision of who I want to be twenty years from now. The sixty-five-year-old Alan Stein Jr. will be physically, emotionally, and mentally fit, closely connected with his children, family, friends, colleagues, and clients, and doing meaningful work in service of others. When I'm presented with any decision—small or large—I ask myself: *Does this get me closer to or further away from that version of myself?* I monitor my time and energy based on this single question.

Vanderkam calls people out for the common complaint that they are "just so busy." She's not dinging them for not working hard. Instead, she's opening our eyes to the fact that just about every single motivated, hardworking person wastes a bucketload of

---

* Though sleep and diet play an obvious role in our physical and mental energy, there are plenty of more qualified people who can discuss these in depth. In chapter 14, I do touch on sleep around the need for rest and its effect on burnout.

time. Think that doesn't include you? Mark a single three-day span, in fifteen-minute blocks, and you'll be amazed how many blocks were totally wasted. "The majority of people who claim to be over-worked work less than they think they do," Vanderkam writes, "and many of the ways people work are extraordinarily inefficient."

One strategy she recommends is literally mapping out each of the week's 168 hours. "There is easily time to sleep 8 hours a night (56 hours per week) and work 50 hours a week, if you desire. That adds up to 106 hours, leaving 62 hours per week for other things." Through that lens, you get a sense of how full the week can be. Once you have a handle on how you're actually spending your time, you'll stop pretending you couldn't find the time for some-thing and accept that you *chose* not to make time for it.

Self-improvement pioneer, entrepreneur, and author Tim Ferriss argues that "being busy is a form of laziness—lazy thinking and indiscriminate action. Being busy is most often used as a guise for avoiding the few critically important but uncomfortable actions." Plenty of people boast about how overworked they are, as if it were a badge of honor. Besides contributing to a dangerous and escalating arms race of who can work more, it isn't even relevant.

In his book *Procrastinate on Purpose*, self-discipline strategist Rory Vaden neatly distills the problem: "Your problem is not that you're too busy. Your problem is that you don't own your situation." Once you do, Vaden writes, "you empower yourself to create your own solution." The stress that we feel at not having enough time is self-imposed. Our tasks may be coming from our boss or client, but how we are managing the time we are given is completely in our control.

Once upon a time, believe it or not, I could dunk a basketball. Those days are behind me, but something interesting about it has stayed with me. When you go up in the air, your body unlocks a built-in fail-safe. Quite simply: *your body will not let you jump higher than you can safely land*. You are protected. I love this concept because it can be applied across the board to what we allow ourselves to take on. We all feel overloaded but it is the rare situation when we can't handle what we've taken on. It just requires a smarter use of our time and energy.

Morning People

Time wasting at work is rampant, as "business professionals now spend half their working hours simply managing their email and social media in-boxes." Half! Of course, we all have to check email and some of our careers have a social media component, but seriously, this number is staggering.

Behavioral economist Dan Ariely, who studies why we do what we do, calls this kind of activity "structured procrastination." We frequently waste our time on minor things in order to put off what we should be doing. Ariely singled out the first two hours of the day as when we are at "high cognitive capacity" and argues that we too often waste those key hours on email, web surfing, or social media.

Laura Vanderkam found that high performers across all disciplines *use their mornings*, when their willpower is full and their optimism highest. If you put a task off to the end of the day, you're risking never doing it at all. You never have more time and energy and openness to new things than in the morning. For as long as I can remember, I've maximized my morning routine because it's when my mood is best, my energy is full, and the soil for growth is most fertile. In fact, I feel like I get far more productivity out of my early mornings than the rest of my day *combined*.

I once asked NBA champion and former Golden State Warrior Harrison Barnes about his time management, which all professional athletes take extremely seriously. You can't even make it to the NBA without being rigorous about how you divide your day, and Harrison got schooled by one of the greats. "I didn't know how early you could wake up and work out until I worked out with

Kobe," he said. "That was like 4 a.m. I'm like getting the crust out of my eyes and . . . he's like 'Let's go.'"*

Clearly, the experience with Kobe had a profound impact on Barnes. It changed how he scheduled his day, even how early the day can begin. Now, he told me, "basketball is always the first thing I do in the mornings." When everyone you're competing against already clears the talent bar, it's those little things that make a gigantic difference. In fact, they're not little things at all.

In terms of using specific times of the day, there is plenty of variance based on individual differences and preferences. For most of my career, I enjoyed and thrived from 5 to 7 a.m. These days, it's usually from 7 to 9 a.m. Those windows might not work for you. Your sweet spot might not even start until 9 or 10 a.m. For as much reverence as I have for Kobe, I don't preach that you must start your day at 4 a.m. That worked for Kobe. Find what works for you.

Color-Coded Life

Though we can never get back our time, advance planning helps us to maximize it. In my career as a performance coach and now as a professional keynote speaker, I've met my share of impressive time managers, but hands down, the king was Texas A&M's basketball head coach Buzz Williams.

I attended a virtual seminar hosted by Coach Williams where he shared his weekly calendar with the group. Looking at it, my head just about exploded. It was this vast, mind-boggling array of color-coded and labeled activities, not just scheduled but explicitly connected to his life and work goals. There were blocks and check boxes for all his work and meetings, but also ones for quiet time,

---

* At a skills camp I once asked Kobe if I could watch him work out. He said I could and that I should meet him the next day at four. When I reminded him there was a camp workout the next day at 3:30 p.m., he smiled and said, "I meant four *a.m.*" (See *Raise Your Game* for the full story.)

reading, communicating with friends and family, even gratitude time. He also had an intricate system of rotation so that each month had the requisite number of variables. It was unbelievable.

"You have to be ten times more clear about your priorities than you think you should," he told us. "When you really start saying what your priorities are, it should be reflected in your daily itinerary." Our schedule isn't just about what we are going to do, it's about the people we are and *want to be*. Though Coach Williams is an extreme example, his calendar demonstrates the kind of control we could have over our time. An hour, or a weekend, or a day off doesn't slip away on its own.

When you are intentional with your time, it will surprise you to find that you actually have more than enough. Mental performance coach Todd Herman calls calendars our "field of play," which is a great way to view it: it is the place where we perform. Herman told me that when he works one-on-one with executives, he asks for them to share their calendar. He needs to see what their priorities actually are compared with what they say they are.

Thin Spread

The #1 reason I'm still not at the Buzz Williams level of time control is because of one word: *yes*. I am a people pleaser who loves saying yes, even when I probably shouldn't! In his book *Essentialism: The Disciplined Pursuit of Less*, leadership strategist Greg McKeown explains how we can all weed out dead weight in our lives. "Only once you give yourself permission to stop trying to do it all," McKeown writes, "to stop saying yes to everyone, can you make your highest contribution towards the things that really matter."

You are no good to the people in your life who matter most if you are indiscriminate with your yeses. You may not realize it, but **every time you say yes to one thing, you are actually saying**

no to something else. Sometimes it's a no to an option you're not even aware of yet.* When you say no to things, new opportunities will show up because you will be available to receive them.

"If we don't plan our days," Nir Eyal writes, "someone else will." Eyal is a behavioral engineer who literally wrote the book (*Hooked*) on how companies can create habit-forming products. Now, in an effort to undo the negative effects of what he has created, he's using his expertise to help people break those same patterns.

According to Eyal, all activities are one of two things: traction or distraction. **Traction** helps us reach our goals, whereas **distraction** moves us away. Thinking of your tasks as either one or the other helps crystallize whether they're worth doing. Throughout your workday, try to **identify your traction tasks and then maximize them**. It doesn't mean there's no time for distraction, and we all need breaks, but make sure you clearly delineate those activities so they don't spill over into all hours.

Juggling

In this day and age, we tend to romanticize those who "have a lot of things cooking." I used to admire and even try to emulate these people, but I have stopped doing so. I now know that if you have too much going on, you are wildly inefficient, and not fully serving anyone, much less yourself. Part of making use of our time is deciding where *to stop* spending time. It means *closing* doors. This is where "no" becomes your most efficient tool.

Dan Ariely has done experiments to show how reluctant we are to close any doors—in everything from shopping to dating— because we are always caught up in the "What if?" game. Keeping options open is practically an American pastime. But Ariely points

---

* In economics, this is known as "opportunity costs."

out that we don't think about "the consequences of not decid-ing." We don't think about all that we lose (time, money, effort) in keeping everything open, which takes "energy and commitment from the doors that should be left open." Put simply: **trying to do everything is actually doing nothing**. You don't gain opportunities by keeping all doors open, *you lose them*. Keeping every door open means going through none of them.

Pillars

You'll be amazed how much time you actually have when you're in intentional mode. In chapter 1, we looked at how stress decreases when we focus on one thing. Well, the flip side is true as well: **our stress goes up when we spread ourselves too thin**. We don't necessarily get stressed by the amount of work and responsibilities we have; we get stressed when we feel we don't have enough time or capacity to do them well.

With our increasingly distracted minds, and an ever-increasing menu of ways to distract us, the ability to block out your time to do a single thing is going to be the valued skill of the twenty-first century. With each passing year and technological invention, this becomes more of a challenge. Famed investor Warren Buffett, who has lived through many cycles of boom and bust, knows how to keep his eye on the ball. He recommends making a list of twenty-five things we want to get done in the near future, and then *crossing out numbers 6 through 25*.

"High achievers aren't completing more tasks," business coaches Dr. Jason Selk and Tom Bartow write. "They're accomplishing the ones that matter most." Have you wondered why prolific colleagues seem to have so many more hours in their day? It's because their hour is not your hour, not really. They *use* the hour in ways that you don't. **Remember: You will never *find* the time; you have to make the time for the things that are most important.**

The All-Nighter Myth

We also need to rid ourselves of this idea that being in a time crunch improves our performance. It's a myth, and I know where you got it because I got it there too: in college. Back then you turned in assignments after consuming a platoon's worth of coffee and candy bars into the wee hours of the morning before they were due and convinced yourself: *Hey, I actually do better under the gun!*

You don't.

Study after study shows that "people were the *least* creative when they were fighting the clock." Researchers actually found that not only do we do worse under time crunches, but we also bring that feeling to the next thing. It's called a **time–pressure hangover**, and those who regularly work this way lose their creativity for the *next three days.*

Putting things off until the last minute—procrastination—is not only a time management issue; it's an emotional one. Procrastination actually has more to do with how you feel about doing something than time management. If you dig into the reason you're putting off the work, you're more likely to remove the obstacle in your way. Plus, when you kill time with meaningless activity, you're actually *increasing* your stress. You may feel like you're putting off the cause of the stress, but you're doing the opposite, feeding it. The best way to fight this urge? In a word: routine.

The Power of Routine

In my mid-twenties I read a book called *The Millionaire Mind*, in which the author interviewed thousands of self-made millionaires to find patterns and commonalities among them. The one that stuck out to me was the outrageously high percentage—over 90 percent—of self-made millionaires who made their bed every morning. (It was especially impressive considering everyone in the group could afford to have someone else do it.)

That was enough for me: I immediately began making my bed and haven't missed a day in over twenty years. It is one of my most ingrained habits, and though it seems minor, that's exactly why I do it. Starting each day with a small act of discipline strengthens that muscle. It sets the tone for what's to come and builds momentum first thing in the morning.

Routines decrease stress by bringing predictability and organization to our days. A routine tells us what we have to do, which decreases our doubting and worry about what we could or should be doing. If your routine is going to the gym after work, then you just go. **Routine is a time and energy saver** because you don't waste time arguing with yourself. (In Alcoholics Anonymous they call this "resigning from the debating society.") Take your waffling, wavering, and rationalizing off the table. If you have a routine and you stick to it, the effort vanishes. It's automatic and you get to the point where it's so automatic that the routine is doing you.

Arkansas head basketball coach Eric Musselman, who has the enthusiasm and energy of a new coach half his age, has a reading–cardio–podcast listening–weightlifting routine that he does seven days a week. Home, away, vacation, workday, off-season and on: he does it. He doesn't even have to think about it, which makes it easier. "It's nonnegotiable. It doesn't matter if I have a million meetings," he told me in our interview. "It's part of my routine that never changes," and it has been consistent for twenty years. Musselman has tapped into the idea that it's actually easier when it's nonnegotiable!

Creating a daily routine will preserve energy you won't have to expend later. Imagine you are a video game character each morning starting with 100 percent (with my kids, I call this my "daddery"). Some of that can be recharged, but it's usually going down until you hit zero and collapse into bed at night. So it's best to preserve our energy for when we need it.

There are plenty of strategies we can use to take energy away from what we deem nonessential activities. Steve Jobs's iconic black turtleneck came from a desire to manage his decision energy. He had to make thousands of little decisions each day at Apple, and he didn't want to waste energy on what to wear. President Obama had only two different color suits for the same reason. Both men had deemed wardrobe energy as nonessential and developed a routine to treat it as such. What activity can you routinize to take away the effort or time it normally takes up?

Know Your Rhythms

Science and technology have revealed so many secrets about the human body, but one of the most fascinating to me is how we can use our natural tendencies to maximize performance. Being attuned to what our body naturally wants to do—like we are with sleep and food—helps us **lean into our natural rhythms** instead of working against them.

As I said, I've always been an early riser. As a young kid, I would spring out of bed well before the Saturday morning cartoons even began and just wait for them to turn on. (My brother Jeremy was the opposite—you could drop a brick on his head and he'd stay sleeping.) As an adult, I began to make use of this inclination to get up early, working in tandem with my body's rhythms. As I developed my routines, I leaned into this habit to make use of it.

Most people follow a circadian rhythm in which they begin the morning at a relatively low energy level that increases through late morning until around lunch; the curve then goes down in the afternoon, and most people feel a crash around 3 p.m. Best-selling author and researcher Daniel Pink calls afternoons "the Bermuda Triangles of our days." If we know about this natural inclination to lose energy in the midafternoon, we should plan for it. Don't schedule activities that necessitate high brain power or energy during this time. Do you have something on your to-do list that looks like mindless busywork? Save it for 3 p.m. Don't waste your fertile midmornings on those tasks.

Studies have shown that these natural rhythms affect even judges, whose job is to literally be as fair and equal as possible. Judges' rulings have been found to "depend on when the case was heard, even taking into account the severity of the crime." (A defendant wants to face the judge early in the morning, or after their lunch break. Before lunch and at the end of the day are the worst times.) If judges can't control their reaction to their body's rhythms, when their entire profession is based on being objective, then you're unlikely to.

Throughout our day, humans also experience an **ultradian dip**, which is "a twenty-minute period of fatigue, lethargy, and difficulty concentrating at the end of our 90–120 minute" cycle. It is during this valley that we should schedule our breaks. Our energy and moods follow a somewhat predictable path throughout the day. One study measured five hundred million tweets across eighty-four countries and found that positive moods peak in late morning and then begin to drop before rising again, peaking around 8 p.m.

Eisenhower Boxes

So how do you determine which tasks are useful and which are wasteful? Here's a really helpful chart that I use. They're called Eisenhower Boxes, and they have helped me simplify my life and take away my stress. The boxes help you prioritize the tasks you want/need to accomplish based upon their urgency and importance. It also allows you to identify the things that you should either delegate or leave undone or delete entirely. I keep an appropriately *full* schedule—a term I prefer over "busy," as it makes me feel in control of my own agenda.

I also have a running to-do list in the notes section of my iPhone. At the end of each workday, before I unplug for the evening, I take ten minutes to review the list and transfer everything over to the primary to-do list, which is the only thing on my laptop's home screen. Reviewing and updating this list every evening allows my subconscious mind to work on it while I sleep. Every

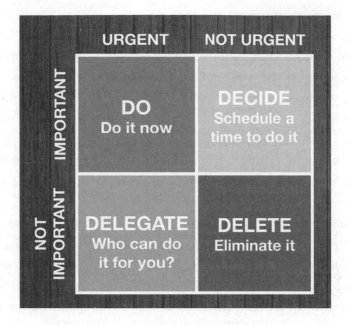

morning when I get into my office, I check my to-do list again and make any additional updates; then I start tackling it. This provides a structure and visibility to my workload that keeps the stress at bay.

Optimize

Being smarter and more dedicated about your time doesn't mean throwing yourself against the wall for sixteen hours a day. It means striking when your mind and body are fertile, and recharging when they're not. Twitter CEO Jack Dorsey has said, "I would rather optimize for making every hour meaningful—or every minute meaningful—than I would maximizing the number of hours or minutes I'm working on a thing." It's not always about the *quantity* of time, which isn't always in your hands (even if you're Jack Dorsey). It's about the *quality*.

We can all be more considerate and judicious with other people's time as well. Jordan Harbinger, one of the best in the podcast game, has a 30,000-foot view of this concept. When I got a chance to interview him for my own podcast, he talked about how he took into account his (significantly large) audience's time. In editing his show each week, he was careful not to leave in throwaway or mundane exchanges, which would be like wasting "750,000 minutes on earth on humanity. That's like an actual tragedy. What could've been done during 750,000 minutes of people's time?" We all need to think about wasting not just our own time but other people's. The fact that Jordan extends that thinking to his audience shows why he's one of the best at what he does.

Sometimes wasting time is necessary, as long as you're aware that that's what you're doing. Happiness expert and author Gretchen Rubin recommends actually *scheduling* unstructured time. It sounds counterintuitive, but it's not. **We need to set protective boundaries around our free time**, around our family time, around our decompression time. Otherwise, those hours will be eaten up— maybe without our even realizing it. If you don't plan on leisure or unstructured time, one of two things happens:

1. You *never* get a break, which overloads you and adds to your stress.

2. The mentality that you "need a break" flows in and out of all your activities.

Our hours won't get drained away and our batteries won't run on empty if we take a deliberate and thoughtful approach to managing our time and energy. Of course, much of the planning that helps us take control of our time is done in advance, which leads us to the subject of the next chapter: prepare.

Action Steps

- As an exercise, **map out** how you spent a single seven-day period (168 hours). Use graph paper or an Excel spreadsheet and record each block; then sit down with the results. What do you notice? What could you add? What can you remove?

- Take a close look at your **morning routine** and how you spend the first sixty to ninety minutes after you wake up. Could this time be better spent? Is there something you're too drained to do at the end of the day that you can move to the morning?

- **Build a Buffer:** Slowing down can be tough if you're afraid you won't live up to your obligations. Build in time between commitments. If you normally schedule ten minutes to get from point A to point B, allow yourself fifteen to twenty minutes instead.

- **Say NO:** But always with kindness, tact, and compassion. Practice diplomatically and politely saying no, because yes is actually a no to other things.

- **What's Your Center?:** Former fitness professional and entrepreneur Ryan Lee told me he has built his entire world around his family, so he has developed an internal scale that he uses to measure whether something is worth doing. He called it the "profit-hassle" scale. He's at a point in his life where if it's high hassle—even if it's high profit—he won't do it. This tool puts your priorities front and center.

CHAPTER THREE

Prepare

So far, I've gone over how focus can lessen your stress and how intentionally managing your time and energy can do the same. This chapter is a natural extension of those two ideas because we can't do either without preparing.

Preparation is a sign of respect. Respect for others, respect for your craft, and respect for yourself. High performers—in sports and in business—take their preparation very seriously. They trust and appreciate the steps. They make their **preparation their separation**.

From 2009 to 2016, I traveled the world running my Cutting Edge Clinic series. These were three-hour strength and conditioning workouts for middle and high school basketball players. A typical session had around sixty players working out and thirty coaches observing. I made a point to always arrive an hour before each workout started. Why? Because what I saw in these players before we began was going to tell me just as much as observing them during the clinic. Maybe even more.

As soon as I arrived, I would casually and inconspicuously sit toward the top of the bleachers and observe the players entering the gym. Within a few minutes, I could easily put every player in one of two buckets: those who were waiting for the workout to start and those who were *preparing* for it to start. The waiting group was usually in flip-flops ("slides") and headphones, sprawled out in the first row of the bleachers, hunched over phones or messing around with friends. The preparing group was already laced up and on the court, doing some type of warmup (stretching, ball handling, form shooting), and building up a solid sweat. By the time I began, they didn't need to shift into competitive basketball mode. They were *already there*.

Do you want to take a guess which group ended up performing better? In a competitive arena, the benefit of preparing when others aren't is so obvious that it's surprising how many don't do it. Of course, this is why it's so valuable.

The best example I witnessed of a player preparing at a clinic happened in Halifax, Canada, in 2010. I was there for a long weekend, running multiple workouts for hundreds of players. But one player really stuck out. Nate, a seventh grader, was a tall and lanky kid who arrived at the gym an hour before every workout. He would be standing outside waiting for the host to open the doors, dressed and laced up, with a ball under his arm. As soon as the gym door opened, Nate hustled inside and got to work. He was polite, enthusiastic, and always "locked in." When each workout was over, he continued to work on his game; at the end, the host had to kick him out of the gym to close up shop! That young man, Nate Darling, ended up coming to DeMatha while I was the performance coach there, playing Division I basketball (at the University of Delaware), and made the Charlotte Hornets' roster as a rookie. Darling started preparing for the NBA a decade before it happened, which is exactly *why it happened*.

> You are not what you do. You are HOW you do what you do.

Irrational Optimism

Larry Bird, widely considered one of the greatest competitors of all time, never lacked confidence. As reigning champion of the three-point contest, he famously showed up in the locker room before the 1988 showdown and said, "Ok, so which one of you is coming in second?"

Bird's confidence came from his preparation. "No top performer has lacked this capacity for irrational optimism," said soccer manager Arsene Wenger. "No sportsman has played to his potential without the ability to remove doubt from his mind." Michael Jordan went to six NBA Finals and won every single one, a feat that most likely will never happen again. Jordan once said that if you feel pressure, "it's because you haven't practiced enough. . . . All I had to do was to react to what my body was already accustomed to doing." Familiarizing is the key. You put the work in so that the bright lights—whether those are the literal bright lights of the NBA Finals or your own personal "bright lights," like a performance review at work—don't faze you.

Legendary boxing trainer Cus D'Amato, who coached both Muhammad Ali and Mike Tyson, famously said that no boxer can be knocked down by a punch he sees coming. Think about that: no matter how powerfully he is struck, his body will be able to absorb it—as long as he is not surprised by it. At the pro level, power alone cannot knock you down. Only being thrown off balance can.

If you look at the most famous knockouts of all time, you'll notice that the knockout punches were rarely the ones that looked the hardest, but rather they were the most unexpected. This concept applies far beyond boxing. *You can't get knocked down by anything you see coming.* Know what's coming. Expect what's coming. Arm yourself and design your environment for what's coming.

KD

I spoke to Kevin Durant on Zoom the afternoon before the Lakers would win the 2020 NBA title during the unprecedented "bubble" season, which Durant had sat out. He was renting a house in Manhattan Beach, California, while he rehabbed in Los Angeles from an Achilles injury that took him down during the 2019 NBA Finals.

In many ways, KD had to start from scratch after such a serious injury, one that some people never come back from. He talked to me about how he had to learn to *walk again*, but he was finally back to playing every day. Despite the frustration that must've come with missing an entire season, Kevin seemed confident and relaxed. He was itching to get back out there, but he was focused on using his time *away* (I wouldn't dare say "off") wisely, demonstrating the mindset of a champion.

When I asked him to describe the biggest lesson he'd taken in during his time away, he immediately zeroed in on preparation:

> I always felt like preparation is the most important thing, for me, as an athlete, as a human being. . . . I broke down every single part of my body in order for me to strengthen and get better so I could get back on the floor. The preparation I had to put in before I got on the court or what I do after, post workout, all that stuff changed as I start to get older and start to experience changes in my body. Preparing for games, shootarounds, building my routine up as a professional athlete has evolved since we started working together.

For those who don't know, my relationship with KD goes way back. When the talented Durant was a rail-thin sophomore in high school, I became his personal performance coach, working to build his strength so he could move to the next level. Two years later, when he joined Montrose Christian, I was among his staff of coaches. His rise to become one of the all-time greats has been a marvel to witness, but it has never been a *surprise*. From a young age, Kevin showed that he was willing to push himself, to prepare in the way others weren't, which—along with his skill—is the reason why he's one of the best.

The best invest their time in the controllable column, maximizing their attention and effort inside those areas. They don't complain or wallow in the things that they can't change. By preparing while others aren't, they maximize their edge. "After twelve years I know my rhythm," Kevin told me. "What I need to do on the floor, how I need to prepare as a basketball player, having a lot of time for myself is good for generating ideas. Being a veteran you learn how to prioritize your time, figure out your routine. I think I'm at that point." Despite two NBA titles, an MVP award, and being hailed as the best scorer in the league, Kevin still used the term "I think" here. This tells you that he hasn't let up.

Locus of Control

Preparation is about locking in our feelings of control. Psychology writer Maria Konnikova was so fascinated by the game of poker that she took a year off from her journalism job to study it and play in some professional settings. Her goal was to write a book about her experience. She found a mentor, practiced online and in small tournaments, and eventually joined the pro circuit. But a strange thing happened on the way to producing her manuscript. Incredibly, with no previous pro experience, Konnikova got so good, and became so successful on the pro circuit, that she had to delay the book.

Konnikova made over $200,000 during her "training" and now has a career as both a writer and a poker player. One of the things she teaches in her book about the experience, *The Biggest Bluff*, is called a locus of control. Put simply, there are two types of loci of control. Those who have an **internal** locus of control believe **they affect events** around them; those with an **external** locus of control believe that **things are happening** to them.

Think about your own locus of control. When something happens, good or bad, do you focus on your role in the matter? Or do you focus on the circumstance and outside factors? Well, study after study found that those with an internal locus of control—remember, just *the feeling* that they affect events—universally perform better in a variety of situations. Even in situations where you are *not* in control, just the feeling that you are has a huge effect.

Because chance plays an enormous role in poker, it's in the margins where players can get an edge; that's what distinguishes the fish from the sharks. The cards fall lucky and unlucky for everyone, but what distinguishes the great from the merely good is not randomness or luck. The winners spend time in these "between the lines" areas (which, in poker, is knowing percentages and your opponents' betting patterns) that can give them an edge.

"People who think they control events are mentally healthier and tend to take more control over their fate," Konnikova explains. Her teacher told her never to focus on or even talk about bad luck, because that is what losers do. After enough times of being reminded of this, she learned to singularly focus on the things she could control. With practice, she mastered the ability to succeed *in those places*.

Clearly, this idea goes far beyond poker. You can focus on what your colleague did wrong, what your client can't see, and what your boss doesn't understand, none of which you can really affect. Those things are there, sure. But what good does it do to worry about them? Work on the area within your control.

Steph Curry practices off-balance shots not for the attention he gets from teammates, opposing players, or the crowd; he's too good to waste time on pure showmanship. He does it because he's increasing the likelihood that he can score from a compromised position or still hit the shot after getting fouled, giving him a chance at a three-point play. Kobe Bryant took the time to study the NBA referee's rulebook so he'd know where the refs stood on the court, and he tailored his game accordingly. They both found ways to excel in the margins by focusing on what they could control and how they could prepare.

Again, the issue is not whether you actually do have control—everyone will have varying degrees of control depending on the situation. It's in the *believing* that you do. If stress is the feeling of the world imposing itself on you, then preparation is how we push back.

Quarterbacking

Podcast host, author, and keynote speaker Ryan Hawk is a former college football quarterback.* When Ryan lost the starting quarterback job at Miami University (to future star Ben Roethlisberger), he transferred to Ohio, where he again took the starting QB job. That experience—of being both starter and backup—has given Ryan unique perspective. He has lived the value of preparation firsthand. It's a skill that was essential as a player and one that applies to every aspect of his current career.

In all of team sports, I don't think there's a position that requires more preparation than quarterback. He has to know what everyone on the field is doing on every play and react accordingly—in seconds. I asked Ryan to describe for me what he was thinking in the moments before the snap, and he explained how he'd have to know not just his team's offensive strategy "inside and out without really thinking," but also the various possible reactions the eleven defensive players might have! Can you imagine holding all of that in your head and having to access it within seconds? Next time you watch a football game, take a moment to appreciate what these quarterbacks are pulling off on *every play*.

---

* He's also the brother of former NFL linebacker A. J. Hawk.

Without studying and knowing all of this complex information in advance, he wouldn't be able to look up in the chaotic, high-pressure situation and make sense of any of it. Only sustained advanced preparation allowed him to know at a glance what gaps he could exploit. In the moment, Hawk had to tap into all the knowledge he spent time learning during the previous weeks. Preparation lowers the stress in the moment because you don't have to handle it all alone. The responsibility is spread out among earlier versions of yourself!

Backup quarterback is tough, Hawk told me, because "you have to really be ready to go knowing that there's a great chance you're *not* going to play." It's an astounding commitment, if you think about it. You're doing all that work for no glory, and maybe for no outcome. And then you have to do it again the next week and the next! If you told a group of students to study all week for a test they may or may not take, how many would study? And if they didn't have to take that test, would they be willing to do it all again the next week?

Next time you see a backup quarterback take over in the middle of the game and do even a passable job, think about the preparation it took to get there. Think about Tom Brady, who was thrown into a game as a young backup after starter Drew Bledsoe went down, and how he turned that into a twenty-plus-year career as the greatest ever. Think about Hall of Famer Scottie Pippen, who was once a skinny equipment manager for the University for Central Arkansas basketball team. He chose to practice each day with the team just in case a spot ever opened up. One summer, a few players dropped off the team just as Pippen happened to grow six inches. Opportunity met preparation, and Pippen's moment came.

Straight Line

One of the great honors of my professional life is having one of my personal quotes painted on the giant wall outside of the Penn State football locker room:

Photo by Michael Hazel

Every single PSU football player passes this quote when he leaves the locker room and heads to the practice field. It reminds them that their habits and their dreams are directly connected. It's a straight line.

The team's head coach, James Franklin, is an inspirational figure. He obviously knows his X's and O's, but it's his mastery of the human element of the game that separates him from the pack. Franklin has an intuitive sense of how to motivate, how to inspire, and how to lead. "If you're not in the .001 percent that are just naturally the best," he told me, "you *better* outprepare people. There's so much confidence that comes from that and so much peace that comes from that."

When I asked Franklin about his stress during game weeks, he said it lessens in direct proportion to how ready the team is. "I don't sleep great Sunday through Thursday," he told me. "Because I'm thinking about all the things that we got to get done. But Friday night I put my head on the pillow and I feel pretty good because I know we've done everything we possibly could to be prepared to go out and play well [on Saturday]." Saturday's James Franklin leans on the work done by Sunday-to-Friday's James Franklin so he can be fully present at kickoff.

Game Situation

Kevin Eastman was one of the Boston Celtic assistant coaches under Doc Rivers for their title run in 2008. In his book *Why the Best Are the Best*, he tells a story about drilling with Ray Allen, who would insist on being at the arena three hours before the game. Eastman was rebounding and passing him balls for a game-speed shooting drill when he looked over to see Allen doing push-ups on the court between shots! To be clear: Allen was catching and shooting at game speed but doing push-ups in the seconds between releasing the ball and receiving the next one. (Most people couldn't do this at all, much less make the shots.)

Allen wasn't some kind of fitness nut: there was purpose behind this drill. In order to stop Allen, who was one of the best outside shooters in the league, defenses were overly physical with him. To get open in games, Allen would have to use his arms to separate himself from a defender to receive a pass, an act that tensed his muscles. So Allen often had to shoot in games with this feeling of tightness. As the games went on (and the shots became more important), Allen's arms would be exhausted and the tightness would be even worse. So with Coach Eastman, Allen was recreating that tenseness in his arms and shoulders so he could practice shooting that way.

As top NBA trainer Rob McClanaghan, who has worked with Steph and KD, among others, puts it, "The main thing about teaching players to be better shooters is to make sure they practice shooting when they're *tired*. . . . You have to be at your best in moments when you feel your worst." Allen was already a knockdown shooter, one of the best alive, but he saw an area of improvement and he put himself through the ringer to accomplish it. I think the average performer comes up with excuses as to why they didn't do their best; competitors like Ray Allen anticipate those issues and work to overcome them in advance.

Where It's Going

"Rebounding isn't brain surgery," Dennis Rodman once said, "but there's more to it than being able to jump higher than the next guy. **A lot of the work is done before you ever even jump.**" Rodman, perhaps the greatest rebounder of all time, trained himself to understand the trajectory of the ball, to predict where the ball was going to bounce, and to position his body to be there. In *The Last Dance*, the documentary about the Chicago Bulls dynasty of the '90s, Rodman explained his near-obsessive preparation:

> I used to have my friends late at night, 3, 4 in the morning, go to the gym. I said, "Shoot the ball." I said "Shoot over here, shoot over there. Shoot over there." I'd just sit there, react, react. I practiced a lot about the angle of the ball and trajectory of it. Even for certain players. Bird, Magic, Michael—how it was going to spin and thus how it was going to bounce.

With Detroit, and later, Chicago, Rodman would watch his teammates—and opponents—during shootarounds to see the rotation and trajectory of each player's shot, understanding where and how they would likely miss. Whoever is in the right position to rebound a ball after it hits the rim may seem random to the untrained eye. But Rodman knew it wasn't. And this knowledge was a way for him to get an edge.

Coach Mike Jones at DeMatha Catholic, one of the most competitive high school basketball programs in the country, would have his starting five practice breaking a full court press (being defended from one end of the court to the other) against seven defenders, two more than are allowed on the court. Other times he would put rules in during a scrimmage, such as *no dribbling*, which forced them to be more efficient at moving the ball.

He didn't do this to make his players miserable. The opposite, in fact. Jones wanted practices to be so difficult that the game itself was a relief. He also adhered to Bobby Knight's maxim: *Before you can win, you have to know what loses.* "I think we're going to win," Coach Jones would say, "but if we were to lose, what would be the one or two reasons why? Did we get outrebounded? Did we not contain their guards?" He would get the players to answer those questions so they could plug those holes *in advance*.

Pre-commitment

If we're talking about the ways previous versions of yourself can help your future self, we have to talk pre-commitment. A **commitment device** is a useful tool for winning the battle for self-control, a method of setting yourself up with rewards or punishments *in advance*. If you want to quit smoking, meet a deadline, complete a task—build in your incentives **ahead of time**, when you're thinking more clearly than you will be in the moment. You need to prepare for the busyness, the distraction, the temptation. You wouldn't conceive a battle plan while you were under fire; you'd do it before the shooting starts.

A simple version of this would be to put fifty bucks aside to spend on whatever you want if you turn in that work project ahead of time. There are various websites (like stickk.com) that will help you set up a "commitment contract" and will follow through on the reward or punishment. For example, some will donate money to a cause you hate if you fail to meet your goal.

Anytime you leave your ATM card in your hotel room when you go gambling or take an Uber *to* a bar, you are setting up a commitment device: making your future decision when your self-control is highest. One thing I do after signing up for a challenging athletic event is post about it on social media right away. I use my social media followers as accountability partners.

One of the most powerful examples of the Ulysses pact I've ever heard of comes from Adam Davidson's book *The Passion Economy*. He tells the story of a father of young kids who was trying to quit smoking. After years of failure, he undertook an extreme version of the pact. He sat his kids down and said that if they ever saw him smoking again, "they should no longer respect him." The thought of losing the respect of his children was the largest possible loss he could conceive of and it worked: he never smoked again.

Stu Vetter, the former head coach at Montrose Christian, often said he tried to "make high-pressure decisions during times of low pressure." For example, he would decide before the game his exact strategy for dozens of scenarios like what play to call if his team was down four with fifteen seconds left. He didn't want to have to draw up something new in the heat of battle when the team's emotions were high. Coach Vetter would keep these scenarios on laminated index cards and pull them out as needed. If the team was down one with four seconds left, inbounding the ball under their basket, he would pull that card out. Before the players took the floor, he would remind them: "You've got this. We've run this play a hundred times in practice!" A situation that would normally cause distractingly high stress became just another play to run.

Stress peaks in unfamiliar or overwhelming situations. We can't always attack it in the moment, so the wisest move is prepare before the high-stress moment arrives. If you do, it just might not show up at all.

Visualization

"The game happens up here before it happens anywhere else," all-pro NFL wide receiver Courtland Sutton has said, pointing to his head. "If you can see it before it happens, you're ahead of the game." Sutton called it "seeing everything twice." Athletes and performers have long embraced the power of visualization—picturing success before it happens in reality.

In the 1960s, Australian psychologist Alan Richardson ran a three-week study to see if visualization actually improved performance, using the game of basketball. He used subjects with little experience with the game, and his findings were jaw-dropping. There were three groups: a group that practiced free throws every day (for twenty-one days) but never visualized, a group that practiced free throws on just the first and last day but never visualized, and a group that only practiced on the first and last day *but visualized every day in between*. Remarkably, this third group—which practiced only two days but visualized the whole time—improved almost as much as the group that practiced every day!

A similar study "found that simply imagining lifting weights increased strength in [a] test group by around 35%." Various other researchers through the years have put visualization to the test and found equally astounding results. Why does this work? Because, when done properly, your brain understands visualization as practice, even if it's all happening in your head. By pre-visiting the moment in your head, you are familiarizing your mind with the situation and allowing your body to adjust to how it will feel. It's something of a magic trick.

"The basket stays stationary," Kobe wrote about his turnaround jumper. The shot has a high degree of difficulty because you jump before you can see the basket, so you don't really have time to aim. It's a split second, and for Kobe, "muscle memory just kicked into work. I didn't have to see the rim to make a bucket." Why? Because he knew in his mind where it was.

Hall of Fame point guard Isiah Thomas used visualization off the court to prepare against Magic Johnson's Lakers in the NBA Finals. "When I was walking down the street for, say, lunch, I'd imagine those individuals in front of me. I'd imagine going around them." L.A. Clipper Reggie Jackson said that during the years he was off the court from injuries, he rediscovered his passion by living out the game in his mind. Brain scans show that during visualization, parts of the brain light up that are associated with doing the activity itself. Even though your conscious mind may know it's not real, your brain and body are still benefitting from the experience, strengthening memories and connections, laying the groundwork for future performance.

"Players get confidence from feeling prepared. It's like putting a suit of armor on," Jill Ellis, NCAA's winningest coach and two-time World Cup champion, said. In order to give her players the confidence to take on challenges, Coach Ellis would show them video clips of their previous successes. Then she would get them to visualize that clip over and over again, even spending time in practice on this. Ellis knew the value in the activity because the players would take that picture with them onto the field. We may not have video evidence of our successes, but try imagining yourself in your successful moment. Visualize it regularly. Carry that image with you the next time you have to perform.

Brown M&Ms

In the early 1980s no rock band put on a show like Van Halen. Before anyone in music was doing complex stunts, they would rig lead singer David Lee Roth up to contraptions that would allow him to fly over the stage while also setting off various pyrotechnics. Traveling from city to city, Roth and the rest of the band needed to trust that wherever they played, those in charge of the stage show had rigged everything properly. The problem? There just wasn't the time for them to check everything. The band's contract had explicit instructions on how everything needed to be set up, but how could the band know if the venue crew had carefully read it? Their performance—and sometimes Roth's life—depended on it.

Their solution was genius and has become a legend, though for the wrong reasons. Roth invented a way to check if the contract had been carefully read. He included in the instructions, somewhere deep in the document, the demand that a bowl of M&Ms be put in the band's dressing room but that *all the brown M&Ms had to be removed*. Failure to comply meant the band would not play but still be paid in full.

When Roth arrived for a show, if he saw a bowl of M&M's without brown ones, he knew the crew had read everything carefully. If he saw a bowl of M&M's with the brown ones not removed, he knew they'd just scanned the contract, so he couldn't trust them and the band wouldn't play.

Ironically, for decades this story was used as a knock on how spoiled Van Halen (and rock stars in general) could be, but that's because people didn't understand the purpose of the clause. Roth needed to perform his best and devised a way to make sure everything was prepared for him to do so. It makes sense to trust others, but never blindly. If your preparation can be undone by someone else's *lack* of preparation, find a way to check it before the big moment, so you don't go crashing to the floor.

Stress Test

When I give a keynote, I'm not dangling from the stage (at least, not yet!), but I do plan for problems to arise. It's not that I'm a pessimist. I do this so I don't get thrown off worrying about how to handle a malfunction or curveball. So I *plan* for my audiovisual equipment to break, for the microphone to cut out, for my allotted time be cut in half right before I go onstage, for the fire alarm to go off during my presentation, for too many or too few people to show up. Before I get up there, I know what I would do if any (or all) of those things happen. If they do, I'm ready. And if they don't, I'm not exerting brain space worrying about what would happen if they did.

Stage fright can actually be abated with practice. How? By getting onstage more often. That's right: **do the stressful thing enough that it stops being stressful**. "When we engage in a new situation, our brain is hyperactive," writes research scientist

Anwesha Banerjee, "but as we engage ourselves more and more, the brain gets a lot less active. The brain gets habituated." In a literal sense, we get "over" it, as in we react less to what once spiked our stress level. Too often, we get nervous around things we never do, so we never do them. But this creates a negative feedback loop; if we break that loop, we'll find that our experience of that situation is no longer stressful.

St. Louis Cardinals performance coach Jason Selk (along with Tom Bartow) wrote that "most of the difference between the highest achievers and the average achievers is in **how they think and how they prepare**." That's right. Someone who works with the greatest players on the planet doesn't believe that talent outdoes preparation. Why? Because everyone in the Major Leagues is talented—that's the baseline. That's why it's called the Major Leagues! Preparation becomes separation.

When Michael Phelps's goggles broke and filled with water during the 200 butterfly at the Beijing Olympics, he still won (with his eyes closed!), because he had visualized this exact thing happening in practice. Similarly, when future Hall of Fame kicker Adam Vinatieri used to practice with the Patriots, Coach Bill Parcells would mess up the ground Vinatieri had prepped or he'd block the sun to put the ball in shadow. These annoying distractions were purposeful because they gave the kicker more confidence on game day.

Solo Feats

Free solo climber Alex Honnold has accomplished some of the most amazing feats of climbing ever done on earth, including ascending the three-thousand-foot El Capitan in Yosemite National Park *without a harness or rope of any kind.*★ That's taller than two Empire

---

★ If you haven't seen Jimmy Chin's Oscar-winning documentary on Honnold climbing El Capitan, *Free Solo*, do yourself a favor and watch it: it's life changing.

State Buildings stacked on top of each other. In order to achieve something so mind-bogglingly dangerous—a single mistake is instant death—Honnold stakes his life on preparation. He does numerous run-throughs (with ropes), so he knows exactly where every single step will be, which gives him the confidence on climb day.

"[He] has always insisted that he does feel fear," one journalist noted, "he just prepares to the point that he knows he'll be able to accomplish his goal by mentally rehearsing everything that could happen." The preparation is what keeps him at ease. Fear never totally disappears, but each practice run is like a rock hammer chipping away at stone. "There is no adrenaline rush," Honnold told *60 Minutes* about his climbs. "If I get a rush it means something has gone horribly wrong."

Extreme ice climber Will Gadd has a similar mindset. He preps his climbs for *years* in advance. Gadd literally prepares for all the ways a climb can wrong, a process which he calls "the positive power of negative thinking." If he breaks down every possible worst-case scenario, he's much more confident in the moment. Negative thinking can indeed be a type of preparation: when you walk your kids across the street, you act as though a car may go speeding by at any second. That's how Gadd treats his climbs, so when those few serious problems arise, they are a breeze. Just kidding; I'm sure they're still insanely difficult. But by pre-drawing a mental map of all the ways there are to die, he makes sure he doesn't.

If your arena isn't free solo or ice climbing, you can still prepare for the stress by taking out the surprise element. **Pre-create** the circumstances that might throw you off so they don't. Have a friend throw obnoxious questions at you while you run through your PowerPoint, or ask your spouse and kids to act like a distractingly bored audience as you rehearse your presentation. If these things happen, you're prepared. If they don't, your brain is not dwelling on the fact that they might.

Kobe and Phil

Kobe Bryant and his Lakers coach, Phil Jackson, may have seemed like night and day. One was a competitive basketball assassin, the other a Zen basketball philosopher, but their approaches meshed on the way to five NBA championships. Both men understood how preparation served as an antidote to pressure. This is why Kobe used to get to the Lakers' court before it was open. Jackson remembers finding him sleeping in his car in the parking lot of Staples Center when he arrived in the morning. Kobe spent many hours in empty gyms and stadiums, far more than in the games themselves. This immersion helped Kobe internalize the feeling of being in those places, so he became as comfortable there as he'd be at home on his couch. That way, when he was surrounded by twenty thousand fans, he wasn't fazed. He wrote:

> There's something about being in a big arena when no one else is there. It gives me a sense of nirvana and also prepares me for the game. When I jogged out of the tunnel and the fans were screaming and it's loud, the noise didn't impact me. Mentally, I was able to remember the stillness of the earlier moment and carry that with me.

"You build things from practice that you can take to games," Phil Jackson used to tell his players. "And, if you remember the poise and execution training that's really an important part of our program, then you can take that to the Finals or to any critical games and perform properly." You do what you can in the time before the moment so that the moment doesn't overwhelm you.

Are you waiting or preparing?
It's better to prepare for an opportunity that never arrives than not be prepared for one that does.

Investing

My friend Brian Levenson, who runs Strong Skills, a premiere coaching and training company, put it succinctly: "We need to be humble in preparation . . . which frees us to be arrogant in performance." Once we're out there, there is only so much we can do. But before we get there, there is *so much* to be done.

The problems, Brian told me, arise when performers "can't adjust [and] can't pivot." Brian's book, *Shift Your Mind*, is about this very concept, the ability to not always be the same thing: we need to know when it's time to be selfish and selfless, when to be focused on the future or the present. Earned confidence, he said, comes from the fact that "you've already seen yourself in that space or in that environment, you visualize, you've given yourself some space to think about the future." This specific type of confidence is called poise, and it's the topic of the next chapter.

Action Steps

- Author and business leader Keith Gerson told me about his practice of firing himself on Friday and rehiring himself on Monday. It's a brilliant exercise. Try it. Ask: **Would I hire me right now? Would someone else?**

- You may not be free soloing or ice climbing, but think about your **worst-case scenario** at work. What would it look like? How can you prepare for it now?

- The flip side to the above mental exercise is this: *Pretend that next week you will be presented with a fantastic opportunity in your work, something you've been striving for.* If that were to come your way, are you prepared to seize it? If not, what could you do to get ready for it?

- Next time you have to perform at work, **pre-create the circumstances** that *might* throw you off, so that they don't. Have a friend or colleague throw as many challenges at you as possible while you rehearse your keynote (interrupt you with a question, turn the lights on and off, or unplug something you need).

CHAPTER FOUR

Poise

At one of his talks, iconic motivational speaker Wayne Dyer pulled out an orange and asked, "When you squeeze an orange, what comes out?"

The audience hesitated, unsure what he was getting at.

Dyer encouraged an answer: "Would apple juice come out? Grape juice?"

Audience members giggled at the seemingly ridiculous question. Then someone said, "Orange juice."

"Right," he said. "Orange juice. Why?"

"That's what's inside," someone answered.

"Exactly!" Dyer said. "What comes out is what is inside." Dyer took a beat, a moment for the idea to hang there. "So when someone squeezes you," Dyer said, "pushes you, puts the pressure on you, what comes out? Whatever is inside you. That's what will come out."

The first three chapters of *Sustain Your Game* have built to chapter 4. What comes out when you squeeze those who **focus, manage their time and energy**, and **prepare**?

Poise.

What Poise Is Not

Poise is not being numb or lacking feeling. Poise is not pretending or posturing that everything is okay. And poise is not putting on a fake smile to give the appearance of having it all together.

What Poise Is

Poise is an inner confidence that radiates outward. It is the calm within the squall. Poise is recognizable—from the outside by observers and on the inside by those who have it. It's having the composure to not get rattled by challenge and adversity. And poise is self-reinforcing: the more you have it, the more you believe you deserve to have it, and then you have even more.

Self-Control

When I was younger, I used to get quickly bent out of shape when things didn't go my way. Whether it was a small inconvenience (a delayed flight), a slight annoyance (inept cashier), or a small adversity (flat tire), I almost always reacted in a way that didn't serve me well. I was easily bothered by disappointing news and was quickly frustrated by people who tested my patience. This was during my playing days, and my frazzled mindset plagued me on the court as well. If a referee missed a call, my frustration would linger for several possessions. In almost every area of my life, I made it a habit of letting the little things get to me. It was self-defeating and it was exhausting.

It took years of internal work, heightened awareness, and a more enlightened approach, but I stopped viewing things as happening to *me* and began accepting that things just happen. I shifted my focus off the actual event and instead focused on my response.

My friend Derin McMains, who is the mental performance coach for baseball's San Francisco Giants, once told me that "our emotions are designed to inform us—not direct us." That is such a powerful truth. *Emotions are information, not instructions.*

There is nothing inherently wrong with emotions like anger, sadness, frustration, or disappointment. A problem only arises if we then allow those feelings to dictate our actions, if we partake in destructive behavior because of those emotions. As I've said countless times to my twin sons, "It's okay to be upset at your brother. It's not okay to punch him!" One is natural and acceptable. The other is voluntary and damaging.

One of the most important skill sets we can possess is the ability to recognize, understand, and regulate our emotions and process them in real time. That is what we mean by emotional intelligence. For me, any time I am feeling angry, sad, frustrated, or disappointed, I go through this three-step process:

1. I acknowledge how I am feeling and **give myself permission** to feel that way. I don't suppress or resist.

2. I try to dig a little deeper and find the **root** of why I am feeling this way. The **real cause** is rarely on the surface. What's on the surface is almost always a trigger for something deeper, and it takes **self-awareness** to get there.

3. I don't allow myself to react on impulse, as that usually will stack a negative behavior on top of a negative feeling. Instead, I take a few beats, and **decide on a response** that will move me forward and improve my situation.

Your response is your own. You can't always control the input, but no matter the situation, you *always control* the output. That's the essence of poise.

Wanted Man

Streetball legend and basketball entertainer Grayson "The Professor" Boucher knows a little something about pressure. The Professor's mystifying dribbling skills and playmaking moves have made him a global sensation, garnering him the adoration of fans, pick-up players, and NBA superstars. Grayson is most famous for his sick handle, his ease and fluidity dribbling the basketball. I love that word—*handle*—because it is also the word we use to describe the way we carry things, as in "He really knows how to handle himself" or "He can handle the pressure."

When the Professor steps onto a basketball court, he not only wants to win and perform well, he wants to blow everyone's mind. He has to draw a wow out of them. Considering that this is literally what everyone is expecting, his success at doing it is all the more impressive. In addition, each player on the court is also gunning for him, looking to show him up. During our interview Grayson told me that every time he goes out there, someone is bound to have the game of their life against him. That's just the nature of being number one. "They're thinking 'if I play you, you're supposed to beat me,'" he told me. "'But if I beat you, I'm famous.'" That unequal equation just comes with being the best, and those who stay on top find a way to make it work for them.

When I asked the Professor how he managed pressure, he deftly juked around my word choice. "You feel that *tension*," he told me. "You feel people after you on a whole other level. I wouldn't say I feel it as pressure because when I get in my element to play ball I'm having so much fun." Notice how Grayson took control of the emotion, saying "I wouldn't say I feel it *as pressure*." He chose how to feel it. By using words ("tension") that allow him to view a pressure situation as positive, Grayson changes what it becomes.

Grayson also has a larger viewing public to think about. Because of his popular YouTube channel (Professor Live) and video platform, *everything* he does on the court is filmed, and of course bystanders regularly film him as well. In the 2020s, there's no such thing as a private audience. Because of Grayson's notoriety, the stakes are always high, even when he's just playing pick-up. A game is *never* just a game. He has to not just perform well, but to do so entertainingly; on top of all of that, he has to act as though it's no big deal. In these videos, the poise *is* the substance. "Breaking the ankles" of your opponent with a dribble move is hard enough; now try looking *natural* while doing it.

It takes a lot of hard work to make anything challenging look so easy. I can't do what Grayson does (pretty much no one can), but in my field I have to relentlessly rehearse to the point where everything I say and do appears natural (and unrehearsed!). This is one of the reasons I closely study stand-up comedians. Elite comedians appear as though they are riffing in a room with friends—but that's not what's going on at all. In fact, they are carefully working the audience, guiding them along, while simultaneously hiding the fact that they are doing so. When the Professor goes behind his back and puts the ball through the legs of an opponent and scores, he makes it look like just another two points. Celebrating or swaggering after would defeat the purpose. *Act like you've been there*, the saying goes. Grayson acts like he's *always* there.

Grayson has what sounds like the opposite of stage fright; he's *most comfortable* on the court, which he thinks of as his world. "If I play in Madison Square Garden," he said, "you might be a little anxious getting out there but after jump ball and one or two possessions, it's like you're in the driveway playing by yourself again." When I watched his videos later that day, I tried to look for how he was managing the kind of attention, pressure, and focus that his work requires. And I saw none of it: the only thing I observed was pure joy.

Standing in the Ocean

ESPN broadcaster Jay Bilas, a friend and mentor, preaches the school of mental toughness. (His entire book was geared around the concept.) Mental toughness has nothing to do with the macho, tough-guy attitude that some bring to their work; that's more about show than substance. Rather, it's the ability to reframe your perspective, adjust your mindset, and have unparalleled clarity about the task at hand. Mental toughness, like any skill, can be improved with purposeful practice.

I had the pleasure of interviewing Sue Enquist, iconic UCLA softball coach, who has won eleven championships, one more than UCLA icon John Wooden.* Though she's no longer on the field every day, she is still the consummate coach, working as a motivational speaker and bringing together players, parents, and coaches through her ONE Softball organization.

When I spoke to Coach Enquist, I was struck by her relaxed confidence. She possessed a demeanor that obviously would have a calming effect on young players. We spoke about the necessity of poise, which she defined to me as being "peaceful in the moment of calling." *The moment of calling* is such a beautiful way to describe performance. Enquist spoke about these ideas as they connected to two of her daily practices: meditation and surfing.

Surfing is not just a leisure activity for Coach Enquist. It's a way of life and a metaphor for how to live. Getting in the ocean, "relinquishing all control, because you never know what's coming" helps remind her how to approach everything else on land. This is a liberating place to get to. We can do nothing about the wave; all we can do is respond to it. She is such an admirable model of how confidence doesn't have to look arrogant or combative; rather, it can be an engine for peace and positive thinking.

---

* She is also the only person in NCAA softball history to win a title as both a player and a head coach.

Dr. Jonathan Fader, a sports psychologist for the New York Mets and Giants, as well as for CEOs, fire departments, and actors, coined the term "objective optimism." (It's like the old saw: "it's not bragging if it's true.") Objective optimism is a clear-eyed assessment of the situation, but one where you **give yourself the benefit of the doubt**. Some of us tend to imagine things going horribly wrong when we can just as easily imagine the opposite. And if it's something we're prepared for, which is more likely to happen?

Coach Enquist actually used a type of objective optimism with her players. One example she shared with me was that of a nervous batter in the on-deck circle, worried about striking out. She would teach the player to rewrite that future and "project success" by thinking about "how good it will feel when I get bat on ball and I'm standing on base." Instead of worrying about striking out, which leads to imagining the out, which leads to it happening, write a different story. Then bring that story to life.

Poise comes from knowing and trusting your abilities, and so Dr. Fader tells us to simply review the evidence. This is not rose-colored glasses or blind faith; how you feel about your abilities literally *improves those abilities*. It is a positive feedback loop where attitude and performance feed each other. Poise and inner calm are part of a self-generating system. Having it creates more of it and so on.

Picturing

Dr. Fader also teaches that positive visualization works because it **changes your behavior**. If you expect to get what you want, you behave differently—which gets you closer to what you want. In his book *Life as Sport*, Fader uses the example of looking for a parking space in his crowded New York City neighborhood. Fader experimented with visualizing an open spot near his building. What he was amazed to find was that, much of the time, it worked.

Now, why did it work? Did visualizing a parking spot magically produce it? No, of course not. But by working toward that reality—by *expecting* that reality—he subtly changed his behavior and was more attuned to his environment. This led to his noticing cues, responding quickly, and ultimately grabbing that highly coveted spot.

You can't choose what is thrown at you. But what you notice, what you care about, and what you let affect you is entirely in your hands. The best athletes and performers know this. "Being mentally tough," Fader writes, "is really about having a great filter. Every elite athlete . . . works at their filter . . . metabolizing results they don't want."

This is why Kobe's short-term memory was such an asset on the floor. He wasn't eliminating his doubt; he just didn't give it the keys to the car. We all have yapping voices in the back seats of our minds, but the best know how to tune them out. "Elite performers in sports and business haven't come up with a secret way to *eliminate* anxiety surrounding these situations," Fader writes. "They just know how to recognize the level of anxiety they're in at the moment and then manage the physical effects of it." It's why high performers never shirk from the spotlight or the responsibility. They've figured out how to block out what they need to, zero in on what matters, and perform at the highest level.

Outside In

Poise and confidence don't always need to originate from the inside. Sometimes they can *start* from the outside. Just like we can imagine a parking spot and then find one, we can do something externally to change ourselves internally. Whether it's a haircut, new suit, leather jacket, tattoo or piercing, there are countless external choices people can make to influence their inner selves. How we feel about ourselves is a two-way street: sometimes we act according to how we feel, and sometimes we feel according to how we act.

Psychologists have determined that "our posture and the way we conduct ourselves while carrying out different actions can influence the way we feel and the results we achieve." In fact, smiling before you feel happy can actually improve your ability to feel happy! Your mind processes the smile, and since it's a two-way channel between body and mind, your mood changes accordingly.

Entrepreneur and author Todd Herman wears glasses without lenses—but it's not a fashion statement. His book *The Alter Ego Effect* explains how—in moments of crisis or high stakes—you can devise an imagined version of yourself and then *become* that self. He teaches professional athletes and other performers to tap into an alter ego, "a mental picture or model in your mind, an image, of what you want to be moving towards," and then bring that person to life.

"We tell ourselves the story of who we are, absorb what people think about us as we age, and those ideas harden," he told me. Todd admitted he was once a scrawny kid with depression issues and low self-esteem. "We all did it as children, dress up as our favorite superhero," he said, "pretended to be our favorite sports star on the driveway. It was our way of acting into something bigger than what we thought we were." We mature out of that, he explained, but there are plenty of reasons to use those same skills, that same creativity, in the adult world.

The alter ego "is our way of taking back control of our narrative by actively creating and feeding this persona." Over time, Todd did exactly that, transforming himself into a confident, in-demand author and coach. He understands that identity is intimately tied to behavior, and he uses that knowledge to motivate people to tap into the self they want to be.

Leeway

Take a moment to think about this question: When you are at your most self-critical, whose voice do you hear?

Next question: Is it your own?

Those who have trouble remaining poised tend to be hardest on themselves. During pivotal moments their inner critic lowers their confidence and increases their stress. It's important to have standards but also equally important to give yourself some leeway. **This is absolutely not a sign of weakness.** In fact, giving yourself room to fail creates a cushion that those in the "hustleholic" crowd don't have. For me, trying to hide insecurities, fears, and weaknesses causes way more anxiety than owning them. Simply: it's okay not to be okay.

Sometimes poise involves going easy on yourself, showing **self-compassion**. "Self-compassionate people aim just as high as self-critical people," psychologist Susan David says, "but don't fall apart when they don't meet their goals." The dialogue you have with yourself is more important than anything you say to your coach, teammate, boss, colleague, or even loved ones. It is the history you write about yourself, the ongoing conversation going on in your head, and the script you will follow in the future.

The Coin

Quick math: if a coin lands on heads five times in a row, what are the chances it lands on heads the sixth time?

Take a moment to think about it. Then read on.

Trevor Moawad is a mental conditioning coach who works with Super Bowl champion quarterback Russell Wilson, the NBA's Memphis Grizzlies, top CEOs, and US Special Forces. He is a proponent of **neutral thinking**, which "emphasizes judgment-free thinking, especially in crises and pressure situations."

Moawad teaches that "we elevate the past. We give it too much importance." This is something we are all guilty of doing. We all project the past onto the future. When we imagine an upcoming event, we often just superimpose our previous experience onto it, expecting things to play out similarly. In doing so, we bring along those judgments, assumptions, and conclusions. Those things keep us stuck, unable to change the future because we act as though it's already determined.

Neutral thinking is characterized by a calmness that is neither toxic positivity (which can veer from reality) nor negative thinking (which never helps). It's intentionally **detaching emotion**, and viewing the situation as neither good nor bad, neither right nor wrong. *It just is.*

I think of it as being the flipped coin. Going back to the question at the start of this section: What are the chances of a coin landing on heads after it has already landed on heads five times?

50-50!

The odds don't change because *the coin doesn't know what just happened.*

Past failures cannot affect your present if you don't let them. It is your choice whether or not to bring the past into the present—whether that's a childhood failure or what happened five minutes ago. Neutral thinking is what gives the confidence to Steph Curry to keep firing away, no matter what his shooting percentage is that night. Each shot is its own moment, a chance to execute mastery, and it is wholly disconnected from the missed ones. He is the flipped coin, indifferent to how he just landed.

Remember athletes' boring answers about taking it "one game at a time"? That's neutral thinking! The reason they are able to execute day after day is because they take each game as it comes. They're not trying to account for every missed shot and every lost game, because that would consume them. It would be impossible to get out on the court or field night after night, and play at such a high level, if they were beating themselves up over every turnover, screwup, loss, or failure.

High performers internalize the idea that the past does not determine the future. The best three-point shooters on earth hit four out of ten shots, meaning they miss more than they make. The same goes for hitting in baseball: the best batter who ever lived—Ted Williams—got a hit 40 percent of the time in one season, and people are still talking about it *eighty years later.* If shooters were concerned with their percentages, they'd be afraid to shoot, a choice that would (a) be selfish and (b) hurt their team. So they don't let themselves feel that fear. They don't think about it. They shoot again and again because *each shot is the only shot.*

Hand on the Stick

It's hard for us to even conceive of the kind of poise that a professional athlete must develop. Scientists once measured the blood flow in the brains of professional athletes during a game and compared it with those of regular people who were just *imagining* they were playing at the professional level. Guess what? The regular people (who, again, were pretending) were *more* stressed! Stress is a relative concept: what's stressful for Kevin Durant is different from what's stressful to you or your accountant or your child. It's not just athletes' bodies that are streamlined, impressive specimens. Their minds are, too.

We all are trying to close the gap between what we can do in practice and what we can do in the moment. Often, we are our own biggest obstacle in closing that gap. John Foley was a former Blue Angels lead solo pilot who now works as a consultant and leadership speaker. He applies lessons he learned in the air to help people at jobs that may be less dangerous but no less stressful to them.

As Foley put it to me, you can practice for thousands of hours on a flight simulator, but "at the end of the day it's getting in the jet, and it's actually getting your hand on the stick" that is going to make or break you. "Hand on the stick" could mean a job interview, giving a presentation, or pitching a client. Poise is the ability to transfer the ease with which you practice—or as much of that ease as possible—to the performance space. Foley explained that this is as much a physical challenge as a mental one. Your mental foundation is what allows your physical gifts to flow out of you.

"The ability to block out distractions is critical," he told me, which he calls "compartmentalization." If you do not have control over the mental aspect, then you will simply not be able to produce. This is true for athletes, musicians, stand-up comedians, actors, and really anyone: if you don't work on taking each thing as it comes, then you will not be able to produce what you are capable of. In sports, when you fail in the moment—not because of a lack of skills but because of a lack of poise—there is a word for it: choking.

Choking

Cognitive scientist Sian Beilock is an expert on choking. In her book on the subject, *Choke*, she clarifies that choking is not just doing badly—it's doing worse than we normally would "in response to a highly stressful situation." Sports psychologist Dr. Michael Gervais says it's called choking because we are "choking off *access to our craft*." We choke when the environmental and self-imposed pressures of a situation overwhelm our skills. Shooting free throws in an empty gym and shooting them with one second left at the end of a close game are physically identical actions but vastly different situations. Poise is bringing the confidence of one to the pressure environment of the other.

Rick Aberman, a psychologist who directs peak performance for baseball's Minnesota Twins, explains that coaches can help their players by watching their language and only speaking to players in positive frameworks. This is not because the players can't take criticism. It's because when you instruct someone to avoid a particular action, it will actually *increase* the likelihood they will do that action! "When the coach reviews plays from a game," Aberman explains, "and only focuses on what *not* to do next, it's a recipe for players to choke."

Pointing out the mistake plants the idea of it in the player's brain. Thinking too hard about what not to do is a great way to *make sure* you do it. So even saying "Don't cross your feet" (when playing defense in basketball) will unconsciously trigger a player to cross his feet. It's why it has never once been helpful to say to someone, "Don't panic." All anyone hears is the second word.

Whatever we bring to the forefront of our minds—whether to embrace it or reject it—we end up doing. "When athletes think about themselves screwing up, they are more likely to do so," Beilock writes. "The ability to control your thoughts and images during performance is crucial." Poise is having an understanding of which emotions are productive and which aren't, what to listen to and what to ignore, and which messages to yourself are most likely to be helpful. If you notice, there's one common denominator to all of these actions: they are within your control.

The Jones Rule

DeMatha Catholic High School, where I once worked as a strength and conditioning coach, is the alma mater of current NBA players like Markelle Fultz and Victor Oladipo and retired veterans like Adrian Dantley and Danny Ferry. I remember once watching DeMatha, ranked #2 at the time, get upset by a much lesser team, a surprising occurrence. What struck me as I watched was not the loss itself. It's what I noticed about Coach Mike Jones throughout the game.

If you only had your eyes on Coach Jones, you would not be able to tell that his team was getting crushed by a lesser team. Though Jones is by no means a stoic person—he shows emotion when he needs to—he was able to maintain poise during that loss because his players needed to see it. He understood that his behavior through that game would last longer than the game itself. It would carry over, and as a coach, teacher, and leader, it is just as important how you lose as how you win. Probably more so.

At one point DeMatha made a run and went up by three. Ninety seconds later they were down again by five, and Coach's demeanor *never changed*. I think of this as the Jones Rule: many of the most effective coaches are the ones you can watch and cannot tell how their team is doing. (The Spurs' Gregg Popovich and the Patriots' Bill Belichick seem to be believers in the Jones Rule.) It doesn't mean they don't care; it means they won't let disappointment or emotions take over.

MJ's Face

In the 2020 Chicago Bulls' documentary *The Last Dance*, there are repeated scenes of Michael Jordan in an enclosed space, sometimes a locker room or stadium corridor, with something like thirty microphones, boom mics, and cameras shoved in his face. The reporters are packed five-deep, cornering him against a wall or locker, shining lights in his face, and barking questions about his future, his teammates' troubles, sometimes his personal life. MJ went through this day after day after day—for *years*—during the prime of his career. He was the most recognizable athlete on the planet, the face of his team (and league), and he accepted that this kind of attention came with the territory. Growing up, I saw Jordan on TV all the time but I never really thought about what it was like from his side of the cameras.

In the documentary, viewers get a look at these press gaggles from MJ's perspective, who was often exhausted from playing forty-two minutes in an NBA game, being the best offensive and defensive player out there, and carrying his team to victory. When you look at the scene, you can't help but notice the unparalleled frenzy around him. And then you look at MJ's face. Unchanged. Total composure. Sometimes a slight smile, and always calm, like he was having a one-on-one conversation.

Now, we know from hours of behind-the-scenes footage of Jordan in practice, on the bus, and with his teammates that this was *not* his personality all of the time. He was poised in public, strategic in how he showed his face to the world, to young kids, parents, management, sponsors, and fans alike. He did so many admirable things on the court, but his ability to maintain composure day after day in that environment is almost more impressive. In an uncomfortable position, when it mattered, he was his best self.

Self-Talk

In *Raise Your Game*, I explained how "your comfort zone is your cage," and one of the main reasons is we don't stretch if we stay where we are. We will never stand on the great stages of our profession if we don't push ourselves. And in order to make it out there, in that new, uncomfortable space, we have to believe that *we belong there*.

In an interview with *GQ*, Jalen Rose explained why he had "irrational confidence" as an NBA player. *He had to have it.* You couldn't convince him he wasn't Magic or Michael, he said, because that's what he saw when he looked in the mirror. Night after night he played against the best of the best: "How am I gonna sit in a locker room with a uniform on and some shoes laced up chasing my dream and don't feel like I'm about to go out here and score 30 on MJ?" he said. "I might as well not suit up and not play the game." In Rose's mind, confidence was a requirement for entry at his job.

Dr. Michael Gervais has spent many years teaching mindfulness to pro athletes, including a decade with the Seattle Seahawks. He's a big proponent of carefully managing our self-talk. "Confidence comes from one place and one place only," Gervais has said. "What you say to yourself." We are all drowning in our self-talk. One study found that "we internally talk to ourselves at a rate equivalent to speaking four thousand words per minute aloud." What are we saying to ourselves over and over again? How does that affect our behavior?

Our reactions to stress and our self-talk in these moments are in our hands. If the tense situation arrives and the feeling of stress comes on, are we at its mercy? Or is there a way to make it work for us?

That's the idea behind the final chapter of this section.

Action Steps

- **Slow Down:** Journalist Carl Honoré is one of the pioneers of something called the Slow Movement, which counters the idea that "faster is always better." Honoré offers a strategy to stay poised during high-pressure situations: take a break and "during this brief time out, imagine yourself looking back on this 'crisis' a year from now and notice how insignificant it will look then." This helps you remove the immediate emotions from the moment, giving you a big picture view that helps put things in perspective. Almost nothing is as important as it seems at the time.

- **Consult Your List:** Create a handy list of positive attributes you have and examples of times when they served you well. (You can keep it in the notes app on your phone.) When prepping for a pressure situation, consult your list. Remember your successes. Visualize these moments.

- **Mirror Work:** In her book *Presence*, Amy Cuddy explores how we can change our confidence from the outside in through our body language. Find a mirror in your house and practice confident gestures and postures. Do any lift your mood and self-esteem? Practice working them into your natural behavior.

CHAPTER FIVE

Using Stress

When I was twelve years old, I got my black belt in Tang Soo Do. The test had three primary components: forms, which was like a dance of choreographed moves that required memorization along with perfect footwork and technique; sparring, which was fighting an opponent; and jujitsu, which tested the ability to free yourself from a variety of holds from an attacker. These included getting grabbed from behind in a bear hug, being put into a bent over headlock, and having a wrist grabbed by two hands.

Even though it happened over thirty years ago, I still vividly remember being a scrawny preteen and having four two-hundred-pound grown men attack me as part of my black belt test.

So how did I even stand a chance given the vast disparities in size and strength?

Those of you with martial arts backgrounds know the answer. I used their size, strength, and momentum against them, strategically utilizing angles and leverage to my advantage. That's how I could negate the massive discrepancy in physical stature.

The goal in jujitsu, judo, and other grappling-based martial arts is to use an opponent's strength against him. The size of your opponent, which may feel intimidating, can become *your advantage* if you understand how to use it. As the great Bruce Lee said: "One should be in harmony with, and not rebellion against, the strength of the opponent." The other guy's size and strength can become *your* tool, if you know what you're doing.

Now, why I am talking about Bruce Lee and a black belt test I took decades ago? Because the same principles can be used when dealing with your emotions. For four chapters, we've explored ways to alleviate stress, but there are times when the energy is so undeniable that we have to figure out how to work with it.

That's when we need to use the powerful energy of stress in our favor.

Signal and Tool

Alicia Clark is a psychologist and the author of *Hack Your Anxiety: How to Make Anxiety Work for You in Life, Love, and All That You Do*. She works to help people turn stress into a springboard to their best selves. Though we've been hearing for years about the dangers of stress and anxiety, Clark teaches that these feelings do not have to be obstacles or problems. Anxiety can be a powerful tool: it is both a signal that you care and the fuel to get you through it. I spoke to Alicia during the pandemic, when she was managing her own busy patient load, parenting a senior in high school and one in college, and living her own stressful life.

She explained to me that Dr. Hans Selye "discovered" stress in the 1930s while injecting rats, looking for a new hormone. Selye defined stress as "an environmental demand for change," and he actually labeled two types of stress: **distress** and **eustress**. It tells you a lot about our society that one is a word everyone knows well and the other is one that you've likely never heard before. **Eustress** is the scientific term for the kind of stress that can be channeled in a productive direction. Stress can actually be a performance enhancer, if (a) if we accept it as such and (b) we know how to use it.

Alicia explained that we need to change the idea that we are victims of our stress. The first step? Deciding who's running the show. "If you can toggle somebody into taking control," she said, "and feel control, that lowers the stress right there." Remember: our emotions are just here to inform us, not to direct us. In reality, stress is neither good nor bad; it's neutral. How we react to it, judge it, and what if anything we do in response to it, that's what matters. The difference between a stress that is enhancing and a stress that is debilitating is *our reaction* to it.

Perception

One of my least favorite phrases is "It is what it is." I've heard it more times than I can count, usually said without much thought. What's my problem with this mantra? It's not true! How do we even know what "it" is? We don't. What matters is what you **perceive "it" to be**.

Our perception is our reality. Two intelligent people can view the same situation, circumstance, or result and have two polarizing experiences and perspectives. Don't believe me? Go post something you believe to be true on Facebook and just wait. It doesn't matter what it is; you will immediately see pushback and varying opinions. Seeing things differently is what humans do.

Why do some players feel that taking a game-winning shot is stressful, while others view it as the opportunity of a lifetime? Why do some people get nervous for a job interview, while others feel excited for a chance to show their potential? Why are some people petrified of public speaking (77 percent according to one study), while plenty of people (including yours truly) find it to be one of our favorite things to do? The answer is perception.

Game Day

NBA writer Chris Ballard has interviewed hundreds of players and offers some key insights into their mindsets in his book *The Art of a Beautiful Game*. "What the great NBA competitors have in common is that they see pressure not as most of us do—*Oh, man,*

I better perform—but as an opportunity," he writes. He heard this from a variety of NBA stars, from Manu Ginobli, who claimed the "responsibility" was his favorite part of the game, to Kyrie Irving, who said he enjoys and looks forward to the pressure. Were Ginobli and Kyrie born this way? I doubt it. They have trained to react this way because it's beneficial to their job.

Stress doesn't have to be an obstacle. In fact, it doesn't even have to be stress at all.

It can be something that drives you. Think about the Wall Street types on the trading floor or trainers in the corners of a UFC fight: in those environments, the stress of the moment is an energy that drives them. "Recent research is showing that work strain, when managed correctly, can actually have a positive impact on productivity and performance," the *Harvard Business Review* noted. Your mind and body communicate back and forth. Sometimes you think yourself into acting a certain way, while other times you act your way into a new way of thinking.

Leaning into Your Fear

The fight to push down our fear, stress, or anxiety can actually be counterproductive. If your heart is racing and your blood is pumping, trying to calm down is like "slamming on the brakes when a car is going 80 miles per hour. The vehicle still has momentum," psychologist Adam Grant explains. "It's easier to convert it into a different emotion—one that's equally intense, but propels us to step on the gas." This is why "calm down" is not a helpful way to talk to someone who is excited. In the history of human existence, has saying "calm down" ever gotten the person to calm down? Nope. Not once. You're better off trying to help them channel their energy productively.

It takes practice to get into this mindset, and that's why it's a separating skill. Studies have shown that "the ability to view stress as a challenge instead of a threat" is among the top three most relevant traits for success at work. We are not always in control of what is thrown at us, or even what our bodies are doing, but those who can jujitsu their stress, using its power as a "tailwind instead of a head-wind," end up succeeding more than those who can't.

Just Right

Now, while I'm arguing that some stress can be good, the key here is "some." There's a moderate amount that is optimal. Too much stress can paralyze and overwhelm you, but not enough, and you're just not engaged or activated. Alicia Clark taught me about something called the Yerkes-Dodson curve, named after the two scientists who discovered it. The curve shows the trajectory of how stress affects our performance. The middle—the top of the curve—is where we thrive. The medium amount of stress is ideal because that's where we are primed to use the energy in a way that drives us forward. Too little and we're bored and unmotivated; too much and we can't be productive.

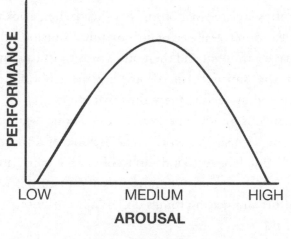

Yerkes-Dodson curve

Renaming Stress

The most important things we ever say are not spoken aloud. **They are what we tell ourselves.** Clark is a big proponent of watching what language we use and being aware of how that language affects our feelings and reactions. (Think back to how the Professor used the word "tension," not pressure.) "We have wiggle room in how we label our experience," she told me, "and the more neutral or positive we label it, the better we'll feel." Language plays a huge role in whether a feeling helps or hurts us. We may call it nervous energy, but that's just our labeling. It's not nervous energy; it's just energy! It is neutral, malleable into whatever we want it to be. We can choose to call it anticipation, butterflies, or panic. *It's up to us.* When we're leaning in to kiss a new mate or waiting for the tip-off of a big game, that energy is considered positive. What's the difference? As far as the body is concerned, not much. The key difference: *what we call it.*

Yale psychiatrist Andy Morgan, who studies US Special Forces, found that "how you frame something in your head had a great deal to do with your neurobiological response to it." Those who were able to reframe the threat in their mind as a challenge "had 23% fewer stress–related symptoms like headaches, backaches, and fatigue." Ideas don't really exist in our mind outside of language. We don't have a thought and then put words to it: **the two things happen at the same time**. Words are the embodiment of the thing, so we end up feeling the words that we use.

For instance, some people love to talk about "grinding things out," but when I hear the word *grind*, I think of a machine that's gone rusted. But I have friends and colleagues who embrace the word. They attach a positive emotion to it, equating it with giving their best effort and getting things done. Who's right?

Both of us!

The perception of stress is no different. I choose to view stress as pressure, and I believe that pressure is a privilege. I believe it to be the foundation of strength. I didn't always feel that way, which just goes to show how malleable it is for anyone. Now I welcome stress because it brings opportunity and growth.

Stage Fright

Harvard business professor Alison Wood Brooks has done studies that show how stress and anxiety change based on what we tell ourselves. It's a process she calls "anxiety reappraisal." Brooks's experiment sounds like a blast or a nightmare, depending on your perspective. She took a group of subjects with stage fright to a crowded karaoke bar and had them get up there and sing. All the subjects arrived nervous, as expected. But Brooks measured whether or not having them change their language—calling their nerves "excitement"—made any difference. She had one nervous group tell themselves over and over, "I am excited," and tested them against a control group who just sat with their nerves and their regular self-talk. The results were eye-opening. The decision to tell themselves that the feeling they were experiencing was excitement helped them convert the energy into something positive, even useful.

Worry, anxiety, stress: these are all just **signs that you care**. "If you aren't nervous," Steph Curry has said, "then it doesn't matter enough to you." I've spoken all over the world, in front of massive audiences, to iconic brands like American Express, Pepsi, Starbucks, and Under Armour. And yet I still get a little flutter of butterflies right before I take the stage for a speaking gig. There's no way to avoid or ignore it, so I try to reframe it: *I care about my work, and I care about this audience. I'm excited for the opportunity. Let's do this!*

Nowadays, that self-talk is just automatic for me. If you practice changing the language of your feelings, you'll be amazed how much the feeling changes too.

Stretching

A reporter once asked Muhammad Ali how many sit-ups he typically does in a workout. Ali's answer? Fifty. The reporter was taken aback, surprised that it wasn't more. A champion heavyweight boxer surely can do more, no? Ali explained it was fifty because he only started counting after *they started hurting*. The ones before the pain didn't even register to him. Muhammad Ali understood the power of stress.

Ali was right: the reps you do *after* the burning starts are the ones that matter. "Stress is absolutely mandated for growth," WNBA performance coach Stu Singer told me. "We have to get into a stressed state . . . you have to stress the muscle to failure and then it begins to grow." This is as true for the body as it is for the mind and the spirit. A person who has never experienced stress is a person who hasn't evolved. When you get pushed to your limit enough, and then over it, you create a new limit.

One of the first principles I learned as a young strength coach was the process of stress, recovery, and adaptation. SRA states that in order for a muscle to grow, it must be *appropriately* stressed first— followed by adequate time to recover—in order for it to adapt. This stress must exhaust the muscle's capacity to contract through the time under tension. If the resistance is too little, the stress will be insufficient. If the resistance is too much, the stress will cause injury. You need to stress the muscle with sufficient resistance so the individual muscle fibers break down. The fibers will repair during adequate rest and rebuild themselves stronger. If you repeat this sequence progressively and systematically over time, you will become stronger. In fact, nothing else is even possible! This SRA principle applies to all types of performance. **Get to the discomfort, because that's not the end of the work. It's the beginning.**

Action Steps

- **Watch Your Language:** Your impression of stress is changeable. It takes a shift in perspective and a change in language. What other words can you use to describe that feeling you get before a performance?

- **Self-Test:** Choose an activity that would normally make you nervous (public speaking, small talk with a stranger, blind date) and prepare for it in advance by using Alison Wood Brooks's method for the karaoke subjects. Repeat: *I am excited. I am excited.* Think of the energy inside of you as positive. Do a debrief afterward: **Did it help? In what way?**

- **Stress Benefit:** Next time you find yourself overloaded with stress or anxiety, take out a piece of paper and write down *three things* you can learn from what you're experiencing. It could be something about the triggers, the root problem, or even the strategy that helped alleviate it. Record it in real time.

PART II

PIVOT—Avoiding Stagnation

Our career paths (as well as our relationships and lives) are rarely on a straight trajectory. We have times when we're climbing and times when we're falling. Then there are the in-between times, when going through the motions, we feel stuck. This is **stagnation**, and no one is immune. The word *career* comes from the Latin word for "wheeled vehicle," which reminds us that the experience we have at work should have motion and a direction. Your career should never feel like it's stalled.

Stagnation comes from the mindset that you're doing "just fine" and are "good enough." This mentality deflates growth and development; it derails performance, stalls productivity, and undermines fulfillment. In some ways, it's worse than doing poorly because it's static. When things are bad, we tend to take action, or at least are motivated to do so. But feeling like things are okay is a sneaky trap. It means you're treading water instead of actually swimming.

The book you're holding is a product of my own efforts to break stagnation. Years ago, at the height of a successful career as a basketball performance coach, I felt my passion starting to wane. I'd hit a wall. While I still enjoyed working with players and teaching coaches, and my love for basketball will always be part of me, I was becoming less and less interested in the latest training exercises, techniques, and methods of on-the-court training. As this was happening, I found myself fascinated with principles of leadership, accountability, and communication, what I thought of as off-the-court training. The brief forays I'd had into that space tapped into something invigorating, and I wanted more.

After some deep self-reflection, I knew I needed to make a change, to shake things up. I felt in my bones that just going through the motions would be cheating the game I loved, the players and coaches I cared for, and myself. And I wouldn't allow that.

I decided to take the principles from the basketball performance world and apply them off the court. My desire was to inspire, empower, and teach. In essence, I would still be a performance coach, but I would coach a different part of performance, to a different audience, in a different way. The mere thought of taking on this new challenge, working on a new skill set, and serving a new audience relit my fire.

Part I was about performing in the moment. Part II will focus on your current day-to-day life. What is working? What is not? How can you make the next five years an improvement on the last five?

As I discussed in *Raise Your Game*, the first step toward improving yourself is self-awareness. You don't know where to go until you know where you've been; you don't know what to do next until you know where you're at. Because we are often blind to things right in front of us, it's helpful to use tools to find these answers.

Self-Evaluation Boxes

A simple graphic I've used is shown on page 93. The original exercise contained a list of adjectives (which can be found online). You select those from the list that are "known to self," separating the ones that are common knowledge and the ones that you keep to yourself. You then ask a few people you trust to choose a few

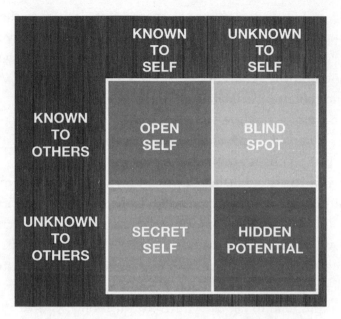

Self-Evaluation Boxes (known as the Johari Window)

adjectives from the list. Any adjectives you didn't include go into the "blind spot." The adjectives that are left over are your "hidden potential."

The Sagging Middle

In his book *When*, about the importance of timing, Daniel Pink writes about how beginnings and endings have their own natural momentum. However, it's the pesky midpoint that "numbs our interest and stalls our progress." When we arrive, we are full of energy and hope and anticipation. When we depart, we are emotional, nostalgic, and reflective. But the middle? It's harder to care. And it can be a slog—if you let it. Because the middle is where the work happens.

Pink emphasizes that it's in our hands whether these midpoints are **slumps** or **sparks**. If we hit the wall and see it as a sign to stop pushing, it'll likely be a slump. However, if it alerts us to the need for change, then it can be a spark. Picture a workday where you haven't been productive. Too much distraction, too much busywork, not enough focus. You look up and it's already 3:30 p.m. At this moment, there are two widely different responses.

The spark: *I already lost the whole day; I better get working!*

The slump: *I already lost the whole day, might as well take off early and call it a wash.*

Stagnation accumulates slowly until you look up and you feel like you've lost the drive you once had. It may initially rear its head as something minor like complacency, blaming others, or rationalizing low performance. Then it spreads. As we adapt to where we are in life, in a job, in a relationship, the excitement tends to fade. It's called the **hangover effect**—and it's real. Even the once most exciting jobs tend to fall back down to earth once you've adjusted to them.

When we lose our drive, it might seem like it's happening *to* us and there's no way to break it. But our helplessness is an illusion, a story we tell ourselves. **We can change that story.** "If you're bored, you've got to challenge yourself more and push yourself out of your comfort zone," writes renowned mental skills coach George Mumford. "We need to be wary of being on a plateau and not moving on to the next vista because we're daunted by the path it takes to get there." Mumford worked with Jordan and Kobe, and he understands that our approach to our work is more important than the work itself. We just have to find new pockets of inspiration during those times when we are sluggish, run down, and tired of the day-to-day.

So stagnation is real, and the issue is: What do we do about it? Riding it out is sometimes an option; it may go away. But once it becomes obvious that it's not, it's time to take action.

CHAPTER SIX

Take Control

Chris Brickley is one of the most sought-after trainers in the NBA, but he doesn't even think of himself as a *trainer*. He considers himself an *influencer*. That's because Brickley does so much more than work out players or put them through drills. Having worked with LeBron James, Russell Westbrook, James Harden, and CJ McCollum, Brickley has been called "the most in-demand basketball influencer in America" and "one of the most renowned names in the community."

Chris has a lean athletic frame and tattoo sleeves on both arms. He was a top high school player who went on to Northeastern (backing up future NBA player J.J. Barea) before becoming a walk-on under Rick Pitino at Louisville, which is *not* easy to do. After college he was the youngest assistant coach in Division I ball and then he ran player development for the New York Knicks. Fast-forward to today: Chris is on call 24/7 for his roster of all-star clients and living in the same Manhattan building as the gym he uses so "players know that I'm home and available at all hours to help them." When they're in New York, they know where to find him. By making himself so accessible, Brickley empowers his players to take control of their game during off-hours and off-season in a way that keeps them sharp.

Chris has forged strong relationships with many of the top players in the NBA (not to mention a few hip-hop stars looking to up their games). Players are drawn to his ability to connect on levels that go deeper than basketball. He's someone his clients can truly trust on and off the court. Even the most accomplished players in the world face the danger of hitting a wall, he told me, and they need someone who knows the proper way to respond to that feeling and *use* it. "During the season they sometimes are like 'Man, I can't make a shot,'" Chris told me. "It takes a different level of communication and having that trust and sitting down with the player during their dark time, when the media's killing them, and getting them to think positively." Because so much of the game is mental, Brickley adjusts his sessions to make sure he and the players address mindset as well as physicality.

"It's an entire lifestyle," he said regarding his role, "really being there for these players, genuinely, to help them get through what they need to get through." Whether that's injecting positivity, redirecting their focus, upping their motivation, or just helping them reconnect with their love of the game, Brickley understands that NBA players are still human beings. They deal with their own doubts, fears, and boredom. Again, these are among the most highly skilled and motivated people on the planet, and even they are not immune to feelings of stagnation. So why would we be any different?

Don't forget this age-old truth: **If nothing changes, nothing changes**. Change is a requirement of growth and development. Unfortunately, change is hard. It causes discomfort. We are all creatures of habit, and any time we alter our routine it makes us uneasy. This is unavoidable. So we need to change how we view discomfort. We need to embrace it. Becoming comfortable with being uncomfortable is among the most important skills you can develop. It's the difference maker.

Hands on the Wheel

Data suggests that a staggering 70 percent of the workday is un-productive. I can hear readers right now: *That's crazy. Not me. I'm always grinding away.* Maybe, but the numbers don't lie. If someone stopped you at any point during the day and asked what you were doing, it's far more likely that you'd find you were wasting time rather than making the most of it. Sure, some of it is meetings we don't want to be in, or conversations we got dragged into, but so much is within our power. We too often relinquish control of how we spend our time and energy, blaming our situation, superiors, colleagues, underlings, clients: everyone but ourselves.

Entrepreneur and CEO coach Jerry Colonna asks perhaps the most important question when it comes to stagnation: **"How are you complicit in creating the conditions of your life that you say you don't want?"** It really is the ultimate question. What can you control or change in your life that you are *choosing* not to? This is the organizing principle for chapter 6.

Everyone is given certain conditions and limitations, but focus-ing on those parameters does you little good. We tend to overem-phasize those because it allows us to pretend that our situations are not our fault. But the only way to boost yourself through a period of stagnation is to focus on **your role in the matter**. Recognize how you are stuck. Take agency in where you are. *Control the controllables.*

Routine

Let's start with our habits and routines. If we don't like where we are, the best place to start is with those things we do all the time, sometimes without even thinking. Studies have found that nearly **half of our day is routine**, a whopping figure when you think about it. We don't so much do our routines as *our routines do us.*

When it comes down to it, **we are our habits**. It takes anywhere from twenty-one to sixty-six days to instill a new habit, depending on its difficulty. But there is no habit you have that can't be wiped out if you truly want to. And there's no new habit that you couldn't instill if you put in the time and discipline.

I recently saw a post on social media about a guy who gets up at 4:30 a.m. every day to run before work. He shared the fact that his colleague was impressed, telling him, "Wow, I wish I had that motivation."

His response: "Motivation? This has nothing to do with motivation. It has to do with *discipline*. I'm not *motivated* to get out of bed before dawn more than the next person. I've strengthened this muscle called discipline." He trusts the systems in place. There's plenty of times you need that autopilot to take over. We can't be motivated every second and rarely at 4:30 a.m. That's why routines are important. *No one* is always in the mood.

Goals are fine, but they are given far too much stage. Look, there's nothing wrong with having goals. We all need a North Star, but the problem is that a goal doesn't really help us with the *how*. The methods we use to get there are way more important than the goal itself. The reason? As author James Clear explains, just about everyone has goals. The person who reaches the top of the mountain and the one who doesn't *both had the same goal*. But only one got there. Base camp is filled with people who have the same goals, but that won't tell you much about who is going to end up standing at the peak.

3 Steps to Change

- Awareness—that a change needs to be made
- Understanding—the impact this change will have
- Reconditioning—yourself to the new behavior, habit, or routine

Systems

My friend and colleague James Clear, entrepreneur and author of
Atomic Habits, told me that you're either driving your habits or
being driven by them: there is no third option. "People are building
habits all the time," he said. "Whether they're thinking about it
or not." Clear runs a place called the Habits Academy. Its tagline?
"Professionals are the architects of their habits. Amateurs are the
victims of their habits."

This is why Clear preaches the **power of systems**—which is
a framework to build, improve, and execute your habits. Think of
it as the scaffolding around the building. It's connected, unified,
and purposeful. Systems are also constantly updating, which make
them more useful than goals. Clear points out another issue with
goals: they are finite. You achieve them and then what? You need
something in place that is always growing. Systems are more like a
lifestyle, expanding as you evolve into the person you want to be.

The best way to get a habit to stick, Clear teaches, is by creating an identity that helps shape the desired behavior. "It's one
thing to say I'm the type of person who *wants* this," he writes.
"It's something very different to say I'm the type of person **who *is***
this. . . . You might start a habit because of motivation, but the only
reason you'll stick with one is that it becomes part of your identity."
It's the difference between telling yourself you're going to start ex-
ercising or you're going to become someone who exercises. Are
you going to stop smoking or become a nonsmoker?

Coasting

Stagnation is dangerous because it doesn't always look or feel like a
slump. It can be just getting by. Sports are a useful world to look at
because all professional players are sitting atop a highly coveted spot.

If they stagnate, they're gone. US Soccer gold medalist Lindsay Tarpley Snow told me that avoiding stagnation as a player came down to "knowing that if I wasn't willing to put the work in, that somebody else was. And that has always kept me motivated because those are things that I can control." Any professional athlete who thinks making the team is the end of the journey will find themselves out of a job.

Just knowing that competition is there, that you have something others want, can be a strong motivator in any workplace. Lindsay is retired from soccer, but in her new role as businesswoman, motivational speaker, and entrepreneur, she learns the same lessons from the market. If you're not producing, whether for your coach or your customers, someone else will gladly take your place. Getting there doesn't mean you automatically get to stay.

Smaller Pieces

You have to start somewhere, and starting with a small routine change is better than being too intimidated to start at all. I think plenty of people know that they have to make changes but get overwhelmed by the sheer size of such a project that they give up entirely. If this is you, recognize that you can only do one thing at a time. **Start with one**.

Personal trainer and life coach Keri Lynn Ford taught me the word *micro-commitments*, which is a great way to approach the mountain of change. If we assemble enough of these smaller actions, we can then merge those together to reach the larger goal (the macro-commitment). Micro-commitments are like taking steps into the pool—determining depth and temperature—rather than just diving in. "They allow us to establish that self-trust and foundation," Ford said. "That's the place on which we build upon . . . these new, healthy automatic patterns take route and those are the things you do without thinking about it."

It is much easier to replace a habit than to stop one cold. Keri called this process "pattern interrupt," and it's about hijacking your automatic tendencies. For instance, you can't just stop eating unhealthy; you have to start *eating healthy*. That takes micro-commitments: shopping for yourself, getting educated on nutrition, being conscious about what you buy, learning how to cook certain dishes, and keeping track of your meals.

Keri also taught me that changing negative habits requires that we reassess our "breadcrumb trail," which is how small habits lead to larger ones. An example of a breadcrumb trail would be going out on weeknights, which leads to drinking, which leads to a bad night's sleep, which leads to an unpleasant or wasted morning, which leads to decreased motivation. Things seem to unfold almost automatically, but that pattern can be reset.

If momentum is getting you stuck in your habits, you can use that same principle to create something positive. Set up your breadcrumbs toward what you want to achieve and who you want to be. Keri recommended that the person who wants to start going to the gym more should buy a backpack, fill it with workout clothes, and leave it by the front door so they'll be more likely to grab it when they leave the house. Lay down a series of micro-commitments and breadcrumbs to break your way out of stagnation.

Powerful Words

The two most common choices we make throughout the day are yes and no. So it's no coincidence that the key to breaking stagnation rests in these small but powerful words. Yes and no are where we exert our power and control over our lives. If we start saying yes to more things that can improve our situation and no to the energy vampires that drain us, we can make lasting change. We can transform from someone whom the day is happening to into someone who is in charge of his own day. We can easily get stuck in a pattern where we feel like we have to say yes to some things and are just in the habit of saying no to others. We also don't like to start saying no to something that we have said yes to for a long time. This makes us a victim of our own momentum.

I am so tired of the cliché that *winners never quit*. Yes they do! They just happen to quit the right things, or more accurately, they quit the things that aren't right for them. This seems like an obvious point that gets missed, but quitting isn't bad: it depends on what you're quitting! Sometimes improving involves **addition by subtraction**. You gain something by rejecting something else.

Let's use the relationship example. Would you consider it quitting to break up with someone who just wasn't right for you? Or are you giving yourself (and them) the opportunity to find someone more suitable? We need to start thinking of jobs and whole careers the same way. Author and entrepreneur Seth Godin has noted that high performers don't avoid quitting. In fact, they're good at it! They "quit fast and often when they detect that a plan is not the best fit, and do not feel bad about it." He suggests that "knowing when to quit is such a big strategic advantage that every single person, before undertaking an endeavor, should enumerate conditions under which they should quit."

Don't get too attached to a choice you made if you know in your heart that it is not working for you. By sticking with it, you are closing doors that you don't even know about. This is called **the legacy problem**, which is when "we would rather stand by a fix that is not working than start looking for one that does." This can be summed up by my least favorite answer: "Well, that's the way it's always been done."

We are also at the mercy of the **status quo bias**, which is a natural "aversion to change. . . . Even when confronted with compelling arguments for a fresh start, the human instinct is to stay put." This can be summed up as "sticking with the devil you know." Stagnation is so common because we all suffer from these tendencies toward inertia, even when they are clearly not working for us.

Taking the Chance

Twitter cofounder Evan Williams never let the fact that he was just a teenager in Nebraska affect his chances of success. In the early 1990s, before anyone knew what the internet even was, he made an instructional video on how to use this new World Wide Web and drove around trying to sell it to local businesses. A couple of years later he read a marketing magazine profile on a guy who impressed him. So he did what all young adults would do in that situation: he drove to meet the guy and ask for a job—*in Florida*.

Williams eventually made his way west to California, where he did some online writing, which he called "blogging." With a group of friends crunched in a small apartment, he helped launch the self-publishing revolution that would culminate in Twitter. The common denominator of each of these steps is that Williams *took control* of his current situation. It wasn't about landing in the right place at the right time with the right people. He created **all three of those things on his own**. It's not a coincidence Williams ended up developing a tool that would empower so many others around the world. He understood that by focusing on things in his control, every step of the way, he could expand not just his world but everyone else's.

Office Life

So far, we've addressed how stagnation is a result of losing control and being run by our habits. I know what some of you are thinking: *I hear you, but my boss won't let me advance, my manager won't let me play to my strengths, my job doesn't give me the chance!*

There's no doubt that those who work within a classic corporate structure can feel they have limitations to their success, but I want you to first consider these questions:

1. Are you sure about what those boundaries are? Have you tested them?

2. Have you maximized your growth within those boundaries?

3. Have you ever taken steps to expand them? What were they?

In the conventional nine-to-five life (more like eight to six-thirty these days), with corner offices and discrete titles, it's very easy to stagnate. If you're operating within a lockstep culture, you can lose control over your advancement. As an employee in these situations, you have to take the initiative. Try scheduling a meeting with your boss/manager and give them a version of this speech:

> I know I can add value to this team. I love this organization, I want to contribute, but I'm spinning my wheels in my current role. It doesn't light me up and I wonder if there's an opportunity for a different place for me here.

Approach it with humility and honesty, and any leader worth their salt is going to hear you out. And if not, then you know you tried and that it's time for more drastic changes.

Wherever you stand on the corporate ladder, think about the ways you can exercise your autonomy. As author and business consultant Marcus Buckingham puts it: "People don't find their ideal job—they *make* it." You can't sit around complaining about how or why your talents aren't being used. That's on you. "Sustained success comes only when we take what's unique about you and figure out how to make it *useful*," Buckingham explains. If we don't commit to this, no one else will care.

The rules are different for those of us who are our own boss, or who move from project to project. You may technically have more control over your day-to-day, but that doesn't mean you won't face periods of stagnation. Freelancers, distance workers, entrepreneurs, and others who aren't fenced in by the typical office boundaries still get stuck in their habits. Stagnation at these jobs is easier to do something about. You don't need permission to make a change or take a chance. If you're stagnating, it's only your fault, so the questions become: Do you have the courage? Do you want to stay with what's easy and safe? Or do you want to take things to a new level?

Traps

Instagram founders Mike Krieger and Kevin Systrom are not just role models because of their success. (The company is now worth $102 billion.) How they got there—and how they continue to view their work—is inspiring as well. They didn't let inertia or the comfort of wealth let them fall into the stagnation trap. Krieger told an interviewer that back when he was running Instagram day to day, at the start of every year he asked himself, "Is this still what I want to be learning?" The fact that Krieger framed it as this question around learning tells you a lot about him. His partner carries that same mindset. When the two decided it was time to move on from Instagram, Systrom said, "I wanted something hard. **I wanted to be bad at something again.** Maybe it won't be as big as Instagram, it probably won't be . . . but maybe it'll be just as fun to learn along the way." He wanted to be bad so he could relish the progress and self-discovery that comes from getting better.

It's not just talk. When Krieger and Systrom were first offered one *billion* dollars from Facebook for their eleven-person company, it wasn't the money that ultimately made them say yes. "The thing that mattered the most to us was that they wanted us to keep running it, independently, like we had been doing," Systrom said. For those who think these guys are full of it, feel free to look up the gigantic offers they *turned down* because it would have meant relinquishing full control of Instagram. They knew where their job happiness came from, and no amount of money was worth giving that up.

In Charge

I remember one time when I was playing basketball in middle school, I kept complaining about how slippery the court was, using it as an excuse for my poor play. Thankfully, my coach put me in check. "Yes, I'm aware the floor is not ideal," he said. "But the other nine players are dealing with it too. They're making adjustments and you're making excuses. It's a lot less slippery on the bench."

The lesson landed.

Today, I loathe complaining and work hard to avoid people who do it consistently. That doesn't mean I never do it. I'm human and fallible, but I am focused on expunging complaining as much as I can from my life.

Complaining is just another way of saying **"My problems aren't my fault."** It takes accountability off yourself, which is unacceptable. Whether something is or isn't your fault is irrelevant. What does that matter? Any time and energy spent assigning blame eats into what you should be doing: looking for the solution.

Most people complain about their job—their boss, their colleagues, their customers—but at the end of the day, **we are in charge of ourselves**. In her book *13 Things Mentally Strong People Don't Do*, social worker and clinical psychologist Amy Morin discusses the ways that we need to **awaken to our power**. In work and in our personal lives we are too often "giving away our power," whether that's through blame, complaining, being overrun by our emotions, or not taking responsibility for our circumstances.

One way we can take our power back is by reframing our language and how we think about our situation. Morin, who suffered the devastating back-to-back losses of her mother and her husband in her twenties, had to learn early on not to allow her negative feelings to dictate her life. After taking the necessary time to grieve, she made a choice to reenter life stronger. But stronger didn't mean blocking out her pain or ignoring her losses. As she put it, "I had to experience the pain while proactively helping myself heal." Morin teaches that mental strength is not about "suppressing our emotions." It's about allowing all of our feelings in so that we can understand what they are telling us.

Strength has too often been mistaken for coldness or a hardness, and Morin aims to upend that entire way of thinking. In our interview, she told me that instead of seeing mental strength as an issue of toughness, we should begin to see it as a means to "take positive action when taking [on] a challenge . . . thinking realistically and knowing you can manage your emotions." Mental strength means stepping forward, even into the unknown, with the kind of attitude and perspective that maximizes your success. It may look risky, but I'd argue that staying miserable where you are is an even bigger risk. We only go around once.

Player Empowerment Era

When I was a kid, even the greatest NBA players didn't have much say about which team they played for: Bird was a Celtic, Jordan was a Bull, Ewing was a Knick, and that's just how it was. There was no talk—ever—of Jordan joining Magic Johnson in Los Angeles to form a superteam. It was nonsensical.

But what has happened, especially since LeBron's decision to join the Miami Heat in 2010, is that the players have more autonomy over where they play, whom they play for, and whom they play with. It began with the stars, but it has trickled down to virtually all players, which has launched what is called the player empowerment era. For a high performer, as everyone in the NBA already is, stagnation and complacency are akin to death. Sports seasons are grueling, and the motivation to get out there every night is not automatic. Money and attention has nothing to do with it. The desire to take control of our situations is universal. The NBA's evolution can teach us something about our own agency.

In the summer of 2016, Kevin Durant shocked the basketball world by choosing to leave the Oklahoma City Thunder to join the Golden State Warriors. The Warriors had won the title the year before and had come within one game of winning it again that year. By joining a stacked team, the same stacked team that had just knocked his Thunder out of the playoffs, Durant made lots of basketball fans angry. I mean, people were *pissed*.

Because I had a prior relationship with KD, people reached out to ask what I thought of his choice. I commended him for taking control of his career and hashing out what was most important for him—not as a public figure, but as a person and a player. That was the decision he came to, and he didn't care what anyone else thought. He knew he'd get blistered in the media, but he didn't let that stop him. Twitter trolls don't have to live with Kevin's decisions. He does. After the criticism, Kevin leaned into this new role as a villain, even showing up to training camp with a Tupac tattoo. KD stayed independent, tapping into his passion and courage. I found his outspokenness to be admirable.

He did it again in 2019 when he went to the Brooklyn Nets (along with Kyrie Irving). Kevin approaches his career not as something that happens to him or is dictated by other people, much less people he doesn't even know. He's always asking: How can I keep evolving and growing? How can I become the best player I'm capable of being? He chose to immerse himself with other great players rather than worrying about if he was the dominant, alpha male.* "That required evolving as a player," he said, "being willing to adapt."

KD knows that stagnation is a toxic force, and he continues to push against it as one of the best basketball players on the planet. He had worked so hard toward winning that first championship, but when he got there (twice), he realized that couldn't be it. There had to be more. He told ESPN, "I realized that, like, my view on this game is really about development. Like, how good can I be? It's not about, let's go get this championship. I want to

---

* James Harden was traded to the Nets in early 2021, transforming it into a full-fledged superteam.

win to experience that stuff, but it's not the end-all, be-all of why I play the game." KD's story shows that stagnation is not an issue of where you are but rather *how you feel about where you are.* In his case, even winning can look like stagnation. So he created a better situation for himself.

On Call

In the modern era, individual athletes have raised training to a new level by upping their off-the-court routines. My former partner, superstar trainer Drew Hanlen, works with five of the top twenty players in the league, including Bradley Beal, Jayson Tatum, and Joel Embiid. Drew is as hands-on as it gets. It's not unusual for an NBA player to have an off shooting night and contact Drew, who will get on a plane, land in their city a few hours later, and meet them at the gym.

Besides passion for the game, Drew says the common denominator among the best is that they're not just "happy to be there. They crave improvement. And they are all coachable." He says that what appears to be a small gap at the highest level is actually a huge gap, separating all-stars from bench players from G League* players. So Drew's players not only tolerate criticism, they *crave* it. "They want to know when the smallest detail is off," he told me. "Most people at the height of their profession don't want that level of detailed coaching and critique," which is why the gap between the very good and the best is so massive.

During our interview, Drew told me the story of Bradley Beal's response to his recent career high of 60 points in a Wizards loss. When he contacted Drew, Beal's first response was disappointment at losing. The next thing Beale did was enumerate three things he could've done better. I could see even Drew was blown away by this. "Imagine the humility it takes for a player to score 60 points in

---

* This is essentially the NBA's minor leagues, previously called the D League.

a basketball game," and having this kind of self-reflective reaction, "instead of pushing it on his teammates, which he easily could've done." Like KD's championships, Beal's scoring a lot in a loss felt like a form of stagnation. It didn't align with his values and his goals.

The Dangers of Safe

Back in 1998, former Duke star and newbie broadcaster Jay Bilas got a call that would change his career forever. Having done mostly local, mid-major-level games, Jay was asked by ESPN to be the sideline reporter for the biggest rivalry in all of basketball: his alma mater against UNC, ranked #1 and #2 respectively at the time. The game was going to be called by Mr. College Basketball himself, Dick Vitale, and Jay was thrilled to have the opportunity.

A week before tip-off, the ESPN producers held a meeting to game-plan. Vitale was out of town for a speaking engagement, and while Jay was not required to attend, he decided to go anyway. He figured he might as well show up to demonstrate how seriously he was taking the job. The producers announced that Vitale recommended that the broadcast heavily feature UNC guard Shammond Williams, who Dicky V had been adamant was the game's player to watch. The lead producer asked Jay if he agreed. I think ninety-nine out of a hundred people in this situation would just agree. I mean, why contradict the most recognizable face in college basketball on your first day on the job?

But Jay did just that.

"Respectfully, I see things differently," Jay said. "I believe UNC forward Antawn Jamison is the player we should focus on. He is the most efficient and effective player in college basketball." As the rookie in the room, on the first question he was asked, Jay decided to offer insight that directly contradicted his Hall of Fame colleague's perspective. He also made a bold claim. Taken a bit by surprise, the producer asked for deeper clarification. Jay explained that "Jamison puts up incredible stats despite actually having the ball in his hands for very little time. I bet you Jamison doesn't have the ball in his hands for a full minute the entire game."

If true, this would be extremely rare. A college basketball game is forty minutes long. What player who is worth watching would only touch the ball for less than a minute? However, the producers were impressed with Jay's confidence and decided to go with it. They even assigned an intern to take a stopwatch and chart how long Jamison actually had the ball in his hands. In the game, UNC decimated Duke, 97 to 73. Jamison ended up with a career high 35 points (on 14-20 shooting) and pulling down 11 rebounds. He was indeed the player to watch.

And how long was the ball in his hands? Fifty-three seconds. Jamison *was* the most efficient and effective player in college basketball. But he wasn't the only one who made the most of that game: Jay Bilas did too. Jay seized his opportunity and cemented an important lesson he's carried ever since: never be afraid to show up and speak up.

The Deadly Comfort Zone

The reason I believe your comfort zone is actually a cage is because it keeps you stuck where you are. The year 2020 really put that idea to the test, as everyone's common routines and lifestyles were put on hold. During the pandemic lockdown, when I interviewed University of Maryland women's basketball coach (and national champion) Brenda Frese, she showed me why she is one of the greatest at what she does. Instead of dwelling on the year that was lost, she chose to view the period as an opportunity.

She spoke about how we can always benefit when we practice "getting comfortable with being uncomfortable," which should be the mantra for all high performers. Frese told me how she raised her children with this mindset and makes sure to impart it to her players as well. Just about everyone will do the work if it remains in their comfort zone. I'm not even sure I would call that work. The way to get ahead is to push up against the boundaries of what we're used to and what is easy.

In 2020 we were all at the mercy of the big picture, hindered in our daily life, and forced to change our thinking. Some came out of that period stronger because they were able to focus on what they could and developed the tools to take that mindset out into the world. Remember: the first step in capitalizing on an opportunity is the ability to *see the opportunity*.

Your Space

The physical world also plays a major role in feelings of stagnation: it controls our mood, our associations, and our self-talk. One of the most pivotal things you can do to break stagnation is to **change your environment**. As James Clear put it, "Environment is the invisible hand that shapes human behavior." This is both a blessing and a curse, depending on whether or not you take control. There are plenty of minor changes to our workspaces that can help break stagnation. With 27 percent of the workforce still remote as I write this—some of whom will never go back to traditional office life—we have the opportunity to completely redesign our work environment.

You want to be in an environment that routinizes what you're trying to do, a place where becoming your best self can happen. Anything you can do to enable that new self (and disable the old self) will be useful. Clear recommends that you tweak your environment to "increase friction" for your bad habits and "decrease friction" for the new ones you want to implement. He offered a seemingly simple tip: at the end of the day, leave a Post-It on your laptop of three key things you need to do the next time you are there. That simple list helps you preview the next day's work and hit the ground running when you return. Instead of opening your laptop and dithering before you get going, you are on a pre-set track.

Nobody works in a vacuum. "Think about the type of person you wish to become," organizational psychologist Stewart Friedman recommends. "If you can find a physical object that somehow represents the image of your future self, place it where you can see it regularly, such as your desk, [which] makes it prominent in your mind." I keep items from my kids to remind me what my priorities are and souvenirs and photos from my time with accomplished athletes to remind me where I've been and what I'm capable of.

You may not be conscious of everything you see, but "a third of your brain is devoted to processing vision." **Your brain is taking it all in.** Whether that's a messy inbox, a disorganized desk (which can lead to procrastination), or an inspirational poster or photograph (nature scenes work best), your work space affects your behavior. I can't stress this enough: just because you don't consciously notice it *doesn't mean it's not affecting you.*

Our environment can be streamlined for focus and productivity. For those intensive work projects, *Hyperfocus* author Chris Bailey recommends "distraction-free mode," which is addition by subtraction. By "removing every object of attention that's potentially more stimulating and attractive than what you intend to, you give your brain no choice but to work on that task." This is the idea behind internet blocking sites as well. Less is more.

If you work from home and have trouble with self-discipline, what can you add/delete to make your work area more conducive to focused work? If you're stuck in a dull cubicle, is there a way to bring some motivation to its half-walls? For those road warriors who spend times on planes, this can be done as well: What can you leave on a hotel night table or in your bag or even wear on your body that gives you a nudge to help perform your best?

Spaced Out

Our environment is filled with so many distractions that we don't even notice them anymore. Some of these distractions are things we carry with us. When was the last time you walked somewhere? And if you did, were you wearing headphones? Did you have your phone? How long since you went on a long ride without watching or listening to something? Steven Johnson, author of *Farsighted*, speculated that the reason the shower is still a place we come up with good ideas is simple: *we can't bring our phones into the shower.* Our minds wander in there in a way that they don't elsewhere.*

We all occupy the digital space as well as the physical space. Think about your computer: Are there items on it or that you have easy access to that are not conducive to high performance? Is there a game you can delete? Can you turn Wi-Fi off to achieve hyperfocus?

If you are stagnating, bored, or unfocused, it could be that "your environment opposes your goal," organizational psychologist Benjamin Hardy writes. Your environment is not neutral. It can either be a motor or a hurdle, depending on how intentional you are about it.

Change your physical environment: Switch up the items around you (e.g., throw out junk food, keep your phone out of your bedroom at night).

Change your mental environment: Alter what you feed your mind and what you choose to watch/read/listen to.

Change your emotional environment: Use demonstrated techniques for improving mood and perspective (e.g., meditation, exercises, cold shower).

Change your relational environment: Protect your inner circle or personal "board of directors" (see chapter 8).

---

* Sadly, I imagine it won't be long until they fully waterproof the iPhone.

Action Steps

- **Streamline:** Take a close look at your immediate work environment. Can you identify two to three things that are not conducive to high performance? Is there a way to remove/change them?

- **Start small:** James Clear taught me about his "2 minute rule" for building a new habit. Don't say *I want to start running*, begin with putting on the running shoes. Once that is internalized, then you can move on to the next thing on your way to building a new *identity* (e.g. as a runner).

- **Routinize:** Is there a routine you can implement at a key part of your day—when you wake up, first thing at your workspace, during a lunch break—that can help break your stagnation?

- **Yes and No:** Some of us get stuck in a pattern where we feel like we have to **say yes** to some things and are just in the habit of **saying no** others. *What might you discover with a new yes? What will you have time for with a new no?*

CHAPTER SEVEN

Reinvent

Reinvention is a provocative word, but it doesn't mean lighting fire to everything and watching it burn. It refers to a process of risk, adaptation, and evolution. It means giving yourself permission to change, to see your world through new eyes, to see *yourself* through new eyes. The thing I love about the verb *reinvent* is that it's a reminder that **you invented yourself the first time around**. And so, we are always in a position to create ourselves anew.

Changing Lanes

When Michael Jordan shocked the world in 1993 by retiring from basketball at the top of his (or anyone else's) game, everyone was stunned. When, a few months later, he showed up swinging a bat in a minor league baseball park in Alabama, we had to pick our jaws up off the floor. Jordan had lost his passion for basketball, and with the recent death of his father, he wanted to fulfill a childhood dream that he connected to his dad. But there was more to the story.

It's hard to conceive of now, but Jordan was only thirty at the time of his (first) retirement. As a successful multimillion-dollar athlete, he had to be pulled by something so strong that he would opt to travel on cramped buses, live in cheap motels, eat fast food, and rise early for batting practice, all to play in the minor leagues of a sport he had given up in high school. But for Jordan, who had spent years as the most watched and dissected human on the planet, the experience was invigorating.

In watching *The Last Dance*, I was surprised by how *not crazy* the decision seemed all these years later. What came through in Jordan's interviews about taking up baseball was how human his desire was, how normal even. He just wanted to be part of a team, one of the gang, and new to something again. Though he had reached the absolute pinnacle of his sport, it felt like stagnation to him. MJ's story shows how personal and relative these feelings truly are.

Steve Magness, a former competitive runner who transformed into a renowned author, speaker, and performance coach, knows a few things about reinvention. "Identities seem permanent, but they are in fact malleable," he wrote. "It may seem like we are stuck as who we are, but our stories can be altered." I understand this idea intimately, as I have gone through my own reinvention. The seed to my desire to be a keynote speaker was planted fifteen years ago when I was working the NBPA Top 100 Camp. The camp brought in a former NBA player and motivational speaker named Walter Bond to talk to the group. I was mesmerized by his brilliant storytelling, impactful lessons, and innate ability to get the audience to think, laugh, and feel. I remember thinking: one day, I want to do *that*.

Ten years later, I started to experience feelings of stagnation as a performance coach, and the thought that it might be time to try *that* eked its way into my consciousness. With each passing month, the voice got louder, until I knew I was ready to shift to a new stage. The reinvention wasn't smooth, and it's still not finished, but I don't know where I'd be if I hadn't taken that leap. The reinvention began with me simply listening to myself.

There was a learning curve as I figured out how to speak differently, adapt to new audiences, meet with and learn from various other motivational speakers, authors, and business leaders, and constantly improve my craft. I had long been a "basketball guy," but

I didn't let others, or even my own past, tell me who I was. That choice was up to me.

Not Your Grandfather's Career

Evolving as a person is an essential part of being alive. Simply put, if you're the same person you are at forty that you were at twenty, then you wasted twenty years. One of the issues in our society regarding career tracks is young men and women are still being asked to choose one before they have any real-world experience, which is crazy if you think about it.

Think about your current job or the industry in which you work. When did you choose it? *Did* you even choose it? Or did you more like fall into it? Are you in a field because it's what you majored in during college? Because your parents encouraged it? Because a friend knew someone who got you in the door? You were an inexperienced person making an inexperienced decision. It might have been perfect for the time, it might have been good for a while, or it might have been a disaster. Nevertheless, *you are not stuck with it now.*

A great metaphor for this is the writing process. Getting started often requires just putting something down on the page. It's not perfect—it might not even be good—but you need to start somewhere. ("You have to write it to fix it," my cowriter likes to say.) Once writers realize where the piece is going, they then go back and change the opening to reflect that. Even if that opening gets deleted entirely, it was important because it led to where things ended up. You are not stuck with where you started, and it wasn't a waste that you spent time there. Each step led to the next.

The concept of a career has evolved over the last thirty years. The world of clocking in at a single job for decades, a world that our grandparents took as a given, is not the only option anymore. We don't need to stay in the same place doing the same thing to feel like we've had a "steady career." Even the idea of working for a

single place is dated: the gig economy, freelancing, entrepreneur-
ship, flex time, and adult education all comprise the new reality.
People can create the careers they want, maybe even ones that don't
exist yet.

Searching for the job that fits your unique skill is a process of
self-discovery and self-invention that has lasting, positive effects.
The National Bureau of Economic Research found that "younger
workers who sample more occupations—viewing each successive
job hop as a chance to discover the kind of work they find most
satisfying—tend to be more financially successful in their thirties
and forties." There are plenty of practical ways to "play the field"
and explore what's out there. The search will give you a better sense
of your choices, and it will bring you satisfaction from *knowing* that
you have found something that fits you.

Out of Order

In the twenty-first century, we no longer have to follow the
conventional path. We don't have to hit the same benchmarks at
certain ages in a certain order anymore—whether that means in our
work, relationships, living situation, interests, skill set, or education.
In *Life Is in the Transitions*, author Bruce Feiler proclaims that "the
linear life is dead." We no longer have to go "through a series
of preordained life stages," but rather we can "experience life as
a complex swirl of celebrations, setbacks, triumphs, and rebirths
across the full span of our years." Your life can be lived any way
you choose.

The average person will move 11.7 times in his lifetime and is
twice as likely to live somewhere other than where he grew up.
Before he's fifty, he will have held twelve different jobs. Millennials (born between 1981 and 1996) will change jobs even more,
staying in a single job an average of four years and having four
different jobs in their first ten years out of college. A pre-pandemic
survey found 60 percent of millennials are "currently looking for

new employment opportunities."* The generations coming into the workforce will continue to be less and less attached to staying in the same job or position as long as previous ones had.

I'm not suggesting you hop from industry to industry, job to job, with no plan or purpose. Your résumé shouldn't look like a random sampling of careers as though you were eating at a buffet. However, it *should* **read like a story of a person evolving**, gaining experience, and honing new skills. Each stop along the way is an opportunity to develop, connect, and explore on the way to the right role for you.

My cowriter, Jon Sternfeld, went from teaching high school English to being a literary agent to being an editor at a publishing house to being an author, each move bringing him closer to where he inevitably ended up. He says he couldn't have just decided to be a writer at twenty-two and turned it into a successful career (even though that was his major in college). He had to go through a series of doors until he landed at the position that was right for him, discovering writing after passing through other steps. Those earlier jobs were necessary stepping stones that helped him hone his skills and learn about what he wanted to be. Like a video game, the final level wouldn't have revealed itself to him if he hadn't gone through all the other levels first.

The Scale

Reinvention isn't a single choice or action. It's a series of them. If you feel stagnant in your attempts to move upward in the same space, look for lateral moves, related roles to your current position, or nearby opportunities. Bruce Feiler suggests we should "cultivate our native curiosity about things adjacent to the work we do now." This might be staying late to work on a project out of your department, taking on a role for no extra pay, volunteering or

---

* We can imagine since the pandemic that this number has only gone up.

interning, or developing a relationship and assisting someone in a position you're curious about. Find ways to spend time with a person who does what you want to do and become "some combination of a bird of prey and a sponge—eagle-eyed for opportunities to learn and avid to absorb."

Another change from previous generations is that you no longer have to choose between stability and passion—if you're willing to do the work. Economist Adam Davidson's book *The Passion Economy* is about how the future of the workforce is not an "either/or" proposition but a "yes and" one. We can have a secure life *and* be passionate about our work. Previous generations couldn't conceive of this, but many of us can now find a way to be paid to do something we love. In fact, Davidson argues, "to succeed financially we must embrace our unique passions." It won't happen right out of the gate, and it won't be easy, but it is possible—if we're okay with taking risks.

Creating the Bridge

My friend Rick Simmons founded the telos institute, a global consulting firm that works with organizations on purpose, strategic change, and leadership. Rick is a brilliant guy with a big heart and an open mind. One of the many things he taught me is the concept of liminal space. Liminal space refers to the in-between, often uncomfortable place between where you are and where you are going. When you are standing at the threshold of the new thing but have not yet begun it, you are inside liminal space. Think of the trapeze artist: he can't reach the next bar until he lets go of the current one. Depending on the perspective, this might feel like falling, or it might feel like flying. When he's in the air, that's liminal space.

These can be scary but also revitalizing moments in our lives. They require risk because you can't get to the next bar without letting go of the current one. You have to let go. *You have to be okay in midair.* You have to reach out without a guarantee of safety.

I read an analogy that compares liminal space to a scene in *Indiana Jones and the Last Crusade*. In order to reach the Holy Grail and save his dying father, Indy has to cross a giant canyon by stepping out into nothingness before the bridge appears under his feet. It's the perfect metaphor, because the stepping has to come first; **the bridge only reveals itself after the first step is taken**. There are so many times in our lives—whether it's work, relationships, or experiences—that until we take that first step, the next step will not appear. It is our own action that *makes* it appear. If we sit around waiting, the bridge will never show up and we'll be stuck on the other side.

Opened Doors

Even with the right mindset and plan, there will be rejections and closed doors. There will be moments of insecurity when you know less than everyone around you: good. It means you're not playing it safe. It means you're stretching, which is how you grow. If you only like to be in situations where you are comfortable and experienced, then you will be doomed to stagnate.

When I spoke to retired soccer star Ben Olsen in 2020, he had a shaved head and thick beard that was just starting to grey at the bottom. (I didn't ask if this was his pandemic look or not.) He was nearly unrecognizable from the boyish guy who was once DC United's star player and had recently roamed the sideline as its head coach. At the time of our talk, his coaching career had just officially ended, and he was in a reflective mood. What stood out to me more than anything was Ben's honesty. Here was a man who rose to the top of a hugely competitive industry—twice—and he still spoke humbly about the ways he had failed and stagnated in his attempts at reinvention.

In 2009, when injuries brought an inevitable end to Ben's storied playing career for DC United, he was given the job as an assistant coach for the club he had given his life to. Six months later, when the head coach was fired, they gave Ben the job. He's the first to say that he fell into the position, that he hadn't really earned it, and that he was put there in an interim role to make the fans happy. (The team's president called Ben "the heart and soul of D.C. United.")

During our talk Ben admitted that the transition from player to coach was neither planned nor smooth. Whereas playing the sport he loved always came naturally, the coaching side of soccer was a struggle. "It was premature," he said about getting the head coaching job. "I was not ready. I wasn't even close to having the foundation or the infrastructure internally to be ready to coach grown men. I didn't know who I was as a leader."

To Olsen's credit, he put in the time to learn "who I was, what I was good at, what I wasn't, what I needed to surround myself with to make myself whole as a coach and as a leader." And it took years. Some people would take the fact that they were an MLS head coach (the youngest in league history) as proof that they had made it. But Ben took it as a challenge. He wanted to earn the job, *even though he already had it*. That's what makes him special.

It was not easy. Olsen's team hit rock bottom early on, garnering the worst record in league history, which was a wake-up call. "Getting punched every weekend, no light at the end of the tunnel" gave him a chance to reboot, reassess, and take inventory of who he was. Olsen used this public failure as an opportunity. He reached out to college, pro, and national coaches who had once guided him as a player. One of his mentors, Bruce Arena, taught him to "make sure he was taking the good out of this [losing] year." Our failures are always going to teach us, likely more than our successes do. If we let them.

Three years into the job, Olsen reinvented himself as a professional soccer coach. In 2014, a year after his last place finish, he was named Major League Soccer's Coach of the Year. He went on to hold the head coaching job for a remarkable ten years, a lifetime in professional sports, where coaches are often the first to get tossed when things go south. Olsen was recently named president of the Washington Spirit of the National Women's Soccer League, yet another reinvention. His attitude is to be as open-minded and as willing to put in the work as he was the last time around.

Learn on the Job

Writing a new story takes time. It means planning and taking steps to inch toward that new version of yourself. Make sure you leave time to plan for that reinvention, which won't happen overnight. Start building your exit ramp with the materials that you have available to you. Don't wait until it's too late. Quitting your current job or leaving your current situation—if you even get to that point—is the *last* thing you do, not the first.

1. Begin with the **end in mind**. Get clarity on where you want to end up and work backward from there.

2. **Talk and listen to people** who do what you want to do.

3. Don't think of yourself. Think of how you can **add value** to a person, organization, or customer base.

Groundwork

As the Chinese proverb says: *Dig your well before you're thirsty*. You need to be laying the groundwork for quite some time before you make any big leap. **Think about it: the best way to make a giant leap is to take a running start.** Daymond John was a waiter at Red Lobster when he began the fashion label FUBU. He wanted to buy a particularly stylish beanie, and his mother scolded him for choosing to pay twenty dollars for something he could make himself for two. The comment set off a lightbulb in John's head; that's exactly what he would do. Phil Knight was a CPA for years *after* he started what would become Nike, using his paychecks to fund his new venture. History is filled with these stories, and it's important that we don't cut ourselves loose from something stable based on nothing but a dream.

Golden State Warriors head coach Steve Kerr has one of the best jobs in sports, but he didn't just luck into it. He *made* it happen. After Kerr's playing career ended, he worked as a basketball analyst for NBA broadcasts. He was mapping out his post-playing career, taking the time to "talk to both coaches of the game I was covering and study the game film to prepare for the telecast," Kerr shared at a recent leadership event I hosted.

Kerr then had a stint as a general manager for the Phoenix Suns that was less than ideal, but it was an excellent learning experience. It gave him a sense of what he *did* want to be: a head coach. He returned to being an analyst to lay the groundwork for a coaching career, spending those years preparing for a future coaching job that was years away. He told us he got ready by "turning to not only my coaching mentors for advice but also reaching out to coaches who I didn't know," like Bill Parcells, Pete Carroll, and Jeff Van Gundy. Van Gundy, who's also been both coach and analyst, encouraged him to start thinking of ideas of how he would run his future team. "Start writing them down because by the time you're ready to interview for a job, you should be able to have all your thoughts down on paper," Van Gundy told him.

Kerr took the advice, telling us, "I literally spent two years on a document that I was going to present at a coaching interview." There were the expected thoughts on offenses and defenses, but there were also management, leadership, and culture issues that he really took the time to consider. Kerr went back to this document regularly, organizing his thoughts and plans so that by the time he interviewed for jobs, he didn't talk or think like a coaching candidate. He talked and thought like a coach! He had a firm understanding of what he wanted from his team before he even had a team "I studied for the test," he said jokingly.

Using the Kerr model, think about what future role you would love to have. In what ways can you prepare? Whom can you talk to? What planning can you do now so that you are ready for the opportunity when it comes.

Springboard

Jon Gordon is among the greatest reinvention success stories I know.

As a motivational coach who has worked with MLB, NBA, and NFL teams, college programs, major corporations, and schools across America, Gordon is an in-demand speaker. He is an infectious presence with the unique ability to light a fire under so many different types of people and organizations. One of the most inspiring things about Jon is that he didn't begin his career anywhere near his current role. He began as a restaurant owner and manager who had the desire and the calling to be something else.

I interviewed Gordon through Zoom during the 2020 lockdown, and his energy and enthusiasm just jumped through the screen. In a stark white room, he was perfectly centered in the frame in a simple black t-shirt. His books were carefully and evenly laid out—front covers showing—on a shelf behind him; a plain black baseball cap with the word CULTURE printed on it was draped over a tripod in the corner. Gordon is a prime example of how the right method and attitude can lead to successful reinvention. In his late thirties, Gordon decided that his purpose was to be writing and speaking, "to inspire and encourage others as the books I have read had inspired me."

As his restaurant began to make a profit (which is not easy, as anyone in the business can tell you), he used that money to seed his new career. He invested in himself. Gordon picked up the phone and cold-called a famous speaker who advised him to speak on what he was passionate about and "do it everywhere and anywhere. Do it for free if you have to. The more you do it, people will see you and want to book you, and the better you get, you'll get booked more and more." He did exactly that, speaking for free in order to gain a following, reputation, and experience. Gordon estimates that he gave around *eighty* free talks, building his brand and business along the way. Now he's a legend in the community and an inspiration to so many people who are looking to make a change in their lives but may just be too scared or lost to get started.

Old Tools

I know some readers are thinking: *I've been doing my job for twenty years. I'm a vice president of my company and make a six-figure income. What do you mean, I'm stagnating?* First of all, put your money away. It has nothing to do with satisfaction.

But maybe you've settled into a comfortable rhythm—you have become so used to your role, so stuck in the groove, that you're just on autopilot. And maybe you're afraid to admit it. You have to break the temptation to stay in **mental cruise control**, adjusting so well to the situation that you don't realize that you've stopped growing.

As a teenager, Steph Curry had always been a good shooter, but his father, NBA player Dell Curry, knew that as his son got older, his unorthodox form would be a problem. Steph shot from a very low release point, and his father knew it would be too easy for better or taller players to block his shot. So Steph spent the whole summer before his junior year in high school reteaching himself how to shoot, changing his release point. It was a process that required him to fail over and over again at the one thing he'd been phenomenal at.

Picture it: after years of being the best at something, a fifteen-year-old Steph Curry willingly changed how he did it because his future ceiling demanded it. This is one of the greatest leaving your comfort zone examples I can think of. Steph would not be who he is if he hadn't done this difficult and emotionally painful thing. He could've stayed with his low release point—which had been working so far—and still been the best shooter in his school. But he saw a bigger world and did the work in order to one day succeed there.

Karl Weick is a renowned organizational theorist who used the term "mindfulness" to describe the ability of organizations to organize themselves. In one of his studies, Weick learned that far too many firefighters were injured or killed when they unnecessarily held on to their tools while trying to escape a fire. In studying the phenomenon, he saw a principle that applied to everyone else. **We all have old tools and strategies that we hold on to long after they're useful, even to our own detriment.** "There are no tools that cannot be dropped, reimagined, or repurposed in order to navigate an unfamiliar challenge," Weick writes. "Even the most sacred tools. Even the tools so taken for granted they become invisible." Reinvention involves letting go of something that was once integral to your identity but no longer is. Whether it's fear or habit or old-fashioned laziness, you need to drop your old tools in order to free yourself up to move forward and pick up new ones.

Telling a Story

We all tell ourselves a story about who we are that, over time, hardens into place. This isn't always bad. It depends on the story and how you feel about it. For some it can be motivating, as Dr. Bob Rotella shares in his work with LeBron James. Early in his career, LeBron didn't want to just be successful; he had his eye on being the greatest of all time. Rotella understood the power of LeBron's self-narrative, so he didn't discourage it. "I knew that this desire to be the best would empower him," Rotella wrote. "The way he chose to think about himself would drive him. . . . That's why the way he saw himself was his most important talent." All of LeBron's actions, through the ups and downs, hero and villain periods, were driven by this desire to be known as the best.

But identity can work both ways. If the story of who you are is no longer working—if it's the source of your stagnation—then you need a new one. Author and entrepreneur James Altucher has crashed and burned so many times in his life—going from rich to broke and back again—that he has made a name for himself doing exactly that. In the documentary about his successes and failures, *Choose Yourself*, he encourages us to "not be imprisoned by the constant stories society tries to enslave us with. These are just stories that are told. I can choose not to believe them." Identity is the story we tell ourselves about who we are. What story are you still telling? How is it not serving you anymore? Which one do you want to be telling?

Business has plenty of examples of companies who benefitted by changing their story. If you had told me ten years ago that Burger King would be serving a veggie burger, *and it would be selling*, I'd think you were crazy, but the world changed so they changed. Mark Zuckerberg began Facebook as an exclusive social media site for the Ivy League. But the site took off when the original Facebook team rejected that plan so the company could become literally the opposite: the club that everyone was allowed into. Twitch, a video gaming app that is one of the hottest things on the planet right now, actually began as a twenty-four-hour live platform in which gaming was a very small component. Slack, the office text channel, wasn't originally meant for public use at all; it was invented by employees at a floundering online gaming company just so they could communicate with one another.

On the flipside, there are brands that blew it by holding too tightly to their story. Kodak (digital film), BlackBerry (smartphone), and Zune (music player) all owned their respective territories first, way before anyone else. They had more than enough of a head start to become the long-term leaders in their respective fields. But they refused to change as the times and customers demanded. They wouldn't let go of the old story, so customers let go of them.

The Role of Belief

Sometimes changing your story has more to do with what you believe to be true than what is actually true. After a string of losses, the 2019 St. Louis Blues decided to adopt the '80s pop song "Gloria" as their unofficial anthem. The team had been in last place in the NHL, yet for some reason, from the moment they started playing the song in the locker room, they *could not* lose. And with every win, they just kept feeding this belief that the song was leading them to victory. Soon enough, it was picked up by the local media, the fans, even the stadium public address system—all the way to the Stanley Cup championship. Did the song help? Did Laura Brannigan's explosive pop melody have special powers? Well, all that matters is that the team believed it did. *So it did.*

Sports, especially baseball, are filled with strange superstitions: from what color shirt players wear on certain days, to pregame meals (Wade Boggs ate chicken for years), to the number of times they hit their cleats with the bat and in what order. You don't have to believe in magic to see that the power of these rituals comes not from any supernatural force but rather from the *belief that they work.* They offer a feeling of control over one's environment.

Believing in something makes it more likely to happen—because you unconsciously make it so.

Becoming an Adjective

I'm a huge fan of comedy, especially stand-up, which I often study for my presentations. I consider stand-up the epitome of public speaking. No music. No slides. Just the comedian, microphone, and a crowd. The comedian must move the audience—to laugh, to think, to anticipate—with nothing more than the spoken word. He has one goal—to make a group of strangers (often intoxicated, sometimes surly) who have paid money and are expecting to laugh, laugh. I study comedians verbally (tone, inflection, pace, pauses, volume, rhythm) and nonverbally (facial expression, hand gestures, physicality, blocking/staging). My goal is not to tell jokes, but to master my craft and emulate the most effective techniques for affecting the mental and emotional state of an audience.

In the early 1980s Judd Apatow was a funny kid with a love for comedy. He had grown up studying the greats, even interviewing a few as a high school kid in Long Island. Young Apatow was witty enough to write some killer jokes for professional comics. But when he got up onstage himself, it was just . . . crickets. His love for comedy did not make him a great stand-up comedian. I'm sure it was a brutal realization for him as a young man. He had dreamed, done all the work, met the masters, and yet, it wasn't going to happen.

But instead of giving up, Apatow reinvented himself. After years of hustling through television writers' rooms, he got the chance to create his own television show—*Freaks and Geeks*. It was a cult classic boasting a murderers' row of young talent (James Franco, Jason Segel, Seth Rogen) that was canceled after one season; then he made another one, *Undeclared*, that was canceled after two. Again, Apatow didn't get dejected. He adapted to a yet another form and tried something new: movies.

That's where he found his flow, with a string of hugely successful films he either directed or produced: *The 40-Year-Old Virgin*, *Knocked Up*, *Superbad*, *Bridesmaids*. Now among the most influential people in Hollywood, Apatow has helmed some of this era's biggest comedies, has discovered a new class of stars, and almost single-handedly popularized the "bromance." By changing his own story, he has altered the course of comedy. Apatow has so many imitators that he's even become an adjective: *Apatovian*. (FYI: I would love to become an adjective: Steinian? Steinish?)

Had Apatow begun his career by planning on making ground-breaking comedy films that changed the course of movies, it's unlikely he would have succeeded. He had to get there organically by following his passion, studying the greats, doing the work, and learning from his failures. It happened for Apatow because of his talent, of course, but also because **he was open to the power of reinvention**. "You can't connect the dots looking forward," Steve Jobs said in his famous commencement speech to Stanford in 2005. "You can only connect them looking backwards. So you have to trust that the dots will somehow connect in your future. . . . This approach has never let me down, and it has made all the difference in my life."

Action Steps

- NBA head coach Tom Thibodeau once said, "Before we adjust anything, we have to first make sure we are doing it the way we have taught it." Before you go all in on reinventing, be sure you're maximizing the current game plan.

- Think of an aspect of your job you excel at and/or enjoy. Is there a way to **follow that thread** into a new position or a new job entirely?

- **Write a New Story:** As an exercise, tell a new story about yourself that will happen over the next five or ten years. It can be short, but write it out and keep it somewhere where you can check in on it regularly.

- For those who are looking to strike out on their own but don't know where to start, **find a problem** in the world. "The intersection of personal passion and problem solving is where good ideas are born and lasting businesses are built," says radio producer Guy Raz.

CHAPTER EIGHT

Reach Out

At an event I was speaking at in Utah, I met Larry Yatch, a veteran Navy SEAL who once worked in the Middle East. After a decade with the elite group, an injury led to his retirement, and now he speaks as a leadership consultant. We spoke to the same audience, and he had some valuable lessons from his time in the field with the highest stakes possible. One point he shared that stuck out was how aligned SEAL members have to be with one another. The planning must be synchronized down to the millimeter and millisecond, a kind of precision that most people can't conceive of. "Success is fully dependent on your ability to coordinate action with other people," he said of his time as a SEAL. In those situations, it's literally life and death. Though we are not facing those same dangers, our success and failures are also aligned with how well we work within the context of our teams. In this chapter, I'll cover ways to make use of your teams and how they can break your periods of stagnation.

The Charity Stripe

If you've ever watched an NBA game, you've noticed something that happens when a player goes to the free throw line to shoot foul shots. After the first shot, hit or miss, the teammates who are lined up to rebound will usually step into the paint and give the shooter a fist bump or low five. This ritualistic moment is a perfectly distilled version of the team concept.

Think about it: being at the foul line—especially in a high-stakes, high-pressure situation—is an isolating experience. The player is alone in a way he never is at any other point in the game. The foul line is "a place where the weight of isolation is enough to bring you down." All eyes are on him. It's a "free" shot, as in it's not being defended, so people think it's easier than it is. The fans are specifically cheering or booing (or distracting) just that one player. At this moment, the ritual of physically connecting with your teammate sends a powerful message: *I got you.*

I love the simplicity of this gesture and think it can be applied elsewhere. **Are there ways you can do this for your teammates when they're in a solitary or stressful situation?** It is a powerful moment of connection that helps both the receiver and the giver.

Working Alone

In the twenty-first century, it's easy to feel isolated at work. Depending on your situation, you might have limited interaction with colleagues, clients, superiors, and subordinates. You may communicate through email, talk through screens, and have lunch every day in front of your computer. All of this might be convenient, but it can also be uninspiring, lonely, and draining.

The coronavirus pandemic brought this issue to the forefront of most of our lives. The extended lockdown triggered a period where just about everyone had to work from home, but it also led to a larger discussion of what an office even is and what it should look like. I believe this period will prove to have a permanent impact on how and where people work.

With the rise of video conferencing, collaborative documents, open-source computing, and the work-from-home (WFH) culture, millions of workers now view themselves as independent satellites operating on their own. Though it has brought conveniences, this culture of distance work is driving us further apart.

It has happened socially as well. We might have more "friends" online, but how many actual friends do we have? Sociologists found that we tend to view other people online as "objects" instead of human beings. This obviously hurts our ability to feel empathy and is a reason why online comments can be so cruel. We may be more "connected" in a social media sense, but are we connected to others on an emotional and spiritual level? Is shooting an email to someone in your department as impactful as sitting down with him for five minutes? Don't we need that physical connection?

Working alone, you may go the whole day without seeing anyone, missing out on the chance interactions that make today different from yesterday. Offices bring opportunities to be with close colleagues but also to interact spontaneously with people, grabbing coffee in the break room, getting out of your car in the parking lot, or stopping to chat in the hallways, so-called functional inconveniences. Steve Jobs famously put all the bathrooms for the entire Pixar company in the ground floor atrium to encourage "arbitrary collisions of people" from different departments, because he believed it encouraged creativity.

Our interactions at work are not just a side effect (or nuisance) of being in an office. They're a benefit. In a study of the fifty best places to work in the United States, there was only one feature that was shared by every organization in the top fifty: "quality relationships." Across all industries, the thing that makes the most people happy about their workplace is the connections with the people there. Think about your favorite jobs you've ever had: Weren't the people part of what made it so great?

There's also evidence that these relationships help improve our job satisfaction and keep us engaged in our work, both of which improve performance. We shouldn't trade that all away just because we can. With the world moving toward automation, digitization, and AI, connected relationships are more valuable than they've ever been. Don't sell them short.

Your Health

"Social connection is such a basic feature of human experience that when we are deprived of it, we suffer," writes author and scientist Leonard Mlodinow. Mlodinow explains that "social pain"—hurt feelings—affects the same part of the brain that physical pain does. When you say someone "hurt your feelings"—you are not being metaphorical. Your body actually feels pain in the same way!

In addition, the dangers of lacking social connection are significant, comparable with "the effects of cigarette smoking, high blood pressure, obesity, and lack of physical activity." Those who reported fewer social connections than their peers were more likely to die prematurely, and isolation has been tied to depression and anxiety, to sickness and weakened immune systems, to obesity, and to shorter life spans.

It's not just the presence of other people that benefits us; other people make us feel useful. A Canadian study a few years back gave a group of senior citizens with high blood pressure forty dollars to spend each week and then tracked the effect their choices had on their blood pressure. The results were staggering. After only a few weeks, the groups who chose to use their money on *someone else* noticeably lowered their blood pressure compared with those who bought an item for themselves. The health improvement wasn't minor, either; it was as comparably positive as a change in diet! Other studies have found that giving money away improves mood more than spending on oneself (it's called a "helper's high") and those who spend time doing volunteer work live longer.

One of the most famous (and longest) studies on the positive effects of social relationships, the Grant Study, is currently directed by Harvard psychiatrist Robert Waldinger. The study began following a group of students in the middle of the Great Depression and tracked them throughout their lives.* Waldinger's conclusions? Our mental, physical, emotional, and spiritual health are all tightly wrapped up in our relationships, far more than we realize, *more so than even our physical choices.* Building a network of people who care about you, inspire you, and make you feel valuable isn't a luxury. It's a life-and-death issue.

Your Circle

It's strange how accumulating "friends" and "followers" has become a numbers game. Our worth is now measured by how many online connections we have, though outside of networking I'm not sure how beneficial this really is. Your inner circle should remain manageably small, which allows for deeper and more meaningful connections. Just like you need to be conscious of what you put in your body, you need to be careful of who you let into your inner circle. There's only so much time and energy we have, and if we're spread too thin in our relationships, we're not benefitting from any of them. It's like multitasking where you're doing so much that you're doing nothing: are you "friends" online with two hundred people but actual friends with none?

Lastly, are you keeping a friend out of habit? If you have decided that someone in your life is a drag on you, don't just resent them or talk about them behind their back. Do something about it. In *Harvard Business Review*, Scott Gerber recommends being proactive: "Start by making a plan to lessen your time investment in people . . . that make unrewarding demands on you until you can fully withdraw." Your social network should be like a garden— cultivate positive growth and weed out the dead plants. We all have relationships that are dying on the vine, and it could serve both of you if you just clip those suckers off.

---

* A young John F. Kennedy was one of the subjects.

It may sound harsh but it'll give both of you the time and energy for something—and someone—new. We think of romantic relationships as the type that we consciously begin and end, while friendships are the relationships that start and end more subtly. But there's no reason that this should be true! I'm not suggesting you have to explicitly break up with a friend, but you can make a conscious decision to pull back from the friendship and find a respectful way to do so. Best to clear the brush so new things can grow in its place.

Rubbing Off

In *The Buddha and The Badass: The Secret Spiritual Art of Succeeding at Work*, Vishen Lakhiani recommends to "align yourself with the people you need to make your vision a reality." He calls this "attracting your allies." While it's important to be able to lean on others when in need, the people in your life should also bring out and reinforce the best parts of you, the parts you're trying to cultivate. If you feel like you're stagnating, maybe your social group or work colleagues are contributing to the inertia. It's vital that we form stronger connections with people who encourage the version of ourselves we want to be.

As James Clear put it, "Join a group or tribe where the desired behavior is the normal behavior." Find a circle that challenges you, because you are going to absorb and reflect the behavior of those you spend time with. You will do it purposefully, out of a desire to belong, and unconsciously, out of habit. From friends, we pick up patterns of speech, moods, beliefs, behaviors, and other friends. Think about the people outside your family whom you spend the most time with. What behaviors do they each bring out in you? Are these desirable or undesirable? Do they lead to the best version of yourself? Asking these questions will ultimately allow you to be more diligent about with whom you spend time.

My former business partner, trainer Drew Hanlen, told me that everyone should "find a couple of people who push you, challenge you, encourage you and are there for you at all times—good and bad." He recommends surrounding yourself with people who "will also tell you the real." Drew works with some of the most skilled and visible ballplayers on the planet, and he's seen both the benefits and the drawbacks of inner circles. Who can give you that extra boost? Who is just another weight on your stagnation?

Accountability

One of the biggest benefits of being part of a team is having a built-in accountability system. Your team can help you see your blind spots, hold you to a high standard, and call you out. These are people who care about you enough to tell you what you need to hear even when it's not something you *want* to hear. Don't insulate yourself away from those who tell you the truth. "Every billionaire suffers from the same problem," wrote entrepreneur and inventor Marc Andreessen. "Nobody around them ever says, 'Hey, that stupid idea you just had is really stupid.'"

There are athletes, businessmen, and artists I once looked up to who clearly bought into their own hype and failed to improve, likely because no one ever challenged them. This is the death knell for any career. It is also a cautionary tale for those who surround themselves with yes-men who function like an insulated padding around their lives. They never have to hear a critique or receive a new idea; they feel protected but are actually signing up for a lifetime of stagnation.

Our friends and coworkers can also operate as mirrors. UCLA Bruins basketball coach Cori Close advises that you should "ask a lot of questions of the people around you [which] will give you a window into your wiring." The people who spend the most time with you have insights into your behavior that can prove valuable. In some ways, they know you better than you know yourself.

Your friends or colleagues can reinforce the best version of you by becoming accountability partners. If you're trying to develop a new, positive habit, let them know about it, respectfully enlist them in the process, a strategy that has been shown to work. Offer to do the same for them. Remember: holding someone accountable is not something you do *to* them; it's something you do *for* them. It is a form of love.

> **Want a powerful way to hold someone accountable?**
> Initiate the conversation by saying, "I believe in you and I know you are better than what you are showing." This approach will increase the chance of their being open to receiving your feedback in a positive way.

Contagious

It is essential that you protect your mental and emotional currency the same way you would protect your family and property. Put a fence around yourself and don't let anyone in who—intentionally or not—pollutes you, endangers you, or weakens you.

We are affected by those in our circle far more than we realize. Social psychologists James A. Fowler and Nicholas Christakis determined that "if you became happier, any friend within a one-mile radius would be 63 percent more likely to also become happier." This principle especially holds true for negative feelings, which are harder to shake than positive ones. We are influenced by the emotions of our friends and colleagues on even physiological levels. Stressed-out people release a smell that others unconsciously pick up on, which contributes to their own anxiety. "We can also pick up negativity, stress, apathy like second hand smoke," writes Shawn Achor, "simply observing someone who is stressed—especially a coworker or family member."

One reason the effects of these "contagious" people in our circle are so insidious is that *we don't even notice them*. We take in their behavior like the air we breathe. Emotional contagion theory suggests that you align with people in your life by mirroring their tone, body posture, and moods. And because they are imitating you right back, the two of you fall into a feedback loop that is hard to break. We all know that we're more likely to laugh or yawn if we see someone do it, but the same is true for all the other behaviors as well. It's happening on a level we don't even notice, and that's how it gets inside us.

Mirrors

Of course, we can't always control whom we work with. However, it's still important to be conscious of their impact and, when we can, make adjustments. Daniel Goleman, the psychologist who popularized the idea of emotional intelligence, found that "in seventy work teams across diverse industries . . . members who sat in meetings together ended up sharing moods—either good or bad—within two hours." Most amazingly, this shared mood was not connected to the subject of the meeting at all! It was just the mood they brought into the room; colleagues naturally imitated one another's emotional states.

Goleman found examples of this dynamic in the sports world, too. "Quite apart from the ups and downs of a team's standing," he wrote, a team's "players tend to synchronize their moods over a period of days and weeks." A team's mood will go up and down in ways that aren't related to wins and losses! We think satisfaction comes from victory, and that may be true, but it goes the other way as well: victory is a result of teammates sharing positive connections.

The truly great players are also looking for teammates (and opponents!) who bring out the best in them. They know that rising to the next level isn't something you do on your own.

Action Steps

- **Your Crowd:** "Surround yourself with people who remind you of the future, not the past," Benjamin Hardy recommends. Your friends/acquaintances are an integral part of your environment. Make a list of those who you feel add value to your life. If someone in your life is *not* on that list, can you find ways to minimize your association with him?

- **Social Media Audit:** Look at your follows on social media; these people are a part of your mental environment. Do they fill your bucket with inspirational, educational, helpful, and meaningful content? Or do they post gossip, negative opinions, and useless garbage? Unfollow and unfriend anyone who isn't adding value to your mindset.

CHAPTER NINE

Expand (Your Circle and Your World)

There's nothing wrong with the familiar, but if your social circle is made up exclusively of the same people for going on ten, twenty years, it could be contributing to your stagnation. It's vital that your inner circle is just as committed to consistent growth and development as you are. If you keep pushing to move forward in all aspects of your life and your friends don't, those relationships may be holding you back in ways you don't even notice.

Just maybe . . .

- You're playing a role for those friends because that's what you're all used to.

- You're afraid to try new things because of their judgment.

- You revert to the self you were when you first met them. (Sometimes we grow along with old friends, but sometimes we don't.)

- Your similarities or shared experience brought you together, but that was a long time ago. Are you the same people you were when the two of you met?

Circles and Mirrors

It is common for us to seek out versions of ourselves. Early in life, and again in new situations, this is one of our main drives: **Who is like me? How can I connect with them?** But our social lives can become their own kind of echo chambers. As organizational psychologist Tanya Menon explains, "When we're in trouble, when we need new ideas, when we need new jobs, when we need new resources—this is when we really pay a price for living in a clique." Sometimes old means tried and true. Sometimes it just means tired and done.

The comfort zone of our social circles can be confining. It doesn't mean there's something wrong with our friends or that we need to cut them all out. But social connections are an area for growth that gets neglected. "The modern world gives us more op-portunities than ever to forge relationships with people who do not look, act, or think the same way that we do," writes economist Tim Harford. Yet what do we do? "We keep our social networks nice and tidy by seeking out people just like us."

Think about the way the online world sorts itself into like-minded groups and belief systems. Just having access to new people and ideas isn't enough, especially when all we look for is mirrors. This is why seeking out diversity—of ethnicity, race, age, gender, thoughts, and perspectives—is so essential.

Ties

It's common to resist the introduction of new faces in our lives because they don't seem like "our kind of people." But that's exactly why we should let them in. We have no idea what the relationship might offer, and that's a good thing! There are tangible and intangible gains from injecting new life into our social circles. One example of a tangible gain is that most people get their jobs through what are called "weak ties," like friends of friends or indirect connections. The reason? Our strong ties, those we're closest to, know the same people we do and have heard about the same opportunities we have. People we know less well are more likely to hear about something we haven't or know someone we don't. So new people increase our opportunities. However, there are the less tangible gains: new people introduce us to fresh ideas, novel experiences, and—you guessed it—yet more people.

But don't take my word for it.

Durant's Circle

When I interviewed Kevin Durant, he spoke candidly about how valuable his inner circle was to the person and player he has become. And that's not because it is made up of people who always make him comfortable or are just like him. That's not what he's looking for. KD makes a point of associating with "people that look at life from a different perspective, who've been through things, who've experienced different situations in life with different people," he told me. "I enjoy people who have traveled the world. I want to hear those perspectives as well."

Plenty of people in KD's position might (and do) keep themselves in a bubble in order to feed their ego, but Kevin is a real searcher. He saw getting to the NBA as the start of a journey, and he continues to treat it as such. He doesn't want his world to remain small because he knows that leads to stagnation, which will ultimately be a developmental hindrance, a mood destroyer, and a career killer.

I can't help but think of that scene in *The Last Dance* where Michael Jordan is stuck in a hotel room watching TV, with no one to talk to but his bodyguard. This was what his life was like on the road. His world had to remain tight and controlled, and though it wasn't really his fault, I'm sure his mood suffered. (How much gambling with his security guards could he really do?) Now, MJ was MJ, and that was a different time, but it's an instructive comparison. Kevin makes an intentional effort to keep his world fresh and diverse, which makes him such a fascinating figure. He's looking to be informed, surprised, and challenged. It's what makes him not just an impressive athlete, but an impressive person.

There are plenty of people who "make it" and then spend all their time in their comfortable bubble. But the true greats know they gain from pushing themselves out of their comfort zones, as performers and as people.

Echo Chambers

When we spend time in the same groups, we also fall prey to dangerous habits like **groupthink**. This is a state in which individuals stop thinking for themselves and care more about being agreeable than useful. Then all the differences collapse and flatten so "group members unknowingly end up talking about information they share rather than information that is unique to each of them." Groupthink happens when the individuals are too intimidated to be themselves or express dissent. When I first started coaching, I remember hearing the maxim "If everyone on this team is thinking the same, then some of them aren't actually thinking." That's groupthink.

It is not only dangerous for the individual, but it's also ineffective for the group. It's actually been shown that the best way to solve problems in a group isn't through brainstorming at all: it's through disagreeing! That's right: dissent and debate yield more creativity and productivity than straight brainstorming sessions. This is why before the military or CIA approves an operation, leaders bring in a "red team," which is a group that tries to poke holes in the plan and see what hasn't been thought of. This built-in "devil's advocate" strengthens the mission because it ensures groupthink didn't take hold during the planning. As former champion poker player and consultant Annie Duke puts it: "We already know why we're right. What we need help with is why we are wrong."

Now, this doesn't mean you should be argumentative with colleagues for no reason, but it does mean you should be open to contrasting opinions and perspectives. That's where the good ideas come from. Scientific breakthroughs happen less often in the laboratory than we'd think. I don't know about you, but I always pictured the great scientific discoveries happening in a sterile white room and with someone in a lab coat way smarter than me popping up from the microscope and saying "Aha!"

While I'm sure this does happen, it's less common than we assume. The highest percentage of these discoveries actually happen *in meetings*, specifically where researchers have to defend their work. Across virtually all scientific fields, discoveries have come about not through solitary lab work but when "groups of researchers would gather around a desk and talk through their work . . . because they were forced to respond to challenges and critiques from their fellow researchers." Because science is about getting to the truth and less about agreeing or appeasing, defending your work is baked into the process. (It is why science moves faster than other disciplines, like, say, politics.) The friction of various ideas and viewpoints creates a spark—a chemical reaction, if you will—and that spark itself leads to discovery.

Another thing we have to avoid is getting trapped in our own "filter bubble." A filter bubble once referred to the information and news we consumed online, but it can now mean all of our interactions and exposure. We only meet others like us, read what we agree with, and hear opinions that match our own. The longer we stay in our respective filter bubbles, the harder it is to break out of them and the more likely we're going to stagnate. We should make room for novelty in our lives, even if that appears in the guise of something uncomfortable. Remember that it's the stretching that makes us grow.

Curveballs

Entrepreneur and best-selling author Josh Linkner says it's important for us to be "heads down" and focused in our work, but not to forget to have "heads up" time when we are aware of the world around us, because we may get inspiration from places we wouldn't normally look.

In his book *Range*, journalist David Epstein splits knowledge workers into two groups: the generalists, who have a firm understanding of a variety of subjects, and the specialists, who *only* know their subject to the exclusion of all else. Wherever he looked, he found that it's the generalists who end up being more productive, happy, and creative. The problem is that "experts can become so narrow-minded that they actually get worse with experience, even while becoming more confident—a dangerous combination."

Range is filled with fascinating examples of how only knowing one thing well can be stagnating and how having your feet in other areas can be inspiring. Epstein includes a study of accountants that showed that when a new tax law was introduced into the code, it was the *veterans* who struggled with it, while the newcomers were able to adapt. Why? The ones with more experience were too rigid in their thinking, almost stuck in place. They couldn't adapt the new idea into their present framework. The same thing happened to experienced bridge players who had trouble when a new rule was introduced to the card game they knew so well. We sink so deep into the mud of our specialty that we can't even move around anymore. One way to break out of this is to put our toes into fields where we are newcomers, which might help build skills in our own field. Spreading into new areas—ones where we are not the alpha—helps us grow intellectually and emotionally. It reminds us that there is always more to know.

I've delivered keynotes, workshops, and team trainings in health, medicine, business, hospitality, academics, tech, sports—and have gained from each of those disciplines. The more we drop ourselves into new worlds, expand where we're willing to learn from, the less likely we'll get stuck. In order to polish my speaking game, I study both stand-up comedy and hip-hop music to improve my timing, tempo, and stage presence. If I only studied other motivational speakers, I'd just be bouncing around my own filter bubble.

The best coaches and players don't just study their own sport. Eric Musselman, who has held nearly twenty different basketball coaching jobs, told me he uses videos of shortstops to teach his players reaction time, of tennis players to teach lateral footwork, of wide receivers to teach precision cutting. His openness to take from anywhere is what makes him such an asset. He told me that back when he was an assistant, he would talk to his mother a good deal about his work and whether he was satisfied where he was. When he felt like it might be time to make a change, she'd ask him, "Have you learned from this system?"

If he answered, "yes," she'd say, "Move on. Go learn from someone else."

New Eyes

The key is to see your work with new eyes. In Buddhism the ability to do this is called "beginner's mind." I love this phrase because it embraces the idea of being new to something instead of covering up those deficits. Beginner's mind is a way to break free from what we think we know, to get back to the open and childlike way we approached things before we thought we had it all figured out.

One of my favorite examples of this: In the 1940s, Edwin Land was inspired to invent the distinctive Polaroid instant camera after his three-year-old daughter wondered why she couldn't see the photograph he had just taken right away. Her question got him thinking: *Yeah, why not?* Kids aren't afraid to think outside the box because *they're not even aware there is a box*. According to Paul Harris, a Harvard child psychologist, question asking peaks around age five (by then kids have asked about forty thousand) and then the frequency starts to decline. One reason? School doesn't encourage questions; it encourages *answers!*

It's not easy to get back to this inquisitive state, and one of the best ways to do so is to teach. Teaching helps to put us in the mind of someone who knows less than we know. It forces us to break down and explain and simplify our craft. Studies show that if you group two math students of varied ability together, not only does the poorer student do better (obviously) but the *stronger student does as well.* Teaching forces you to think in new ways about old things. Look for opportunities to teach your expertise wherever you can. You'll be surprised what you learn in the process.

Another way to see things anew is to bring in someone with a new perspective. Basketball was invented in the 1890s but the jump shot didn't become a popular way to score until the 1950s. That's sixty years of basketball without a jump shot! And there were hold-outs even then. In 1963, Hall of Fame Celtic Bob Cousy said, "I think the jump shot is the worst thing that has happened to basketball in ten years." (In fairness, Cousy hadn't yet seen Steph Curry— who wouldn't even be born for twenty-five years.)

A few things changed in basketball that allowed for the intro-duction and popularization of the jump shot, but a key one was that the younger generation entering the league liked using it. Because the old guard had learned to play by shooting a set shot (two hands, feet on the ground), they thought that was the way the game ought to be played. They couldn't see what the attraction or the benefit was to getting in the air, which just sounds ridiculous from a modern-day perspective. As Nick Greene puts it in the hugely entertaining *How to Watch Basketball Like a Genius,* "The first jump shooters bludgeoned conventional wisdom with every leap, and the move gradually blended into the game as their willingness to ignore their elders increased."

New perspective is how all things evolve. One study found that bringing an outsider on to a largely homogeneous team actually doubled the team's chances of solving a challenging problem. This happened not in spite of the friction caused by the outsider but *because* of it. The groups where everyone came from the same background "were ineffective and complacent," running over the same old ground and wondering why they didn't get anyplace new.

I leaned heavily on this concept when I made the pivot from the basketball training space to the corporate speaking space. Any time an organization thought my lack of corporate experience was a negative, I confidently flipped it around. I would tell them, "The fact that I have not lived in the corporate space is a major asset—as I will help you shake things up with new ideas, new perspectives, and new strategies!" I think far too many people, especially those in leadership positions, are more concerned with appearing smart than actually making smart decisions. Thus they avoid situations where they aren't the alpha. This is as destructive to success as it gets. Someone who can teach you isn't a threat! They are a gift.

Rivals

You can also learn a great deal from your competition. In *Decisive*, Chip and Dan Heath highlight the example of Sam Walton, who as the chair of Walmart, among the most successful companies on the planet, could have acted like he had his business all figured out. But he didn't. The Heaths explain: "Throughout Walton's career, he kept his eyes out for good ideas. . . . 'I bet I've been in more Kmarts than anybody,' Walton said. Again and again in his career, Walton found clever solutions by asking himself, 'Who else is struggling with a similar problem, and what can I learn from them?'" Walton didn't shut out the idea that his competitors might know something he didn't, even though he was wiping the floor with them.

If you look at the bigger picture, your competition is actually a collaborator. Both of you are pushing you to do your best.

Competition can be motivating because we end up "using that as fuel for our motivation." Gavin Kilduff, a social scientist who studies rivalries, found that long distance runners do better when a person they consider a rival is in the race. The presence of the other runners pushes everyone to go faster. "Endurance athletes can tolerate greater muscle fatigue in competition" than they can in practice. The presence of competition literally *brings out the best* in them.

Kilduff found similar results in professional basketball, baseball, and football: there was a positive correlation between a team's record at the end of the season and the performance of their chief rival. (Maybe Celtics fans should root for the Lakers too?) Think of a boxer training against various sparring partners. The stronger the partner, the stronger the session, the stronger the performance. And hip-hop? C'mon! Although they aren't nearly as popular today, the rap battles of the 1990s and early 2000s kept rappers sharp and on top of their respective games.

There's even something called "supportive rivalry," in which the competition is *purposefully* built in to make everyone better. In the wrong hands, this can lead to the negative kind of conflict, so for it to work, there is one element that's required: mutual respect. The Norwegian Olympic ski team has had phenomenal success with the supportive rivalry model. Though it's an individual sport, and only a single person can medal, the team's skiers are open to sharing details about the course with one another. Though the giver in this scenario is hurting his own medal chances (a teammate's better time will knock him out), the culture of giving reverberates back onto everyone. The giver today is the receiver tomorrow, and each member knows it. Coach Mike Jones used competition as a primary selling point when recruiting young men to DeMatha: "If your goal is to play Division I basketball, or better yet to play professionally, then you *need* to play against elite players every single day in practice." Sharpening your skills doesn't work unless you're doing it against hard stones.

Learn-It-All

Former Celtics assistant coach Kevin Eastman, who now works as an adviser to all kinds of teams and organizations, is truly a lifelong student. He shared with me his inspirational approach, in which he tries not to be a know-it-all, but a "learn-it-all." Anyone who has come in contact with Coach Eastman knows he's genuine about this. Every time I see him, no matter the situation, he has a pen and pad out and is taking notes. He even did this while I was interviewing him! Imagine a mind that is so open that he takes notes on the person asking him questions.

If Coach Eastman is on a panel or at a clinic with other coaches and speakers, he'll take notes as though he were an audience member. He told me that this process ensures he's paying attention, and writing it down impresses it in his brain. "It's like I hear it twice," he explained to me. "It's got a greater chance to stick." Eastman also keeps a WILT notebook, which stands for **W**hat **I** **L**earned **T**oday, which he makes a point of writing in each day. When I asked him how he prevents stagnation, he told me, "I know I don't know everything I need to know, and I just have a curiosity gene." His default state is one where he's asking questions, and he can never get his fill. "I never try to waste thinking and learning environments," he said, explaining that everywhere from airplanes to doctors' offices are places to learn something new.

Eastman shared a story about a consulting gig he did for an NBA team where he spoke alongside an official from the Obama administration. When it was time for the team's management group to ask the two speakers questions, Kevin (from the stage) raised his hand to ask the first question. He turned to the Obama adviser and asked the best way to describe President Obama. "Intellectual curiosity," the defense official said. "He was the best question asker in the room." This is the epitome of Kevin's approach. We are taught in school that those who give the best answers will be the ones who succeed. But the most accomplished man in the country was tagged as being the exact opposite: he asked the best questions.

Full Circle Mentor

If you want to get better at anything, find a coach or mentor. He can see things you can't see yet, hold you accountable, know the things you don't know, and teach the things that you don't even know you don't know. The moment I became a speaker, I found a speaking coach. The moment I signed a book deal, I found a writing coach. The moment I started making enough money to save, I hired a financial coach. Mentors are all around us; we just have to be willing to find them and be open to listening.

"Quite often," writes CEO coach Chip Conley, "a mentor is a mirror as he or she (ideally) has an almost alchemical connection with you that can help you see yourself better." Airbnb founder Brian Chesky has repeatedly talked about how he is always looking for ways to learn. "I try to find the top expert in the field," he said, "and ask if they would be willing to give me advice." We may not have access to Chesky's contact list—Sheryl Sandberg, Apple designer Jony Ive, and CIA director George Tenet—but we can benefit from this mindset.

We can also gain by *being* a mentor for someone else. As Brendon Burchard explains, "The mentorship casts you as a role model, and engaging in that role inspires you to call forth the best in you." While having a mentor helps you become the best version of yourself, being a mentor encourages you to *actually be* that person.

Studies have shown that racial and gender diversity (especially in leadership positions) makes everyone more productive. Diversity of all kinds is beneficial, and this includes age diversity. Don't assume that a mentor needs to be someone older or even more experienced than you. Drew Hanlen is fourteen years younger than me, but he was one of my most impactful mentors. As generations mix in the workplace, there has been a trend toward **reverse mentorship**, where younger workers teach the older generation aspects of technology, social media, and youth culture. I'd recommend anyone who feels stagnant in their work try to connect with a younger colleague. Wisdom should not be passed only from the top down, from old to young. It needs to go in both directions.

Seeking out a mentor takes vulnerability. You are putting yourself out there, admitting that you don't know exactly what your next steps are. Kobe Bryant was the king of this. When he was drafted into the NBA out of high school, you would think he'd feel like he'd arrived. But in his mind, that was *step one*. Then, throughout those first seasons, he found players who were willing to talk to him. Kobe cornered Michael Jordan at his first All-Star game to ask about MJ's turnaround jumper. Michael gave him a detailed answer and said if he needed anything, to call him, which he did.

"I asked a ton of questions," Kobe once said about those early years. "I was curious. I wanted to improve, learn, and fill my head with a history of the game. No matter who I was with—a coach, a hall of famer, teammate—and no matter the situation—game, practice, vacation—I would fire away question after question." Some people helped, some laughed him off, and some got annoyed—*Who does this kid think he is?*—but Kobe didn't care. He was willing to be vulnerable because he believed being the youngest player in the league was an opportunity, not an achievement in itself.

Quinn Cook and the DMV

The DMV (DC, Maryland, Virginia) area, where I am from, is famous for its astounding array of high school basketball players, many of whom have gone on to become pros. Kevin Durant, the most famous, has made it a point of mentoring DMVers who make it to the NBA. Members of that group have formed a community within the larger NBA community, sending the elevator back down for others.

One of the players Durant took under his wing was former Warriors teammate Quinn Cook. I've known Quinn since he was in grade school. When I first started working out high schoolers Nolan Smith (national champion with Duke, first round NBA pick) and Michael Beasley (2008 Big Ten Player of the Year, second overall pick), Quinn Cook would tag along and hang out off-court, paying attention to every drill. Young Quinn would mimic us from the sideline until he was old enough to join the workouts.

As a fourteen-year-old, Quinn unexpectedly lost his father, a devastating experience for any kid. But he has used his father's death as a powerful source of guidance. As a high school player, he'd carry a picture of him and his father with him everywhere and wore a t-shirt with his dad's picture over his uniform during warm-up. Having trained Quinn on and off from elementary school through high school, I've seen how he uses his father's legacy as a North Star: Quinn wants every decision he makes to be something his father would be proud of.

Quinn went on to become a McDonald's All American in high school, a national champion at Duke and then . . . was not drafted by anyone. Though disappointed, he refused to let that be the end of the line. As he showed from a young age, he is all hustle and heart, rising through the G League to make it into the NBA and becoming a key player on both the Warrior and Laker championship teams.

When I interviewed Quinn, he spoke glowingly about the community and brotherhood among the DMV players, about the bond that exists whether they know one another or not. He told me how valuable it was growing up alongside older players he idolized, like KD, Nolan Smith, and Michael Beasley, and how he tried "to take advantage of it as much as possible." He watched the teenage Durant "lead by example. . . getting up in the morning when a lot of their friends were going out to party." He saw Beasley and Smith staying in the gym and making sacrifices. We can't become something we don't see, and Quinn had a chance to watch the best.

"I wouldn't have had a *chance* to be half the person I've become without that tutelage and my mentors," Quinn told me. "I know that helped me get to where I am today, so I try my hardest to give back because I know how important that is." Quinn works to reach out to others in his community, whether or not they have anything to do with basketball. He's just that kind of person. Quinn has won at every level, and he humbly credits his coaches, and their lessons about teamwork, to account for that fact. "I could always score," he said, "but I took pride in winning."

Most young athletes—and I've met thousands—are focused on individual production because they think that's what will get them noticed, but Quinn was special. When he was a heavily re-cruited high school senior, Quinn chose Duke even though Coach K didn't promise glory or playing time. He just promised Quinn that he would coach him every day. Quinn was mature enough at a young age, at a time when everyone was trying to give him things, to recognize that having a teacher was the greatest gift.

Brain Picking

I used to politely and enthusiastically ask interesting people if I could "pick their brain." Now that I'm fortunate enough to be in a position where people ask this of me, I realize what a terrible question it is. *Excuse me? You want to pick my brain? Like poke around in there and take what you find?*

The problem with the question is not the intention; it's the framing, which makes it a one-sided exchange. You are making it about *you* and what *you* want. It implies other people are a bowl for you to scoop out of rather than party to an exchange. Seeking out others who do what you aspire to do is important, but make sure you're offering to add value. Coach Eastman calls it "earning the ask."

Also, lose the "I" formulation, as in, "I would love to connect for fifteen minutes." By opening with what you want, you're al-ready making it about you. What's in it for *them*? Give them a rea-son that an exchange will matter for both of you.

Instead of leading with what you want, **lead with what you can offer**. For instance, "In my research, I can see you're currently doing X. So I can customize this demo to be as relevant as possible for you, could you share some additional insight into how you're doing X?" Here are three steps you should follow instead of the "pick your brain" approach.

1. Learn as much as you can about them and their challenges.
2. Determine how you (or your product or service) can add value to them.
3. Clearly communicate this in your pitch.

In the fall of 1999, after graduating from college, I moved back home to the DC area to pursue a career as a basketball performance coach (then known as a strength and conditioning coach). There was a locally renowned trainer named Kevin Maselka who worked with numerous NBA players, such as Patrick Ewing, Allen Iverson, Alonzo Mourning, and Carmelo Anthony. At the time, that was my #1 goal, to train the best of the best. Since I was just starting, and lacked the experience and expertise to train NBA players, I figured the ideal path was to work for someone who did. So I persuaded Kevin to let me work for him.

I use the term "work" very loosely. I was basically an unpaid intern, though I thought of myself more as an apprentice. I told Kevin I was willing to do anything he needed—from sweeping the floor to wiping down the equipment—in order to learn from him and to observe his training sessions. My goal was to add value to him (as well as to his players) in exchange for knowledge. And it paid off brilliantly. In a span of a year I went from cleaning up to spotting exercises to leading warm-ups to training players. I took a role that had a lot of sacrifice up front (mostly manual labor for no pay) in the hopes of opportunity later. Now, things don't always work so perfectly, but if you don't at least put yourself out there, I guarantee there's zero chance of it happening.

Something More

If you focus on TAKING, you'll never have enough. But if you focus on GIVING, you'll never run out. My parents have modeled this for me my entire life. They were both elementary educators for thirty years, my mom a first grade teacher and my dad a teacher then principal. They loved connecting with young people and contributing to their growth, development, and maturity. They relished the opportunity to be role models, to be of service, and to give to their community and society as a whole.

My parents retired in the early 2000s and moved to Myrtle Beach, South Carolina. Within a couple of years, they felt like something was missing. They had each other, plenty of free time, and financial security, so what was missing? **The feeling of contribution.** For their entire lives, what brought them fulfillment was being a part of something bigger. So they went looking for it.

In 2004, my parents became full-time volunteers at a non-profit organization called Fostering Hope, an organization that provides school supplies and clothing to foster children in their area. They un-retired and took on a full-time job—for no pay—because they wanted to give back. Almost fifty years after they first started teaching, they are still contributing to the betterment of their community, and changing lives in a positive way. While many retirees derive happiness from fixing up an old car, playing golf, or enjoying bingo night (all perfectly respectable activities), my parents derive true happiness and fulfillment from making a contribution.

Clearly not everyone is in the position to do what my parents did. However, each one of us can make a point of contributing in our own way. Educator and author Thomas Murray feeds off sharing and contributing. He told me that while he makes sure to give his family his undivided attention, he seizes on (and creates) those special moments where he can contribute to others' growth. "Every day is an opportunity to make a difference in the lives of other people," he told me. "If we look hard enough, those opportunities are vast." He sees it as a way to serve, but it's not just selfless; he views it as path to his own growth. Though the business world too often says so, time is not money. As Thomas put it to me, **time is opportunity for impact**. How do you view your time? Is it aligned with your goals?

Buckets

Each of us has an invisible "bucket," which I think of as a combination of our energy, joy, and fulfillment. Every interaction we have with someone, in person or online, either fills (+) or drains (−) our bucket. To be truly happy and successful, we need to fill other people's buckets and spend quality time with people who fill ours. We are at our best when our buckets are full and at our worst when our buckets are empty.

While giving is noble, make sure you are not doing it at the expense of your own health and satisfaction. You must fill your bucket first, before you can fill others'. This is *not* selfishness. Prioritize yourself and your well-being so you can be the best version of you. You are no good to anyone if you're not taking care of yourself. Remember: it is impossible to pour from an empty bucket.

Shopping Carts

Those of you who follow me on social media have heard this before but it bears repeating. In my view, this is a big deal. One of the biggest. There are few things that are more revealing about you than whether or not you return your shopping cart upon leaving the grocery store. Once you unload your groceries into your trunk, it takes about thirty seconds to roll your cart back. No one feels like doing it. It's slightly inconvenient but really not that difficult. This simple act reveals a great deal about you.

Why? First off, it's an unwritten rule; there's no enforcement mechanism, no ticket-writing officer or store employee who will call you on it. No one is going to videotape you leaving your shopping cart and post it on Facebook (although I have considered it!). So it's really just up to you.

Second, you don't *see* the people who will be affected by it, whether that's the store employee who has to chase it down or the driver who can't pull into the obstructed spot. But your action undoubtedly affects these people. Putting you cart away is simply the small price you pay for living in a society. Abandoning it is an act of selfishness, laziness, and entitlement. What you do with your cart when you're done represents how you see yourself in the larger scheme of society. Is the world here to serve you? Or are you here to serve others? I firmly believe that you are how you behave when no one is watching.

Many years back researchers did a series of tests on seminary students at Princeton that revealed how people really behave when they think no one is watching. The test went like this. One by one, theology students were first interviewed about the need to be a Good Samaritan. After the interview, they were then sent to give a speech on the topic at a building across the street and told that they were running late, so they better hurry. The entire setup was a ruse. The researchers actually planted an actor on the street pretending to be in need of help, either lying on the ground in pain or visibly ill. On this quick dash across the street, every student had to pass right in front of this person needing help. How would these future religious teachers respond?

A full 90 percent of students—people going into the clergy, mind you, people *talking at that moment* about Good Samaritans— flat-out ignored the person in need! They just ran right past him! The study is famous for good reason: so many of us say one thing but do another. We can't really move forward as people if we are not in alignment, with our inner and outer selves pointing in the same direction.

Something Bigger

A while back, after several years as a private performance coach, working one-on-one with players, I craved being a part of a team. I thought back on my years playing in high school and college, and the camaraderie was part of what made those experiences so positive. While I enjoyed the relationships I was making with individual players, I needed the satisfaction and fulfillment from knowing I was making a meaningful contribution to something bigger than myself.

I decided to aim high and target the preeminent program in my area: Montrose Christian. It had a stellar reputation, a Hall of Fame coach, and was practically a factory that produced Division I players. But getting in at Montrose was no easy task.

Every month from 2000 to 2003 I sent letters and left voice messages for Coach Stu Vetter; all of which went unreturned and unanswered. Then finally in the spring of 2003 I caught a break. I made my routine monthly call to the Montrose basketball office, and to my surprise, someone finally answered! This was the first time I actually spoke with a human being. Coach Vetter's lead assistant, David Adkins,★ answered with a gruff "Hello?!"

I was so shocked someone answered that it took me a moment to collect myself. After what felt like an enormous pause, I introduced myself and told Coach Adkins how much I wanted to contribute to his program. Not that I wanted a job or opportunity: I wanted to *contribute*. Coach Adkins must have felt my passion through the phone, as he immediately invited me over to his office to talk shop.

As they say, luck is when preparation meets opportunity. To my good fortune, a couple of days earlier, Coach Vetter tasked Coach Adkins with leading the Montrose off-season conditioning

---

★ Currently the director of player development for the Washington Wizards.

program. He admittedly knew very little about strength and conditioning, so he was curious to hear how I might be of service. After we chatted and got better acquainted, he told me he would bring Linas Kleiza (future NBA and Lithuanian Olympic player) over for a private workout. "If Linas likes your workout," he said, "you're in. If he doesn't, I never knew you."

No pressure.

It was an audition to become a part of the Montrose program. The following afternoon, I took Linas through an hour-long workout and blasted him pretty hard. I felt like it went well, though I got very little verbal feedback from him during the workout. This certainly wasn't abnormal, as it's been my experience that most teenagers take a while to warm up to an adult they don't know. So I had to rely on reading Linas's body language and facial expressions, which didn't reveal much, as he was pretty stoic.

After about an hour, Coach Adkins picked Linas up. He told me the two would talk and he'd let me know. Twenty minutes later, Coach called me. "You're hired!" Coach Adkins said that when Linas got in the car, he said, "That was the best workout I have ever had. When can I do it again?"

That audition resulted in a seven-year stint as the performance coach at Montrose and an opportunity to contribute to a nationally ranked program and work with players like Kevin Durant, Terrance Ross (Orlando Magic), and Justin Anderson (Philadelphia 76ers). That workout was the launching point for so many opportunities in my life, and it began with a desire to contribute. The first four years were strictly voluntary; I never got paid a dime. But the experiences I had, the relationships I developed, and the satisfaction I enjoyed by making a contribution were priceless.

Action Steps

- Be **open to learn** from anywhere: I study both stand-up comedy and hip-hop music to improve my speaking. What other forums and disciplines can you look to in order to get an edge in your own work?

- If you find small talk or networking difficult, prepare some **original questions** that avoid the typical cliché stuff—*What's the most memorable place you ever visited? Who's the one teacher you remember most from school?* It also has the added benefit of making you more memorable and drawing people to you. **Remember to bring value to every exchange.**

CHAPTER TEN
Positivity

Yet. Say it.

Yet.

Yet has power. Yet has wings. Yet is like the stretching of a new blank canvas over your dusty old self-portrait. It might be the most powerful word in the English language. Why? **Because *yet* is a statement of defiance.** It enlivens and reshapes the present. It reframes failure. Yet is three letters strong enough to separate the past from the future.

Part II of *Sustain Your Game* has been about conquering stagnation in your work and life. The first four chapters were about the actionable changes you can make to break out of your rut. The final one is about changing the very way you see that rut.

You don't have to look hard to find negativity, which is everywhere. Some people think cynicism and pessimism are signs of intelligence or wisdom. Don't believe them. They are spinning in their own circles, dealing with their own stagnation. Because negativity is so common, and so easy, you have to fight to keep it from infecting you. And yes, I use the word *infect*, because that's what it's like. It gets into your bloodstream and poisons your beliefs, emotions, and actions.

People who only know me on a surface level naturally assume I am always optimistic, positive, and enthusiastic. Which is understandable, as that's the side of me I choose to share publicly. And that is how I feel most of the time. But I am not that way 24/7/365. I get sad, disappointed, cranky, and frustrated. I have fears, issues, low moods, and insecurities. But I *acknowledge* and *accept* those emotions as real, as part of who I am. That helps me stay positive. Not every second, mind you, but as a person. I am *authentically* positive.

Grudges and Scores

I preach positivity with the zeal of a convert because I have not always been an authentically positive person. I used to harbor massive feelings of pessimism, cynicism, and contempt. I was easily frustrated, annoyed, and irritated, and I was the king of making excuses, blaming others, and complaining. Yet most people in my life never knew my inner anger, as I hid behind a (figurative) "clown mask" most of the time. My bitterness was fueled by my penchant for holding grudges. To put it bluntly, if someone crossed me, I never forgot. I put them on my mental blacklist. I didn't just shut them out, I carried that sense of being wronged into the rest of my life.

At some point I finally realized that holding on to those feelings only hurt one person: me. There's an old saying that expresses this idea brilliantly: "Resentment is like taking poison and waiting for someone else to die." All your negativity toward the world just weighs you down. Then you end up walking around complaining about how heavy things are.

I also have worked really hard to drop my propensity for **score-keeping**, which is similar to grudge holding. Keeping score poisons an ongoing relationship; worse, it encourages you to keep the negative feeling inside as it grows. You just tally up your resentments in your mind and drag each one around like a rock in your shoe. It might be toward your spouse regarding who does more around the house, toward your work colleague over who is getting more credit, or toward a family member who isn't as good at giving as receiving.

As you add all of these up, what are you gaining? Not a thing.

Guess what? Things will never even out. **Just let go of the counting.** Trust me: you'll find your mood lifted and your motivation increased. You will have more energy for the things that matter.

And when you do, you'll see less reason to hold grudges and keep score because what you put out in the world will come back on you. Our internal moods present our external circumstances. It may feel like things are happening to us, and yes, sometimes unfortunate things occur. But our day-to-day? *We create that.*

Positivity is not being naively innocent or clueless to the way things really work. Nor is it just putting on a fake smile and pretending the world is puppy dogs and ice cream (that's *toxic positivity*). A positive mindset is choosing to take the world on the most productive terms possible.

Positive Engine

I feel anger, disappointment, and envy like anyone else. But I've worked hard to develop the skills to manage and process these emotions effectively so that they don't erode my perspective or mindset.

I do this through a process I call **APD: acknowledgment, permission, depersonalization.**

1. I **acknowledge** and own how I am feeling. I don't ignore it, resist it, or suppress it.

2. I give myself **permission** to feel that way! I treat myself with compassion. (I don't get mad at myself for feeling mad, making it worse.)

3. I **depersonalize** it. I recognize that **I am not my emotions**. I am the *awareness* of my emotions.* Emotions are ever fleeting: happy one minute, mad the next. I view my feelings as information. **I do *not* let them dictate how I behave.**

Many years ago I attended legendary coach Morgan Wootten's (formerly of DeMatha) basketball camp. One concept that he drilled into us on defense was to "guard your yard." If you were guarding the player with the ball, you needed to guard one yard to your right and one yard to your left (meaning you would *not* let the defender drive right past you). Your yard was the area you were personally responsible for protecting, and your teammates were counting on you to *not* get beat there.

I've adopted a similar mindset off the court. My "yard" is my immediate surroundings, my colleagues, and my family. I guard my environment. I guard whom I let in. I guard what information comes in. Before I can try to influence others, I need to make sure everything in my own yard is safe, fertile, and protected. I try not to react to things out of my control. I do my very best to stay internally focused on my own effort and my own attitude and let everything else be. While many things that happen to me on a daily basis are not in my control, my response to those things is 100 percent my choice.

I worry only about what I can influence. When someone says something rude, demeaning, or negative, I recognize that is a reflection of them (and what they are going through)—not a reflection of me. So I simply dismiss it and move on. Unless it is being delivered by someone I respect, I pay minimal attention to unsolicited criticism. Remember: no one makes you feel anything. You choose to feel a certain way based on your reaction.

---

* This ties back to Eckhart Tolle's work mentioned in chapter 1.

Chapter 10 will be broken down into three sections, each around a way you can bring more positivity into your life while remaining authentic to your emotions.

1. **gratitude** (positivity about what has happened: **past**)
2. **enthusiasm** (positivity about what is happening: **present**)
3. **optimism** (positivity about what will happen: **future**)

Gratitude

We start with gratitude because it's an emotion connected to everything that has happened up to right now. Gratitude is not about what you have. **It's about how you feel about what you have.**

At both low and high points in my life, when things have been falling in place and when things have been falling right on top of me, I've kept an **attitude of gratitude**. I do this for three distinct reasons:

1. It simply **feels good**. A mentality of gratitude colors everything in my life, often when I need it most. Try to walk around consciously feeling grateful and you'll be amazed at how your mood lifts.

2. I've long lived by the mantra of "That which gets praised, gets repeated." If you want to **have more** to be grateful for, then don't miss an opportunity to be grateful for what you already have. A mentor of mine once told me, "What you appreciate *appreciates*"—it goes up in value.

3. It helps to keep life in a healthy **perspective**. It's so easy to get fixated by what we don't have. Focusing on what we do have provides clarity and balance.

The World's Most Grateful Man

Leadership coach Jon Gordon is the epitome of gratitude in practice. He doesn't just take time out to be grateful, he *lives it*. Gordon understands the importance of attitude as the foundation of success and has seen it work at the highest levels: NCAA, MLB, and NFL. He also practices what he preaches: he's simply the most positive guy I've ever met. You can't talk to him (or even just watch him talk) and not feel his contagious positivity. But here's the key: he's not naturally this way. He *worked* his way to this mindset, which is why he's the best teacher of it.

During our interview Gordon told me that, years ago, at the height of "misery and depression," he read somewhere that you can't be thankful and stressed at the same time. So he put it to the test and set aside time each day to go on **gratitude walks**. Some were ten minutes, some were longer, but he would spend the time saying aloud what he was thankful for.

What this habit did was create a cycle of positive emotions "rather than these stress hormones and the bad stuff that drains you and kills you over time, the bad thoughts and the fears and doubt." It worked, he told me, as "I rewired my brain from negative to positive using the power of gratitude." Because Gordon has experience with the lowest points, his positivity these days is earned and authentic.

Gordon has brought these insights to his work with high-caliber athletes and performers. "You perform at a higher level when you're practicing gratitude," he explained to me. "If you're playing a sport and you're focusing on what you love in that moment, what you're thankful for, you're actually going to perform at a higher level."

Gratitude is another way of playing present because you appreciate what is there instead of focusing on what's not. Most incredibly, even after teaching these concepts for years, Gordon admits that he's *still* not a naturally positive person. He has to *work* at it, and "it's a battle every day." I respect that he was open about this struggle because it reminds us that positivity is not a superpower you are granted. It is a choice you embrace.

Science of Gratitude

Psychologist Robert Emmons, an expert on gratitude, has long taught that the act of being grateful has enormous power. "Grateful living is possible," he says, "only when we realize that other people and agents do things for us that we cannot do for ourselves. . . . In gratitude, we recognize that the source of goodness is outside of ourselves." When athletes thank God for their successes, some people scoff (there's that negativity!) because if there was a God, would he care about sports?

That is irrelevant.

What matters is the player's sense of gratitude and his feeling of appreciation. I view it as his recognition of forces outside of himself. Whether you believe in a higher power or not, we all should take a moment to be grateful to a universe that has worked in our favor, if only for a moment.

Gratitude separates us from our egos, bonds us to other people, and connects us to the world at large. It's undervalued because it's viewed as simply a form of politeness. When our parents taught us to say thank you as children, we rarely put much thought into it—it's just what you did. But Emmons has conducted decades of research on gratitude and has found that "a person who experiences gratitude is able to cope more effectively with everyday stress, may show increased resilience . . . experiencing gratitude leads to increased feelings of connectedness, improved relationships, and even altruism." Most importantly, as Emmons has demonstrated, "gratitude does not depend upon objective life circumstances such as health, wealth, or beauty."

It doesn't matter what you have; it matters how you *feel* about what you have. If you're only focused on what you want, you will never feel satisfied. *Never.* That chase will do nothing but create a sense of emptiness and, yes, stagnation—because you will never get to where you think you're headed.

Putting It Down

When I was a kid, my parents encouraged me to write thank-you notes to anyone who went out of their way to do something nice for me. Whether it was a thoughtful gift from a friend for my birthday, a teacher or coach who helped me during the school year/season, or anything in between, I had to do it. They modeled this as well, and I recall numerous times seeing one of them sitting at the kitchen table handwriting thank-you notes to students, colleagues, friends, and family. As important as handwritten notes were then, they are even more important now, as they are a memorable personal touch in a world consumed by emails, texts, and DMs. I have a bin filled with hundreds of notes I've received over the years, and I read, value, and appreciate every single one of them. "Writing a thank-you note forces you to confront the humbling fact that you have not achieved your success alone," writes Marshall Goldsmith, who dedicates a whole chapter in his book *What Got You Here Won't Get You There* to the importance of thanking.

In *Raise Your Game* I tell the story of meeting Duke's Coach Mike Krzyzewski when he visited Montrose to watch a player of ours. He gave me ten minutes of his time to chat even though he wasn't there for me. Because my parents taught me to do so, I wrote him a thank-you note. And because Coach K is who he is, he wrote me one back. To this day, I remember how that gesture made me feel, and I make a point to write or respond to thank-you notes every chance I get.

Thank-you notes benefit the giver as well. *Alter Ego* author Todd Herman told me he has been handwriting a letter a day regularly for the last twenty years—he's done around five thousand of them. The letters, which include a wax seal with an insignia, are often expressions of gratitude—to loved ones, friends, acquaintances, and famous or inspirational people he doesn't know at all. As he said, people need to be seen. That small act of making them feel seen redounds to both of you.

The Happiness Advantage author Shawn Achor did a massive study of Nationwide and Facebook employees and found that those with a higher social connection score, who went out of their way to express gratitude to teammates, were "40 percent more likely to get a raise or promotion in the next two years." This isn't a reason to express gratitude—if it's done for selfish reasons, then it's not really gratitude. But it shows how impactful this type of positivity can be.

What Comes Next

When I talked with former college football star and motivational speaker Inky Johnson, the first thing he expressed gratitude for was me—for conducting the interview. Now, for anyone else, that might have been too much, but coming from Inky, it felt 100 percent genuine. The man is just an inspiration. "I firmly believe a person's life—and the manifestation thereof—is a result of how they handle the transactions of life," Inky has said. "Transactions" here is not a business term. It refers to the back-and-forth of accepting and sharing that makes up our lives. How we give and receive is who we are.

If there could be an ambassador for gratitude, it would be Inky. As a cornerback for the University of Tennessee in 2006, Inky suffered a traumatic injury to his right arm that ruptured the main artery in his chest, tore his shoulder ligaments, and required extensive surgery. It was life-threatening and left him paralyzed in that arm, ending his playing career. One can only imagine the devastation such an injury had on the twenty-year-old, who had his whole life and career ahead of him. He'd reached the doorstep of the NFL, with eight games left to play in his college career, and just like that . . . he lost it all. But instead of anger and bitterness, Inky turned the tragedy around. He didn't treat it as a tragedy at all. He transformed those feelings inside of him into ones of gratitude, though he confessed getting to that point was "one of the most challenging parts of my life."

As a successful motivational speaker, Inky now shares his story and reinvention with audiences from all walks of life. To this day he expresses gratitude for what came out of the career-ending injury that almost killed him. He told me that he's grateful for the perspective it gave him, the support system that helped get him through it, the opportunity to share his story, and the chance to serve. "Ninety to ninety-five percent of the way I live today is a result of my injury and I'm grateful for that," he told me.

Inky taught me that positive attitude is not something that comes without work. He didn't paralyze his arm, lose his career and nearly his life, and just hop back up like it was no biggie. He had to work to reach the mental space where he could be grateful for what life had thrown at him. "You got to get up and fight for happiness," he told me. "You got to fight for joy. You got to fight to have a perspective to see things on the right side of the coin." People are amazed by his attitude and ask him if he sees negative things at all. "I see them like everybody else," he said. "I just haven't seen how focusing on them can help me become the man I strive to be every day." Remember: **positivity is a choice**.

What You Don't Have

What if I told you there's a game that you don't have to play, but if you choose to, it will make you feel awful most of the time and that eventually you will lose? Are you in?

That's exactly what happens when we play the comparison game. Gratitude is a permanent way to opt out of the draining and unproductive habit of measuring ourselves against others. Besides being about things that don't matter—how we stack up—the comparison game is also rigged. This is because of a bias known as the *availability heuristic*, which means we're affected too much by what immediately comes to mind. Think about it: Who comes to mind when comparing your money and success? **Those with a lot of it!** See? Rigged.

Cornell psychologist Tom Gilovich has shown just how bad we are at objectively measuring "a lot" and "a little" when it comes to ourselves. It has more to do with expectations than reality. Here's one example that I found fascinating. Gilovich discovered that Olympic silver medalists are less happy about their accomplishments than bronze medalists. This doesn't seem to make sense. Silver is better than bronze, second is higher than third. So what's going on here? Expectations! The silver medalist just focuses on what he lost (the gold), whereas the bronze winner focuses on what he just barely got (a medal). On the podium, the winner feels like a loser and vice versa. It's just perspective.

We are not grateful for what we have according to some objective scale. We see ourselves based on our "reference point," which is our friends, neighbors, and colleagues. We are so focused on this reference point—the comparison game—that we make decisions against our own interests. In one study, Gilovich found that when given the choice between making $50,000 while everyone else made $25,000 (option A) or making $80,000 while everyone made $200,000 (option B), *half* of the people opted for option A. They chose to make less money because it gave them the satisfaction of making more than others.

This tendency pops up everywhere: the unemployed are happier if *more people they know are unemployed*, and a lot of wealthy people don't feel they are rich because they compare themselves with the other *rich people they spend time with*. If they happen to hang out with the conspicuously wealthy, they will always view themselves on the low end of the group. They are so caught inside the comparison game that they can't enjoy what they have.

The Closet Problem

The first time we accomplish something, we feel the rush of excitement, the satisfaction of achieving a goal. The second time a little less. Over time, we . . . adjust. That's the problem with gratitude, or I should say *our* problem with gratitude: we get used to things. It's not that we're spoiled. It's just human nature. We're more likely to get a thank-you gift for an acquaintance who helps us once than for our mother, who's been doing it for decades.

Years ago I heard about something I call the **empty closet rule**, which is basically this: no matter how little or how much stuff you have, you will fill the extra space in your house, whether that's a room, a closet, or a drawer. You will—gradually, without thinking—find things to fill it with. The disappointment part of our brain seems to work the same. It's up to us to work against that. Gratitude is not something reserved for those who have the most to be grateful for. There is no objective scale for who should be grateful and who shouldn't. That misses the point entirely. It's up to each of us to find the space, time, and energy for gratitude in our lives.

Enthusiasm

I've always loved quotes. I began collecting them in middle school on a yellow legal pad and still do to this day (though I've switched to a Word doc on my laptop). One of the first quotes I ever scribbled down was from English poet Samuel Taylor Coleridge*: "Nothing great was ever achieved without enthusiasm." It's so simple yet so profound. How are you going to accomplish anything worthwhile without putting your whole self into it?

True enthusiasm comes when what you love, what you believe, and what you are doing are in alignment. Though we think of enthusiasm as something that is visible from the outside, that is not

---

* Ralph Waldo Emerson, whom this quote is often misattributed to, was quoting Coleridge when he wrote it.

what it's about. It's an internal feeling that, when authentic, will likely spill out.

In the same way that gratitude is not about what you have, enthusiasm is not about what you're doing. **It's how you do what you're doing.**

The Trigger

Think of enthusiasm as an always available combustible material you can insert into any situation. It's what you bring to the table before anything else. By beginning with the positive feeling, instead of expecting it to come after the fact, you are shaking yourself out of complacency. You aren't waiting around for something to happen to you to be excited about. Your excitement is what invites it.

Performance coach Brendon Burchard calls this **positive projection**, which essentially means "you get what you look for." With enthusiasm, what you love to do becomes richer and what is difficult becomes a growth experience. This bears repeating: **the feeling doesn't always come first**. Sometimes you have to act the thing in order to awaken the thing.

Former entrepreneur and best-selling author Seth Godin explains it this way: "The way we act determines how we feel way more than the way we feel determines how we act." He compares it to falling asleep, which you first do by *pretending to be asleep*. Some people use the aphorism "Fake it till you make it" to explain this idea, though I don't love the saying. You're not faking it. It's real, you're just *creating* it. You're not waiting for an outside source to trigger it. You are the trigger.

Playing with Heart

A few years ago, during the Women's Final Four, legendary NCAA coach Gene Auriemma went viral with comments about the enthusiasm gap he now finds among young players. He didn't mince words: he reads a lack of enthusiasm as *selfishness*. It's easy to be hyped around your own success, he said, but how do players behave when they're not the center of attention? That tells you what kind of player and teammate they are.

"Recruiting enthusiastic kids is harder than it's ever been because every kid watches [sports] and what they see is people just being really cool," Auriemma said. If a player is not putting her whole self into what she is doing—from the practice court to the team meetings to the bench—"they will never get in the game. Ever." Auriemma has been coaching long enough to know how important it is, as a player, a leader, a teammate, to bring joy onto the court. To be enthusiastic about *team* success. "I'd rather lose than watch kids play the way some kids play . . . ," he said, "always thinking about themselves." Lack of enthusiasm touched a nerve in Coach Auriemma, and I understand why: it's reflective of one's values.

A player who never lacked enthusiasm on and off the court was Hall of Famer Kevin Garnett. KG's energy and enthusiasm level were unparalleled, perhaps in all of sports. "Kevin Garnett plays the game of basketball the way life is supposed to be lived," Celtics broadcaster Sean Grande wrote. "With joy, and with passion, and with purpose. Present in every minute he's on the floor." No one can match KG for floor slapping, defense yelling, bench cheering, and—famously—trash talking.★ Players loved playing with him, opponents loved competing with him, teammates loved traveling with him, and fans loved rooting for him.

"I'm going to roll with a guy who's going to show me his heart," Garnett once said, "and wears his heart on his sleeve and plays with passion over anything." Those comments came after Celtics' teammate Glen "Big Baby" Davis was spotted on the bench crying during a difficult game. While some may have mocked Davis (and Sam Cassell tried to cover Davis's face with a towel), KG stood up for his

---

★ If you have time, seek out opponents' stories about Garnett on YouTube.

teammate. The tears came from a place of love for the game, so KG was all for it. He understood: crying *is* a type of enthusiasm.

Garnett's own enthusiasm expressed itself in this joyous, energetic flame, and it affected everyone. The key with KG was that he was always like that: first quarter, preseason, practice, in the locker room, on the plane. He knew enthusiasm was the burning candle and he never let up. That's what made him one of the game's great competitors and kept him relevant; even after his body started to break down, his heart never did.

One of the reasons for the maxim that "defense wins championships" is because defense is a function of effort and enthusiasm. To play hard defense, you don't need the ball to bounce a certain way and you don't need things to fall into place. Most defense is about how committed you are to it. That's why it's the measure of a champion. Defense is a measure of a team's enthusiasm.

Effect and Cause

Laurie Santos teaches a wildly popular class at Yale University that fills up immediately every semester. It is now held with one thousand students in a concert hall, and it has a waitlist to get in. About 25 percent of all the students at Yale try to enroll.

The topic? Macroeconomics? Hardly. Ancient Greece? Nope.

What does every twenty-year-old college student want to know more about?

Okay, besides that.

Give up? It's a class on happiness. That's right, students in the most prestigious school in the nation, the future leaders and geniuses of America, want to find out how to be happy. Due to popular demand, Santos has since taken the class online so even non-Yalies can check it out.★

★ It's called "The Science of Well-Being."

Santos says our assumptions about happiness have long been wrong. "We often can get in this mode of thinking that . . . [happiness] is the thing you worry about when everything else is sorted," Santos has said, but "the data actually suggests the opposite, that maybe focusing on well-being can make the other stuff that we want to get in life a little bit easier." This is why enthusiasm is so necessary. It is the beginning, the thing you gather up from inside of yourself and put out in the world. The world then responds in kind. The happier are healthier, live longer, have better jobs and a higher salary. But we assume the happiness *came* from those things instead of the truth: happiness *leads* to them.

Ramping Up

Enthusiasm, like gratitude, is something that you create. It is a downhill ramp, a momentum creator. Communications expert Heidi Reeder suggests we should go into our day—and upcoming challenges—with a running start of positivity. She points out that "employees who started the day in a good mood were a little less impacted by negative events with coworkers. . . . A pre-existing positive state adds a little buffer to the troubles that come our way and enhances our appreciation of positive events when they occur."

Reeder calls it having **"positive illusions."** You may not have evidence that your day will be a success, but the point of positivity is that the feeling might cause the result, not vice versa. One reason: a positive mood will draw people toward you, which in itself will improve your chances of success and opportunities because "upbeat moods boost cooperation, fairness, and business performance." Positive and enthusiastic people are magnets, and good things seem to find them. If you don't start from a place of joy, and put that out into the world, I'm not sure why you expect more will ever find you.

Optimism

It's been my experience that the highest performing people are the ones who learn to successfully balance optimism with realism. To me, that's the epitome of strength. Optimism is being hopeful and confident about the future, carrying a belief that things will in fact work out for the best. It doesn't mean that the universe will magically work in your favor. It means that however the chips fall, you're still in the game. Remember: negativity is easy. Choosing to be optimistic takes effort. It is also a courageous act.

The Real

Optimists accept that unfortunate events occur and negative feelings arise. They don't deny, minimize, or invalidate those emotions. He acknowledges disappointment, but believes in his power to move on. The optimist admits fear, but trusts his ability to overcome it. That is **authentic optimism**. Martin Seligman, the father of positive psychology, found optimists "were always looking for causes of their situation that they could control." They're not passive in their optimism, assuming good things will fall in their lap. They are actively searching for the buttons and switches they can get their hands on.

"Despite popular misconceptions," *The Charge* author Brandon Burchard wrote, "optimists aren't just dreamers who don't see the world as it is. In fact, optimists are *more likely to see the world as it is* and take action to address the problem. That's because pessimists don't believe that problems can be resolved." Optimists believe in the power of action.

I wonder if this is why I've always noticed that the positive people I know (like Jon Gordon) also have the most energy. Optimism actually conserves our resources, which is why it has also been connected to longevity. One large study published in 2019 determined that optimists have a life span 11 percent to 15 percent longer than average, and are more likely to live to age eighty-five or older.

Making It True

The problem with pessimism is that it's a self-fulfilling prophecy. "Your brain constructs a world based upon how you expect it to look," author and psychologist Shawn Achor explains in *Before Happiness*. A negative person walks around looking for the negative, so that is what he notices! Preparing for negatives actually creates those very negatives because "negative people literally see a narrower range of opportunities and possibilities." Because of **confirmation bias**—our tendency to see evidence that supports our beliefs—we always get what we look for.

The pessimist unconsciously wants confirmation that things will go poorly, so he finds it. It goes back to Dr. Jonathan Fader visualizing the parking spot and then finding one. You adjust your behavior based on what you expect to happen—which ends up **creating that very thing**. This is why outside shooters have to keep pulling up from behind the three-point line, even if they are 0 for Tuesday. They still believe it's going in, and by believing it, it does!

What you feel, you put out into the world. Then when you go into the world, guess what? It's there!

Can Do

For athletes specifically—from swimmers to wrestlers—research shows that optimists "might actually use failure as fuel to perform even better in the future." Similarly, a study of optimism in salesmen found "insurance agents with a glass-is-half-full outlook . . . are far more able than their pessimistic peers to persist despite rejections, and so they make more sales." These salesmen view setbacks as constructive instead of world ending, which helps improve their chances the next time.

"Because optimists expect their efforts to pay off," social psychologist Jonathan Haidt teaches in *The Happiness Hypothesis*, "they go right to work fixing the problem." Optimism is a belief in our power to affect our own lives. To fight stagnation, perhaps nothing is more important than the trust in ourselves that we can make it better.

Action Steps

- In *What Got You Here Won't Get You There*, Marshall Goldsmith suggests making a list of the twenty-five people who got you where you are today, either in your career or in your life. Then, handwrite each of them a personalized thank-you note showing your appreciation for what they've done.

- **Keep a Gratitude Journal:** For one week, on your phone or in a notepad, keep track of all the things— little and big—for which you are grateful. The purpose of this is not the list itself. The point is to train your brain to **notice such things**, to give them the same (or more) attention than the mistakes and setbacks get. Those who keep a gratitude journal have been found to be "25% happier than those who don't."

- One method of building optimism (or at least cutting down on your pessimism) is what psychologist Ethan Kross calls "distanced self-talk." Speak about yourself and your current situation in the "third person" (use "he" or "she" instead of "I"), which will help you "gain emotional distance." See if this exercise makes you more clearheaded and objective.

(continues)

(continued)

- What are the biggest adversities you are currently facing, personally or professionally? Try to dig deep and get to the root of the real issue. What is causing it? **How are you contributing to it?** Acknowledge that while you may not have control over the circumstances of your adversity, you absolutely have control over your response. Make a list of different responses that could move you forward and improve your situation.

PART III

PREVAIL—Beating Burnout

I'm writing this section in the late spring of 2021, over a year into the global coronavirus pandemic, and though there are signs of light at the end of the tunnel, people are wiped out. Burnout is on everyone's mind. Even before the pandemic hit, burnout was rising, with over 75 percent of workers claiming to have experienced burnout on the job. After a year-plus in some version of quarantine, it's only gotten worse. In fact, despite being home more often, American workers have been working three *more* hours per day during the pandemic. And I think I know why. Read on.

Burnout is used freely to mean worn down, but it is actually a technical term, defined as "a special type of work-related stress—a state of physical or emotional exhaustion that also involves a sense of reduced accomplishment and loss of personal identity." Though it is often used to describe work, it can refer to relationships, to commitments, to activities we once sought for pleasure, and to journeys that we partake in. The term burnout describes a situation when you're giving more than you're getting.

Burnout is the long-term effect of **misalignment**. It's when the activities you dedicate your time to don't match your values anymore, if they ever did. The joy can drain out of something you once loved to do, and if the feeling persists, it may be time to reexamine how you're approaching it. Sometimes getting through burnout requires a revamping of your perspective. Other times it's a message telling you it's time to move on. And then there's everything in between.

Part III is on beating burnout, which is an accumulation of both STRESS and STAGNATION. Burnout means giving your all (that's the stress part) to something that doesn't matter enough to you (that's the stagnation part). How much we care is a major factor of how much we're able to give. Burnout is so prevalent that it almost seems like whoever can cure it will have found the Holy Grail. But I don't think there's a cure so much as there are ways to win out in the end. Prevail.

The word *burnout* was first used to describe an exhaustion of emotional strength around 1970 and is now officially recognized by the World Health Organization as a syndrome tied to a variety of symptoms, including "weakened immune systems and even cardio-vascular disease." Though it will show up differently in everyone, the official description of burnout syndrome has three components: **exhaustion, cynicism, and inefficacy**.

Exhaustion can be emotional and spiritual as well as physical.

Cynicism refers to a negative or detached mood about your work, your superiors, and your colleagues. It's disengagement.

Inefficacy means your productivity is down, you stop believing in your skills, and you don't think that what you do matters.

Here are some sobering statistics: The average US worker works 47 hours per week (49 percent work 50 hours or more, 20 percent work 60 hours or more). Only one in three takes an actual lunch break. A quarter of American workers work night hours (10 p.m. to 6 a.m.), which is the highest in the world, and 27 percent work at least partly on the weekends. In the past three years, employee stress is up 28 percent, anxiety is up 74 percent, and depression is up 58 percent. One of the reasons for the spread of burnout is that with all this time and energy put in to work, an estimated 70 percent of workers aren't passionate about their jobs.

It's one thing to give yourself to your job. It's another to give yourself to something you don't care about, are uninterested in, or detest. This mix of high time and energy commitment with low engagement and passion wipes us out (exhaustion). Then we stop caring about what we're doing during those hours. We don't enjoy who we're doing it with or for (cynicism), and we stop feeling like it has a purpose (inefficacy).

Burnout also doesn't just happen with age. I went through it at nineteen.

As a varsity high school basketball player and then as a freshman at Elon College (now Elon University), basketball was my life. I was a heavily invested athlete whose entire identity revolved around the sport. But during my sophomore year of college, my passion for the game waned considerably. I wasn't miserable enough to quit the team, but I was not enjoying myself enough—or committed enough—to rationalize all the time I was putting in. I reached a point where basketball felt more like a job than a passion. Sure, I'd had dips in high school—especially the end of my senior year—but I always rode those out and bounced back. But when it happened this time, it was more like a crisis. I had to face it: I was burned out.

The person I was and the one I was becoming were no longer inextricably tied to basketball. It wasn't just the time and energy, but the disconnect that was burning me out. Because I *had* to do it, I started to resent it. I was separated from the reasons I had loved the game since I was five years old: the challenge, the camaraderie, the commitment, the competition. Mentally, I turned something I'd once loved and obsessed over into just a job. I'd think, *My job today is to go to practice from two to four.* I was punching a clock, viewing this activity that once gave me joy like someone twice my age who rides a train to a cubicle and can't wait for five o'clock.

I did the bare minimum to keep my scholarship and stay on the team, but deservedly, I rode the bench. And I didn't even care. My immaturity and lack of self-awareness at the time allowed me to blame the coach, make excuses about why I wasn't playing, and complain about the entire situation. But the cold truth was this was all on me. I allowed my burnout to get to this point, and I was the one who chose to hide behind blaming, complaining, and excuses.

As hard as that time was on me, I am grateful for the experience because it was so instructive. Later, when I worked with an unmotivated kid at DeMatha or Montrose, I could say, "I get it, I've been where you are. You're at a fork in the road. I don't recommend taking the path I took." Going from playing every minute in high school to riding the bench at Elon also gave me empathy for those who didn't get in the game. "I know it's tough for you to show up at practice every day and bust your butt," I'd say, "and know there's not a guarantee of more playing time." Seeing that experience from the player's perspective made me a better coach and more compassionate human being.

Burnout is not about work alone, because it can spread to the rest of our lives. If we are disconnected at our jobs, there's a good chance we're not being the best partner, most patient friend, caring parent, or engaged hobbyist. Burnout is like a fire that can extinguish our passion, interest, and energy across all aspects of our lives.

Just like with stress and stagnation, burnout is "a signal, not a long-term sentence." The best thing we can do for ourselves is recognize when burnout is bearing down. If we can spot the early red flags, we can take action before we are fully extinguished. We can make those internal adjustments and pivots. Preventing is always going to be more efficient than solving, so keep that in mind as you read.

CHAPTER ELEVEN
Engage the Process

Over the past few years, the phrase "trust the process" has entered the mainstream. If you're a basketball fan, no doubt you've heard it. "Trust the process" went from a rebuilding strategy of the Philadelphia 76ers to the nickname for its star Joel Embiid to something of a running joke. "The process" was a painful (for the fans) rebuilding strategy for a team that had been losing for a long time.

For the rest of us, the process means the (sometimes uncomfortable, sometimes arduous, always necessary) steps needed to get to where you want to go. I choose to use the verb *engage* instead of *trust*, because it is active. **Engage the process means keep your attention and energy on the steps, not the goal.** "The problem of judging ourselves based on outcomes," performance skills coach Ben Oliva explains, "is that we lose track of the things that *get us* the best outcomes. By focusing all our energy on the outcomes, we end up getting worse outcomes."

Stick with the **how**, and the **what** will naturally flow out.

The process of building a brick wall is laying mortar and carefully stacking brick by brick; if you trust that process, you will end up with a brick wall at the end. There is nothing else that can result from it.

Engaging the process is an outgrowth of the first chapter of this book—focus—because it means deal with what's in front of you. Steve Chandler, performance coach and author, suggests we "shift from doing the whole thing, to simply beginning. Shift from spending hours on something to spending just a few minutes getting it started. It shifts you into the present moment (the only place where the future gets created.)" The reason that engaging the process helps defeat burnout is that it shrinks our world to a manageable size, which gives us focus, victories, and confidence.

Student

Kobe was the ultimate process guy. He was so committed—to studying, to practicing, to learning and gaining an edge, to being a student—even after he was already the best player in the world! As a young child in Italy, Kobe would get tapes of NBA games mailed to him, which he'd watch "the way most children do a Disney movie." As a player, he didn't skip steps, which is why he preached the basics; he once said the way you know you found something you love is if you "love the process."

Kobe treated practice as important (if not *more* important) as the game because that's where the work happened. He knew that without practice, *there is no game*. And he never saw it as a grind; it was always a privilege. "Those times when you don't feel like working," he wrote in *The Mamba Mentality*, "you're too tired, you don't want to push yourself, but you do it anyway. **That is actually the dream.**"

UCLA coach John Wooden—who won an astounding ten titles in twelve years—knew about the power of process. When he watched his players during a game, he didn't even check the score. He'd focus on "if the players were making quick, straight-line cuts . . . or banana cuts." Because he could infer how they were doing based on how sharp they were moving on offense. Wooden trusted the process that much. In his mind, a player cutting correctly would be doing everything else correctly as well. "It's the little things that are vital," he once said. "Little things make the big things happen."

Less Talk

One of the pioneers of the process mindset in competitive sports is tennis instructor and "father of modern coaching" Tim Gallwey. Gallwey's book *The Inner Game of Tennis* has become a bible for so many athletes, and businessmen, entrepreneurs, and all kinds of seekers, since its publication in the 1970s. Everyone, from Seahawks coach Pete Carroll to *Moneyball* author Michael Lewis, has sung its praises.

The essential strategy around Gallwey's work is: **get out of your own way so you can execute what you are capable of doing**. Gallwey's "hands off" approach puts the learner in charge of taking in the information and executing. It can best be summed up by a quote from a Gallwey student: **"It's not that I don't know what to do; it's that I don't do what I know."**

Gallwey came upon his technique almost accidentally as a tennis instructor when he noticed that whatever he was telling his students *not* to do, they were doing. Meanwhile, the things he kept reminding the students *to do* were getting lost in all the instructions. He could see them trying to remember all his guidance, but it wasn't being internalized. So Gallwey experimented—by trying to tell them as little as possible. He would pick up a racket and silently demonstrate a proper forehand. Then he would let the student discover the correct process. He didn't teach tennis as much as "awareness instruction" and focus.

Incredibly, this worked! His students began to pick things up quicker. Not only that, but the students were correcting mistakes Gallwey hadn't even pointed out! Once Gallwey got past his ego (his expensive instructions weren't helping) and saw what was working, he had developed a new system.

Gallwey brings an almost Zen approach to sports. "The first skill to learn is the art of letting go of the human inclination to judge ourselves and our performance as either good or bad," Gallwey wrote. "Letting go of the judging process is a basic key to the Inner Game." His work is to remove the athlete's judgment of the matter, their thinking about what's happening, so the natural movements they already know can have a clear path. The process takes center stage.

The Learning

Bob Richey, head basketball coach at Furman University, has the rare distinction of never having a single player leave his school without a college degree. He's not just an impressive coach but a great guide and teacher of young minds. One thing he said to me, which I can't get out of my head, was, "You can't fire a cannon out of a canoe." It was such a brilliantly efficient metaphor and I understood right away. You need a stable place to launch from, especially if that something aims to be impactful. This was a common theme in our conversation: making sure you're steady where you stand.

Bob is an enthusiastic process guy. He separates recruits into two groups: the gain-minded and the growth-minded. "In order to sustain high performance consistently," he told me, "you have to love the growth not just the gains. You have to love improving . . . not just the results. You have to love the learning, not just the information." This is what engaging the process means—not only valuing the finished project but all the pieces along the way. If you're only interested in reaching the summit, you're going to have a hell of time climbing the mountain.

Only working with the end in mind is bound to burn you out. Why? Because you only can finish once! Even then, it's a brief moment in time before you have to move on to the next thing. The outcome is fleeting, while the process is always. On top of this, **the outcome is not always in our control**. If we engage the process but don't emerge victorious, we can still feel the work was valuable.

Engaging the process means viewing failures as part of what we do, not some setback to get over. Too often we forget that the failures go hand in hand with the work. If we lean into our misses, we open ourselves up to their lessons. The process allows us to believe: *I win even when I lose.* An analysis of high performers found that they were "yet" people. They understood how to properly react to failures. "Even a dramatic career failure can become a spring to success *if you respond the right way*,"* a *Harvard Business Review* study found. Responding to losses as feedback is the distinguishing feature between the good and the great.

Poker players have a term for judging a hand solely based on the outcome: *resulting*. Resulting is a mistake because you've lost sight of your process and have gotten caught up in what happened. Luck can and will fall on anyone, but good process is the difference maker. In poker, resulting is considered a mark of a beginner. The pros follow their process whether they win the pot or not.

What You Know

In writing this book, I have found that if I shut off the judgment brain and just let the process part of my brain cook—*I've done this before, I know how to do it, I trust the system and my instincts*, everything flows much more easily. Just do the paragraph, or the page, or the chapter. I put myself on autopilot, trusting my systems, and it figures itself out. I know where I will land.

Business coaches Dr. Jason Selk (who works with the St. Louis Cardinals) and Tom Bartow use the example of the batter at the plate: Which does he focus on, getting the hit or the fundamentals of hitting? The fundamentals, because "focusing on results—or the end product—actually makes it harder to produce those results." The batter doesn't think about getting a hit; he focuses on his knees, his shoulders, his follow-through. That's the process.

---

* Italics mine.

Steph Curry focuses on his shooting form, not if it's going to go in: that's why it *goes* in. As basketball writer Nick Greene wrote about Steph and his fellow Splash Brother, Klay Thompson, "Their forms are as pure in Game 7 of the NBA Finals as they are during no-stakes, defense-free shootarounds." They are committed to process, which doesn't really change. And any efforts to change it, to force it, even to think about it too much, can throw you off.

Famously, Larry Bird used this knowledge about shooters to get an advantage on the competition. Before the 1988 three-point contest, Bird walked over to his main competitor—Leon Wood—and asked if he had changed his shooting form. Perplexed, Wood said no.

Bird responded, "Well, something looks different about your release." *Brutal.* Right before Bird walked away, he also mentioned to Wood to be careful because the red, white, and blue balls (the bonus balls) were slippery. *So brutal.* Bird won the contest. Yes, he was the best shooter alive at the time, but he also had his competition question his process, which threw off that process. Getting a knockdown shooter to think too much about his form while he's shooting is the best way to undermine him. And the Legend knew it.

W.I.N.

This concept was popularized by Notre Dame football coach Lou Holtz, and I have made it central to my work. W.I.N. stands for **What's Important Now?** If mindfulness or meditation don't sound like your thing, that's fine. Living present is about striving to make things manageable. You can literalize this if you want. When you get up in the morning, ask yourself, **What's the most important thing I need to do today?** Write it down or type it into your phone. When you put your head on your pillow that night, check it off. You have a clear, demonstrable thing to account for your day. This also gives you a little victory to celebrate instead of waiting months or years for the larger ones. That feeling will give you a boost, motivating you to do it again the next day. Pretty soon you'll have stacked up a few days in a row like this.

Focusing on the little steps along the way allows you to get real-time feedback plus the satisfaction (and dopamine boost) of checking off some boxes. Marathon runners don't make it through 26.2 miles by thinking about the finish line. They take each mile at a time. Yes, we need a big picture in our minds to plan, but sometimes we need a narrow window, an immediate box to check, to feel accomplished. All of the big things you want to do in life are made up of the small ones.

It comes down to taking the time to examine yourself. Jerry Colonna sees a parallel in the world of film. "Film is deceptive," Colonna writes in *Reboot*. "What appears to be fluid, ongoing, and always in motion is, in fact, a series of still moments viewed incredibly quickly. Just like life itself." Once we accept that we are a series of choices (of movements), we can stop. We are able to take control of our work, our relationships, and our lives. "Slowing down the movie of our lives, seeing the frames and how they are constructed, reveals a different way to live, a way to break old patterns, to see experiences anew through radical self-inquiry."

Jerry and Larry (and Dave)

Comedians Larry David and Jerry Seinfeld are each worth almost a billion dollars. No doubt about it, as entertainers who started with little, that's impressive. But what impresses me more is that both have stayed on top of their game, long after they could have sat back and coasted. They still care about the work. Seinfeld commits the same effort to each new stand-up routine that he did when he was still a working comic in the 1970s and '80s. He respects the craft that much and he's still motivated to do great work. In a recent interview he said:

> I went out to Long Island yesterday, got home at 7, and then grabbed a sport jacket to run out of the house.
> My wife says, "Where are you going?"
> I go, "I got to go to a club."
> She says, "Why?"
> We're married 18 years. You still have to answer these questions.
> I go, "I need to try out some stuff."
> Real comedians want to go on every single night.

In the early 2000s, a few years after his mammoth hit *Seinfeld* went off the air, he realized that he missed his first love and wanted to be a stand-up comedian again. One of his challenges at the time, which was self-imposed, was that in 1998 he retired all his old material in a very public way (he called his last special, "I'm Telling You for the Last Time").

First of all, let's just take a moment to put some respect on that choice. Can you imagine a rock band doing that? Agreeing to never again play their best songs? Can you imagine anyone doing that? It's hard enough to create something memorable, but to then say, "I'm not going to lean on that anymore. I'm going to do it again." It's a bold move. (Or depending on how you look at it, it's career suicide!)

The point is that Seinfeld believed enough in the work that he didn't want to phone it in, play the hits, and go home. So at around the age of fifty, with arguably the greatest sitcom in history under his belt, and hundreds of millions in the bank, he *chose* to start over. He talked to his friend Chris Rock about this desire to start up again from scratch, maybe looking for some sympathy. But Rock gave him the answer he needed to hear. "Well," Rock said, "at least you know there's only one way to do it."

Brick by brick.

"You either learn to do it or you will die in the ecosystem," Seinfeld has said about his process. "I grasped the essential principle of survival in comedy very young. You learn to be a writer." While inspiration is no doubt part of any creation, Seinfeld's perspective is more athlete than artist, continually putting up the reps. "My writing technique is just: You can't do anything else," he said. "You don't have to write, but you can't do anything else. . . . That sustains me."

His *Seinfeld* co-creator, Larry David, has long given up on stand-up (he used to yell at audiences), but his creative approach is also instructive. David continues to maintain incredibly high standards for his work. Though HBO would rather put a new season out every year, Larry only does a *Curb Your Enthusiasm* season when he feels he has something funny or interesting to say. Sometimes six years pass between seasons *because he doesn't have to do it.*

Sure, the cynic can say, well, he has the money. Yes, but that's not the point. The point is that he respects the work and the process enough to only put out something he can be proud of. Both men are my role models in terms of how to act after you've achieved success. Let it be a platform, not an anchor. Don't insult the craft you love by coasting, *especially* after you could get away with it. Both Seinfeld and David are aware of how too much easy success can burn you out (it'll look like boredom), so they keep that fire stoked by never disrespecting the work.

No Stairway

Brett Bartholomew, who founded Art of Coaching, works with top athletes, US Special Forces, and Fortune 500 companies. He defined burnout to me as "a slow erosion of self . . . giving yourself away and not filling your own cup." Brett is a magnetic speaker who cuts right to the heart of the matter. When I asked him to summarize his "conscious coaching" philosophy, he replied that it's "intense self-awareness [about] where your own b.s. lies, how you can better interact with other people." He told me he keeps a sticky note on his computer that has a list:

- Spousal
- Intellectual
- Physical
- Social
- Financial
- Recreational
- Spiritual

Each day he tries to hit those domains at some point—that is how he judges success.

Shift your focus to the process, micro-steps, and tangible markers of incremental progress. *There is no stairway. There are only steps.* Strive to create positive, forward momentum. Win THIS meal. Win THIS workout. Win THIS sale. Win THIS meeting. Win THIS phone call. You achieve success by winning as many moments and opportunities as possible. How does a team pull off a massive upset when it is the underdog? For one, they do *not* focus on winning the game. Instead they focus on winning THIS rebound. THIS loose ball. THIS free throw. THIS stop. *The process is always in front of you;* the outcome is fleeting, brief, and may be out of your hands.

At the age of four, Wayne Gretsky used to watch hockey on TV with a pen and paper. During the game, he would practice following the puck on the page, tracing its path. Those extra hours watching the speeding puck (on a small, low-definition screen) gave him incredible vision when he was on the ice. Jerry Rice used to toss a football back and forth from one hand to the other in a completely dark room—feeling with his throwing hand exactly where it would land and responding with his catching hand. It allowed him to see a ball fifty feet in the air and know exactly where it was going to come down. Roger Federer would warm up by trying to hit the tennis ball into the ball boy's stationary hand. Stephon Marbury grew up poor in the Coney Island projects, playing basketball indoors with a wire hanger bent into a rim and hung on the back of the door. (He also did jump rope with an extension cord, so every miss hurt like hell.) They were all process people who committed themselves to the steps, knowing that each one led closer to where they wanted to go.

Action Steps

- Turn your latest big project into a series of **microsteps**; write them out. Come up with a small reward (intrinsic or extrinsic) to give yourself as you check each box.

- Even if an idea is "big," **don't shy away from the process**. Reid Hoffman, founder of LinkedIn, former PayPal executive, and angel investor, recommends putting time aside to work "on something that could be part of your Plan B. If you have a business idea you want to pursue, a skill you want to learn, a relationship you want to form, or some other curiosity or aspiration, start on it as a side project and see where it goes. At a minimum, just start talking to people."

- **Work While You Wait:** University of Louisiana baseball coach Tony Robichaux coined this phrase in explaining that one of the problems with youth sports

(continues)

(continued)

is that everyone always gets to participate, which was not reflective of the future these kids will have—in baseball and in everything else. He tries to encourage people in all walks of life to make sure they worked while they waited, not just when the door opened. **What are you waiting on? Is there a way to work for it before the door opens?**

CHAPTER TWELVE

Growth

When you break it down, life is simply a never-ending series of attempts.

Everything we do, every minute of every day, is just another attempt.

Another at bat. Another rep.

Some attempts feel bigger and more important because we build them up in our minds.

But in reality, they're not. Not in the BIG picture.

That interview?

It's just an attempt.

That proposal?

It's just an attempt.

That workout?

It's just an attempt.

That speech?

It's just an attempt.

They are all attempts. Nothing more, nothing less.

Thankfully, every attempt is a chance to learn, a chance to grow, and a chance to develop in some area of life.

That's because every attempt provides us with feedback. We get to choose how to process this feedback, and the perspective we bring to it influences our performance.

We can choose to react to the feedback in a way that serves us and moves us forward. Or we can choose to react to the feedback in a way that cripples us and sets us back. The goal is to get as many attempts as possible, to continually learn, and keep moving forward toward the person we strive to become. This is what I mean by growth.

Engage the process (chapter 11) and growth (chapter 12) are flip sides of the same coin: engaging the process is a strategy to beat burnout when the **big picture is the cause of exhaustion**. Chapter 12 is the reverse: when the day-to-day is weighing on you, take the opposite tack. Pull back and focus on where you're going. **Growth is big picture thinking.**

Ceilings

Before a future NBA player is drafted, one of the metrics discussed is his "ceiling." This is a term for how good the player can be if all things go right—and it's a hypothetical. It's the most optimistic view of his potential. A player's career is a mix of his own commitment to the game, the organization he plays for, the teammates he shares the floor with, the injuries that do or don't occur, and so on. The top players are constantly pushing this ceiling by working on the aspects they can control. No matter where they are on the statistic leader boards or in the contract process, **they commit to growth**.

"The average players want to be left alone," NBA coach Doc Rivers has said. "The good players want to be coached. The great players want to be told the truth." Doc means the truth as in *what they still need to do*. NBA players, especially the great ones, have more than enough people telling them how amazing they are. And I'm sure that feels great. But what they really need is a teammate, coach, or mentor who reminds them of the distance between where they are and their ceiling. Or someone who convinces them their "ceiling" isn't even real.

Top NBA trainer Rob McClanaghan echoes this, saying the great players have something in common: "They walk into the gym looking to learn something new." *Looking* to learn something new. Seeking out the thing that will give them the edge. McClanaghan has worked with everyone up to (and including) LeBron, and he has said that the King "is always looking to add something new to his game." No matter who they are, or how much raw talent they have, "if they don't keep improving, they won't be able to survive long-term."

This is especially true in basketball, where a player's raw athleticism won't hold throughout his thirties, when he still needs to contribute on the court. He needs to up his basketball IQ, build new weapons, and improve his weak spots (maybe his outside shooting or ball handling). When Jordan returned in 1995, after his first retirement, he focused much more on his midrange game. He was obviously still athletic, but he chose to rely less on physical dominance and to play a more cerebral game, which helped the Bulls win another three titles in a row and extended his career into the 2000s. Instead of his explosiveness, his basketball IQ became his weapon of choice. I think people need to recognize how impressive Jordan's decision to *force growth* on himself was. And why it was successful.

Fail Better

The average person tends not to learn from failure because of a **self-serving bias**: when things go well, it was his doing. When things go poorly, someone else screwed up. If you feel like failure is due to other circumstances beyond your control, you're never going to learn from it. The self-serving bias is very common. But in high performers "the self-serving bias that interferes with learning often recedes and even disappears."

While most people are looking to protect themselves from blame, high performers are seeking it out. (Remember Bradley

Beal telling Drew Hanlen all the things he could've done better after scoring 60 points?) A self-serving bias might save you from an uncomfortable conversation or a drop in mood, but when the moment passes, you'll have gained nothing from the experience. Then the experience really is a failure because you took nothing from it.

"Lying to oneself destroys the very possibility of learning," writes journalist and former table tennis champion Matthew Syed. "How can one learn from failure if one has convinced oneself . . . that a failure didn't actually occur." This is not just an immature or rookie mistake. Syed quotes a study that shows that "error denial increases as you go *up* the pecking order." The more you rise, the more you're insulated from criticism—either because of your own choices or the environment you've built. I think everyone recognizes that learning is important when you begin. But not everyone embraces learning after you've reached a certain level.

In Progress

Performance researchers Weisinger and Pawliw-Fry, whom I referenced in Part I, single out accepting responsibility as one of the key skills of exceptional performance. And it *is* a skill. "One of the differentiators of the top 10 percent of performers," they found, "was an ability to *not become defensive when criticized* . . . [and] appraise the criticism as information that can help them." We are wired to protect ourselves, but growth requires working against that instinct.

We are all works in progress. There should always be a gap between your actual self (who you are) and your desired self (who you are working to become). You should never feel "finished." You should never reach your "ceiling." You should never feel you've "arrived." Once you feel there's nowhere to go, you lose the motivation and sense of growth that pulls you forward.

Over Seven Feet

"I enjoy being out on the floor and developing," Kevin Durant told me. "I enjoy conquering that challenge, whatever it is that day. I feel like each day is fresh. . . .That's what keeps me going every day." I've known Kevin for a long time, and that has always been true. He's distinguished—even among the top tier of players—because of his commitment to growth.

I remember Kevin starting to get on everyone's radar his sophomore year at National Christian, a rival of Montrose Christian, where I coached. He had just hit a growth spurt and was around six foot nine inches but with guard-like skills. He was relatively unpolished (compared with who he'd become), but word was he was very coachable and *loved* the work, a true gym rat. Overall, he played hard and smart against us that day, but was slightly overmatched with our more physical and experienced players. While I don't know what was going on in his head, I am sure he knew how important this game was to his national reputation.

Montrose assistant coach David Adkins had met with Kevin and his family a year prior to discuss Kevin maybe attending Montrose. But Coach Adkins told them flat out: Kevin isn't good enough to play at Montrose. (Coach Adkins and I still laugh about that to this day.) So I am sure Kevin wanted to show everyone on the court and in the stands that he was not only good enough, but that Coach Adkins was dead wrong.

Unfortunately (or fortunately, depending on your views of growth), Durant missed two key free throws late in the game that would have given National Christian the win. After those two misses, perfecting his shot became an obsession for Kevin. All these years later, he's considered one of the greatest shooting big men in history. His free throw percentage is in the upper 80s, and in his last two post-seasons, when pressure was highest, it was over 90 percent. In researching for this paragraph, I found there's even a Yahoo question: "Has Kevin Durant ever missed two free throws in a row?" The answer: rarely. I've never talked to him about those free throws years ago, but I'm sure the experience of those high-pressure misses carried him forward. Though he's nearly seven feet tall, the guy just keeps growing.

Burnout is feeling like the day, the task, the job, has maxed out and you're putting in the time and energy (input) for little gain (output). Sometimes this is the nature of the work itself, but very often it's our mindset. In order to not get burned out over a grueling season, professionals like KD lean into what's new, what's different, and what's missing. "I feel like the game is always evolving and I got to continue to evolve with it," he said during our interview. "That's the fun part."

We Beats Me

Growth is not always an individual process; sometimes it happens as part of a group, whether that's a sports team, a military regiment, a business organization, or a family. Danny Ferry, whom I had the pleasure of interviewing, was a former College Player of the Year, the second overall pick in the 1989 NBA Draft, and an NBA champion. Since retirement he has worked in the front office of four NBA teams: Spurs, Hawks, Cavs, and Pelicans.

Ferry has the unique résumé of having played for perhaps the greatest high school, college, and professional coaches of all time: Morgan Wootten, Coach K (Mike Krzyzewski), and Gregg Popovich. All three coaches, he told me, shared one thing in common. They made it like "you participated in something bigger than yourself and contributed to something bigger than yourself." The key, he told me, was that the coaches each got buy-in from the team. This means that the players believed in the team's growth more than their own.

Ferry told me that the best teammates throughout his long career were not distinguished by their numbers, but by their unselfishness,

"demonstrating being part of something bigger than yourself."
They weren't driven by self-glorification, but winning. One of the
great benefits of being part of a team is tapping into this collective
growth, which is a powerful force.

The Source

Advice to the burned out: get clarity on what is causing your
burnout. Are you uninterested in the goal? Bored with the steps? In
need of a break? Craving a new role? Detroit running back and Hall
of Famer Barry Sanders retired early because he was tired of his team
losing, and he saw no future where that would change (this was in
the years before players had more control over where they played).
Michael Jordan retired from basketball in 1993 because winning
was no longer enough. Plenty of athletes have left at the top of
their game because they felt a misalignment between their goals
and their accomplishments. Indianapolis Colts quarterback Andrew
Luck shocked the football world when he retired a month before
his thirtieth birthday. Luck had been plagued by injuries and was
sick of the rehab process, but there must have been a larger internal
reason for his quitting, and I really respect him for listening to it.
Though the public only knows Andrew Luck as a football player,
he's a human being, and he was ready for the next part of his life to
begin, to extend the growth process.

Dr. James Gordon of the Center for Mind-Body Medicine
in Washington, DC, breaks burnout into two different types: exhaustion from doing what you love and a more existential exhaustion from doing "deeply unsatisfying" work. Figure out which
of the two you're dealing with before you take any action. What
parts of the job do you dread? Which parts get you excited? Does
the thought of a nice long vacation immediately relax you? Does
the thought of doing the same job ten years from now keep you
awake at night? These answers hold the key to why you're feeling
burned out and the clues to staving it off.

The Spotlight

In the midst of noise and distractions, high performers have a firm grasp on why they're doing what they're doing. At the start of the 2007–08 season, when the Boston Celtics added all-stars Kevin Garnett and Ray Allen to a team that already had Paul Pierce, the pressure was on for them. Expectations were *high*. In the era before it was common for stars to join forces, the 2008 Celtics were the real deal: a bona fide superteam. The assumption was that these guys *had to* win.

Their coach, Doc Rivers, understood that these high expectations could be used as a tool instead of treating them as an obstacle. "I don't think you should run from pressure," Rivers told them. "I think you should run towards it." In the team's practice facility hung sixteen championship banners, telling the story of the Celtics' historic place in NBA lore. Rivers decided for practices to "put a spotlight on the spot where the 17th banner would go." Throughout that season, that spotlight never went off. The missing banner became a source of motivation and growth for those players. "Pressure is a privilege," Rivers reminded them, which helped his team lean into the expectations. They were all thinking about it, so he had them embrace it. At the end of that season, they indeed raised that seventeenth banner in Boston.

Many of us spend over half of our waking hours at work. Of course, the external rewards are important, but they will never be enough to get you out of bed every morning, onto that crowded train or backed-up highway, to sit under fluorescent lights for over eight hours, to then come home too tired for leisure time, and to do it all over again. The push has to come from within.

Herbert Freudenberger, PhD, a psychologist from the 1970s, was the first to use the term "burnout" in relation to work when he observed a particular kind of strain on health-care workers. (He took the term from its common usage to describe drug addicts.) He found that exhaustion was just one of burnout's three dimensions, along with a feeling of not belonging and a listlessness that spreads into other parts of your life.

Tapping into your need for growth is something you must do regularly, a way to remind yourself why you're doing what you're doing. Where are you headed? How is what you're doing connected to getting there? If you could shine a spotlight on something missing in your life (like that missing championship banner), what would it be?

Down First, Then Up

When it comes to a daunting task, don't just try to get THROUGH it: aim to get FROM it. The process isn't always smooth, it's rarely easy, and you might not feel successful. But it does its work on you. Don't stop when it gets hard because that's when things happen. Remember: Muhammad Ali didn't even *count* the sit-ups until they hurt. Growth requires discomfort, tension, and sometimes even pain.

About six months into the pandemic, I (like many people) felt stagnant, spinning my wheels, living the same Groundhog Day. I realized I needed something to train for. Something to look forward to. Something that would induce an appropriate amount of discomfort.

Something that would force me to grow.

I could go small, just to get going, or go big, hoping to raise my motivation. So I decided to go enormous: hike the Grand Canyon from rim to rim. A friend of mine invited me to join a group he'd organized and got me a spot—with less than two months to train.

I didn't see the trip as a vacation or even an adventure. I approached it as the ultimate growth experience. For one, I coupled the trip out to Arizona with a social media and communication detox, which was tough for me. I was so used to plugging into social media regularly, but I sensed that the experience required a break.

The trip would be an effort to grow out of my own distractibility and dependence on being "connected."

After a five-hour flight to Phoenix, I met the group of fifteen to take the van for a six-hour drive to the north rim of the canyon. The group arrived, jet-lagged and sore, and spent the night in cabins about two miles from the rim. I felt like I had just shut my eyes when it was time for the 3 a.m. wake-up. We were on the road at a pitch-black 4 a.m. to start our hike before sunrise at 5 a.m. in order to maximize everyone's daylight. There were three trained guides who helped to herd us from rim to rim (one stayed in the front, one remained toward the middle, and one brought up the rear). Based on age, fitness level, and experience, the guides estimated it would take the slowest person in our group around fifteen to twenty hours to finish.

The first fifteen miles was a descent down the north rim. It had snowed two to three inches Sunday night, and it was 7° F and pitch-black when we started. We each wore a headlamp for vision and carried our own pack, which weighed twenty to twenty-five pounds. Of course my inner voice was screaming about the cold for that first hour, but I simply chose not to listen to it. Throughout the hike, any time I found my self-talk not serving me, I changed the subject. *That's not helping, Alan, so why don't we say something else to ourselves, okay?* It didn't change the physical difficulties, but flipping that little switch helped. **I control my self-talk**. **I write it, recite it, and repeat it.**

Of the six million people who visit the Grand Canyon each year, less than 1 percent go all the way to the bottom, but I decided to make that my motivation rather than a point of discouragement. It was my seventeenth banner. The trek itself was unusually challenging. The physical exhaustion really snuck up on me, as I'm used to high-intensity training, but this was essentially just a walk. Granted, I walked at a pretty brisk pace, but it didn't elicit the cardiovascular exhaustion of running sprints or the muscular exhaustion of lifting weights. It was a lot of time on my feet, traversing constantly changing terrain, which accumulates on the muscles and on the mind. That pain told me I was stretching—physically and psychologically—so I leaned into it. I welcomed the discomfort, knowing that if it was easy, everyone would hike the Grand Canyon. It became about earning an experience instead of having it handed to me.

The second part of the hike was going ten miles up the South Rim. This unique aspect of hiking a canyon—you go down first and then up, the opposite of a mountain—plays tricks on the body and the mind. Every year, hundreds of people need to be rescued from the canyon because they went farther down than they were able to return. There are signs on the canyon's trails reminding hikers of this, but everyone thinks they can make it. Plenty learn the hard way they can't.

We stayed hydrated and took short pit stops to refuel and carb up, but nevertheless, about 75 percent of the way through, I hit a wall. My calves were so tight it was like someone had bound them with rope. The heaviness in my legs felt like a small child was hanging on to each one. The self-talk—*When will this be over?*—came back with a vengeance, and it took more effort to blunt it. I focused on my heartbeat, my breathing, the majestic cliffs, the deep reds in the canyon, the glorious shock of blue sky, the developing camaraderie of the group. I reminded myself this was a growth experience, not a leisure one. But it wasn't easy.

We understandably got a tad slower from mile to mile, which became mentally difficult to overcome. In the beginning, we were walking at a twenty-minute-mile pace. By the end, a mile took almost an hour, which messed with my head. Four miles left felt doable, until I did the math—which was discouraging. Thankfully, the harder the physical part got, the deeper our conversations got, and we used our emotional connections to fuel us.

When I finished the twenty-five miles in nine hours and twenty minutes, I was entirely spent. My body was drained and my mind was empty, but I felt euphoric, a sense of accomplishment that I carried with me back home. I am a different person now from the one who started that canyon hike. And with a growth mindset, I will be a different person at the end of the next thing, too.

The Right Reasons

I first met the Toronto Raptors' president of basketball operations (and NBA champion) Masai Ujiri over fifteen years ago. I had just started working as the performance coach at Montrose Christian, and Masai was running Radar Hoops, a recruiting site for African players. He brought us three young players from Nigeria, who would go on to play for UVA, FSU, and Xavier.

In the world of high school basketball, there is a crop of men known simply as "handlers," who find young talent, take them under their wing, and provide for them. This ranges from paying for their schooling and giving them a place to live to hooking them up with athletic gear and giving them rides to practice. These young players usually come from one of two places—a disadvantaged background or another country. Handlers see it as an investment; it comes with the unwritten promise that if the kid ever "makes it," the handler will get some future payoff.

To be honest, very few of these people are in it for the right reasons—wanting to provide opportunity and a better life to those who need it most. A few do care about their kids and want to help them find a way out (of whatever circumstance they are in, which is usually the same circumstance the handler came from). They don't want, nor expect, anything in return other than the joy of contributing to the growth of a young person. That was Masai.

My longtime friend and mentor David Adkins introduced us. "Alan, mark my words," Coach Adkins said, "this guy will be running an NBA team one day. He gets it." Coach Adkins was right. Masai always went out of his way to speak to me when he came by. We would chat for a few minutes, and he was always thoughtful and interested. Yes, I said *interested*, not *interesting*. He was curious about my work and what I thought about his players, on and off the court. He was a relationship guy at heart and he was always so kind and so present. I could tell why these kids trusted him and I sensed in him a deep compassion and understanding.

I will never forget two important lessons he taught his kids and, by extension, me. They were both about focusing on growth.

1. **"Star where you are."** Don't worry about your next job or next position; focus on being the best you are capable of where you are at the moment. If you star in your current role, or current job, it will lead to . . .

2. **"Improvement > Advancement."** Self-improvement in itself will propel you forward. Masai believed that the key to advancing in your career boiled down to your rate of improvement, growth, and development. When you get better, better opportunities open up. Don't worry too much about "the game" of getting ahead. Commit to what you can control.

Seeking Rejection

At the end of 2017, comedy writer Emily Winter was in a rut. So she made a resolution at the start of the new year to do something bold: she would try to get a hundred rejections of her work. She would pitch and submit her writing to so many print and media outlets that she'd have a giant pile of nos to show for it. She wasn't a glutton for punishment. Not exactly. Her thinking was that the experience would strengthen her. "If you've never experienced rejection," she explained, "then you're not growing." So she went into the year hoping to create a type of "post-traumatic strength" where all that rejection would create a second skin that made her stronger.

However, something else happened on the way to a hundred rejections. Sure, Winter got a lot of nos, as planned. But she also got yeses, *a lot of them*, and ended the year with "the best résumé that

I've ever had." Winter's unorthodox process gave her an extra type of motivation; since her goal was to accumulate as many rejections as possible, she *had to* put herself out there—*really* out there. And it led to the most prolific and consequential work year of her life. Her story is illuminating because it encapsulates the idea that getting stronger *is* getting ahead. They are part of the same growing process. Both require risk and the ability to face failure.

Eric Weiner, in his book about the happiest places on earth, *The Geography of Bliss*, went to Iceland and found a culture where kids are encouraged from a young age to produce whatever art they want and continue to do so into adulthood. (There's none of that "don't quit your day job" mentality.) "One result of this freewheeling attitude is that Icelandic artists produce a lot of crap," Weiner writes. "They're the first to admit it. But crap plays an important role in the art world. In fact, it plays exactly the same role as it does in the farming world. It's fertilizer. The crap allows the good stuff to grow."

Action Steps

- **Inventory:** If burnout is a disconnect between your values and your work, it may be time for an inventory. On a sheet of paper, write a column of what you think of as your values. In a second column, list the aspects of your job that tap into these values. If you are stumped about column 2, it may be time to change roles and build a new column 2.

- Former Celtics coach Kevin Eastman recommends conducting a **"truth audit"** at least once a year. Be honest about where you are, where you'd like to be, and what you're doing that's "keeping you from getting there."

- Make of list of five failures in your life that felt significant at the time, or which still feel that way. When you are done with that list, go back through it and determine what, if anything, resulted out of those failures. It could be an opportunity, a lesson, a chance at self-reflection, anything. It's impossible to fail without taking something from it—you just have to try to find it.

- Look back at Emily Winter's one hundred rejections project. Can you adapt this process for your own work? Is there a way to force yourself out of your comfort zone and try something new again and again—and court failure—to build up that muscle?

CHAPTER THIRTEEN

Endurance and Resilience

I'm forty-five years old and still in pretty good shape. Granted, I'm no Speedo model, but as a former athlete and professional performance coach, I have taken good care of my body. But at this age, nature does its thing. Many of the physical tasks I could do with ease in my teens and twenties are now a tad bit harder. Legendary comedian George Burns (who lived to one hundred) once said, "You know you're old when you bend down to tie your shoes and think about what else you can do while you're down there." Now, I'm nowhere near that point, but the idea doesn't seem just funny anymore. It has a ring of truth. On some of those mornings when my joints are cracking like popcorn, I think about Vince Carter.

Carter is the only NBA player to play in four different decades. Let that sink in for a moment. He was there in the 1990s and he was there in 2020. He was a teammate of Dell Curry's and played against his sons, Steph and Seth. Carter played until he was forty-three years old, for twenty-two seasons, and until the end, brought it *every single night*. Carter is something of a unicorn in professional sports. When he took his last NBA shot on March 11, 2020,* he was the

---

* The 2019–2020 season was put on hiatus on this date because of the COVID pandemic. His team at the time, the Atlanta Hawks, were not part of the "bubble" that continued the season later that summer.

#3 all-time leader in games played, behind Robert Parish and Kareem Abdul-Jabbar.

Carter is an inspiration to teammates, the young and old, as well as to former players like me because he defied the odds. He's a freak athlete, as all NBA players are, but only someone committed to his own longevity could last into his forties in a high-intensity game dominated by players half that age. Carter came into the league as a majestic dunker and athletic powerhouse; over time he had to adapt his game to become a role player and veteran, a feat not many scoring machines can do. It requires more work, a different skill set, and a healthy dose of humility.

In the summer of 2008 I had the great fortune to work the Vince Carter Nike Skills Academy in Orlando. I was so impressed with how present Vince was throughout the camp, investing his time in connecting with young players and sending the elevator back down to the next wave of future NBA superstars. I don't know if Vince knew at the time he'd still be playing when those guys came of age, but it's a testament to his resilience that he was.

One of the things Vince preached heavily and emphasized daily—to the players and in our private conversations—was his commitment to keeping his mind and body healthy and optimized. It was obvious even then that he understood the correlation between his daily decisions (adequate sleep, clean eating, consistent workouts) and his longevity. He wanted to play the game he loved as long as humanly possible and laid the groundwork early. Vince intuitively understood the type of endurance required to play a long career. His understanding of that in 2008 was the reason that he was still playing in 2020.

In terms of longevity, we are currently witnessing something even more impressive with LeBron James, whose prime has lasted far longer than anyone thought possible. People thought LeBron was in his prime in 2011, ten years ago! Primes simply don't last that long. LeBron went to eight straight finals between 2011 and

2018,* an insane streak, but incredibly, during that run he played two thousand minutes *more* than anyone else in the league. His endurance is off the charts. LeBron deserves most of the credit for this, but there is another man most people don't know who shares in some of that: his name is Mike Mancias.

From 2007 to 2016, I served as the head performance coach at all of the LeBron James Nike Skills Academies. Those events provided me the unparalleled opportunity to work with the top high school and college players, alongside college and NBA coaches, and soak in the brilliance of King James himself. LeBron was always so open and transparent about where he came from, what he did to get to where he was, and what he was doing to continue to level up— even though he was already unanimously considered the summit.

LeBron made it clear that a pillar of his success hinged on how well he took care of his body. His secret weapon in this domain was his trainer, Mike Mancias. Wherever LeBron was, Mike was always nearby. Throughout camp, Mike would warm up LeBron before drills or games, stretch LeBron out when he was finished, and work LeBron out at regularly scheduled intervals throughout the week. I immediately gravitated to Mike, as I figured I had plenty to learn from the guy so highly trusted by the best player on earth.

Mike epitomized an evergreen coaching mantra: connect first, coach second. He worked hard to *earn* LeBron's trust, respect, buy-in, and believe-in through connection. Mike admitted to me that the process was challenging at first, as LeBron had learned to be a bit guarded, understandably so. LeBron had been on the basketball world's radar since he was twelve years old and on the cover of *Sports Illustrated* at sixteen. Can you even fathom how many people through the years have tried to crack his inner circle? But over

---

* "Before LeBron James turned 31, he had already clocked more playing minutes than Magic Johnson or Larry Bird did in their entire careers." (Jeff Bercovici, *Play On: The New Science of Elite Performance at Any Age* (New York: Houghton Mifflin Harcourt, 2018), 15.

time, with a combination of love and consistency, Mike convinced LeBron that he cared about him as a human being first, and as an athlete second. Mike had no hidden agenda, no interest in fame or money or self-promotion. He simply wanted what LeBron wanted—which was for King James to be healthy (injury free) and in unparalleled shape (strong, fast, and explosive).

Recently, LeBron has been talking about wanting to play in the NBA at the same time as his son Bronny, who's currently sixteen and a top high school athlete. If the Jameses pull this off, it'll be the first time in the history of the NBA that a father and son have played together. LeBron's commitment to longevity has been an inspiration to everyone in the league (and elsewhere), who may have thought their best years were behind them.

100 Laps

Rick Simmons, coach and consultant extraordinaire, and founder of the groundbreaking telos institute, stayed on his feet during our entire Zoom interview. His stand-up desk was prominently behind him, so I had little doubt he spent his workday like that, too. In our conversation, Simmons's focus and intensity never wavered. I couldn't help wondering how much being on his feet, with his body telling him that he was "on" for something, contributed to that. I promised myself to try this, if only for a week.

During our talk, Rick told me about an ultra-running event he had recently done in Cleveland: a twenty-four-hour race.

Wait, what? Sound impossible? How about if I told you it was the same one-mile loop over and over? Rick's goal was to get to one hundred laps. "I didn't know true carnage" until that event, he told me, and I got the sense he wasn't exaggerating. That kind of race leaves a lot of bodies lying around. Few things crystallize who you are and what you want quite like running the same loop non-stop for twenty-four hours.

At the end of each lap, the organizers on the sidelines would ask the runners what their goal was (a strategy I applaud, as it's personalized). Rick answered the question the same way, lap after lap: one hundred laps. But at some point in the race, he had what he described to me as an "out-of-body experience." He was watching himself run, almost as if from above, and it occurred to him that the goal he'd set for himself had actually become a limitation!

Once that clicked for him, the whole experience transformed. **He realized his goal had become a limit.** When they asked him about his goal at the next lap, he just yelled: "Do the best I can and feel good about it!" He told me the words just emitted from his mouth, without thought. Rick realized that was the only goal he ever needed. And he continued to answer that way—all the way to the twenty-four-hour mark. His final tally: 112 laps.

The most amazing part of the story is that in the years after that experience, the grueling exhaustion and physical sacrifice, Rick signed up to do the event four more times! This tells me he did it for the right reasons: not for bragging rights or just to tell the story. Rick believed in the growth that comes with that kind of experience. He didn't want to just have done it. He wanted to consistently be someone who *could* do it.

"That becomes the next real hurdle," Simmons told me, speaking about consistency. "It's one thing to raise your game for a moment or a shift, but to sustain that over a long period of time, that is the work of greatness." A twenty-four-hour race is an embodiment of what we're all running. Do we have a set limit? Or are we just trying to do our best and feel good about it?

Endurance isn't about being a flash in the pan. It's not about being hot in the moment. It's about consistency, which doesn't always get attention, especially in today's world where "going viral" is treated as the pinnacle. That attention-getting moment, which is always brief, is celebrated far more frequently than putting in the work day in and day out. Which is more impressive—doing a hundred push-ups today or doing twenty push-ups every single day for twelve years?

My friend ultra-runner Mark Neilan told me that he's met many of these social media fitness influencers, and he knows their secret: they often can only do one rep of the blow-your-mind activity that they post on social. It literally exists just to impress other people. And I don't care what the activity is: one rep just doesn't mean all that much.

Survivor

Arkansas basketball coach Eric Musselman is *a survivor*, like Masai Ujiri, he values growth over advancement. In his long coaching career, Eric has had a total of *nineteen* different stops. In the 2000s he had a string of coaching and assistant coaching jobs in the NBA before being fired by the Sacramento Kings in 2007. After losing that job, he received two more head coaching offers but he decided to do something admirable, even counterintuitive. *He voluntarily left the league.* It's hard to explain to those who don't know the coaching world, but the thirty head coaching jobs in the NBA are the Goldman Sachs, New York Yankees, Apple, and Google of the basketball world. If you can stay, you do stay.

But not Eric.

He turned down those head coaching jobs in order to reset and learn in different environments. Eric has said that "as a coach you always try to get better and improve and learn from your past mistakes. With each year of experience you should become a better coach." He sensed another NBA job at that time wouldn't have taught him anything new. He told me he wanted to "go back in the minor leagues. . . . I don't need to stay at the Ritz Carlton. I don't need to eat shrimp and lobster on the team plane. I'm cool riding a bus from Reno to Bakersfield with my team. I'm fine staying at a Days Inn. I just want to coach basketball."

Musselman has endured all these years later because he has always valued the right things. Everyone understands you have to pay your dues when you're young and new, but Musselman made this decision—to coach in the trenches—after he'd already made it to the pros! He knew he needed to go back in order to go forward.

So he went on to coach in the Dominican Republic and Venezuela (in roofless places where the wind changed the ball's direction and cockroaches crawled freely), in China, and in the NBA's G League. As he did it, he said, "I knew I was evolving as I coached." Some people would see leaving the NBA for the so-called minor leagues as a demotion. But Musselman saw it as a chance to learn; he took lessons from those experiences which built him into the kind of coach who endures. For instance, he told me that in timeouts now, he communicates more effectively because he had to learn to speak to players who didn't understand his language. He mastered body language and facial expressions, and learned how to make diagrams clear and concise. That couldn't have happened without his having to coach in other countries. Musselman viewed his struggles in the NBA not as failures, but opportunities, and he is at the top of his profession (now in the NCAA) because of that commitment to growth.

Response Time

Every obstacle and moment of adversity will reveal opportunities. They may not be obvious at first—and you may have to look closely—but *they are there*. Coupling a difficult situation with a bad response just makes things exponentially worse. Having a system in place, in advance, to overcome it is the best way to tackle anything.

Here is the three-step process I follow any time I'm faced with a major challenge:

1. Give **yourself permission** to temporarily feel scared, disappointed, worried, irritable, or anxious. There is nothing wrong with these feelings. They are normal and natural. Sit with your emotions. **Don't try to suppress them.**

2. As your anxiety escalates and things feel overwhelming, take a moment to refocus your lens and regain poise. **Become a spectator to your own emotions and reframe your mindset. Be present. React properly, in proportion to the challenge.**

3. Once you feel centered, determine what is the **best response** to the situation. Looking through a purely objective lens, what is your best option? What behavior will move you forward? What actions will improve your circumstances? Acknowledge that you don't control what is going on, just your response. And hold yourself accountable.

Standing

In the summer of 2020, I signed up for an ultra-endurance event that struck me as a little bit scary. There have been many instances in my life where I've unconsciously put limitations on myself and what I'm capable of. While I've been a decent athlete my entire life, many of these self-imposed limitations have been physical. There have been numerous times when I've heard about an incredible feat—like running a hundred miles or biking across Europe or scaling a mountain—and my default internal response has been "I could never do that." It bothered me for a long time. So I started to push against it.

Now, I am no longer okay with putting rigid limitations on myself. I am no longer okay with believing I'm incapable, insufficient, or inadequate.

That's why I signed up for Last Man Standing.

Last Man Standing, which takes place every year in Maine, has a simple premise that's in the event's name. At noon, runners begin a 4.2-mile loop through the scenic Maine woods. They have an hour or less to finish; if they do, they start the next race at 1 p.m. If they finish that race in under the hour, they start the 2 p.m. race, and so on. If you don't finish the loop in time for the next race, at the top of the next hour—or if you simply collapse and don't want to—you're out. You get to rest exactly as long as it takes to go from the time you finish a loop to the top of the hour. (For example, if you finish a loop in fifty-five minutes, you get a five-minute rest.) There are no divisions, age-groups, or gender separations. It's literally a contest to see who is standing when it's all over. As long as there are two people running, it's not.

By 10 p.m. that night, I had called it a day after completing a respectable nine laps, a little under forty miles, which is a marathon and a half. Nothing to sneeze at, especially for readers of *Raise Your Game*, who know about my grueling marathon many years ago, which at the time felt like an embarrassment. (I've since accepted how valuable it was.) Though I was nowhere near the leader board—the winner did thirty-two laps—I really wasn't competing against the other runners. I was competing against a long-buried impression of myself. I now give myself permission to try things and am open to the possibility of failing, facing what I once feared. To me, this is the foundation of true resilience.

If I asked you to predict the winner of Last Man Standing, you would never have guessed. Among the superbuff and elite, the winner was an unassuming man in his mid-fifties, with a full-on dad bod. I noticed him throughout the race, just going at his own pace, never changing his tempo based on what other people were doing. He clearly had a game plan, and his quiet confidence was a difference maker. You could see in his eyes he knew he would be the last man standing; he had the experience and expertise to know that this was a mental test, too. Brute athleticism alone wouldn't cut it. He endured because he *ran his own race.*

The Fertile Void

Yael Melamed is a San Francisco–based psychotherapist with an MBA from Harvard Business School. It's a unique combination—therapy and business—so I was immediately intrigued. Yael works to teach something profound and necessary: compassion in the workplace. She envisions a future where companies work to lift instead of damage people's sense of self-worth. Yael is taking on the concept of burnout at its root.

We were introduced through my cowriter Jon and spoke on Zoom in the fall of 2020, during the pandemic. It was an appropriate period to talk, because so many Americans were seeking therapy to get through the challenges of life under COVID-19. So Yael had a full plate, but she exuded such calm and wisdom that, when we were done talking, I thought about scheduling sessions with her.

Yael told me that as the child of immigrant parents with high expectations, she grew up doing what was expected of her rather than what she wanted. In her words, she was "caught on an escalator"—high school valedictorian, honors at Duke, Harvard Business School. Only a few months into graduate school, however, her entire life was turned upside down when she got a cancer diagnosis.

While walking to the campus library, still absorbing the shocking news, she had a vision of her obituary—a scary thought for a twenty-three-year-old. What was even more jarring was how much it depressed her. She thought about the life she was leading, the accolades she had accrued, and realized it was "not the impact I want to leave behind on the planet Earth. It was not aligned with my purpose." Fortunately, the cancer was successfully removed before it had spread, but the experience left a lasting impression. As she explained, the diagnosis was "like a medicine that worked itself on me" and it changed the course of her life and work.

Yael ended up graduating from Harvard Business School, but by then she knew she would only be happy in service to others. So she began to study psychotherapy and, with a foot in both disciplines, she came to a conclusion. She knew how much impact business leaders had on the rest of the world, in the values they taught, the behavior they rewarded, and the environments they created. So that became her focus: working to make people happier and more aligned in an overly competitive, value-draining, and burnout-infested culture. Her friend summed it up nicely: she would help put those who are stuck in their heads in touch with their hearts.

One thing Yael emphasized, in her unique East meets West (Coast) style, was the need to disengage from the rat race. It's so important to have space in our lives, whether we use that time to reflect, to seek inspiration, or to simply break away. It is the unspoken key to resilience: giving yourself room to breathe. Yael referred to these gaps as "the fertile void."

There is so much to be gained from stepping back and getting a bird's-eye view of where we are and where we're going. A car that begins a journey even the slightest bit off course, and doesn't course correct, will end up *hundreds of miles* away from its intended destination! Check in with yourself and make sure you're aligned with who you actually want to be. Look up once in a while, and watch the road.

Exposure

My discussion with Yael got me thinking about the connection between burnout and keeping things inside. If you hold in your emotions, suck up the pain, and just silently bear it, you will eventually break. Those who end up succeeding, who withstand setbacks and manage obstacles, are not putting on the appearance of toughness. They're *actually* tough, which means they are open to being vulnerable.

In recent years, NBA players like DeMar DeRozan and Kevin Love have been open about their mental health in a way that is a welcome change for professional sports. Because of the place pro athletes hold in the culture, it must be hard for them to admit they don't have it all together. Their courage is inspiring, and they have selflessly triggered a wider discussion and acceptance of the feelings we all have from time to time.

Vulnerability and strength are intimately connected to each other, and if you're afraid of being vulnerable (either out of pride or out of fear), you are putting a ceiling on what you can achieve. And you won't be able to endure through difficult phases. Those too afraid of getting hurt end up getting hurt the most. It's time everyone—men especially—gave up the idea that vulnerable feelings make us weak. Real courage is about being open.

Art of the Bounceback

With only four seconds left in the 2012 Washington Catholic Athletic Conference (WCAC) championship game, DeMatha was down one with the ball at midcourt. If we scored, senior James Robinson would become the first player in WCAC history to win four consecutive championships, in a conference that ESPN continually ranks #1 in the nation. Though the circumstances were not ideal, I still liked our chances. James Robinson was, without question, the best leader I have ever coached. Not the best shooter, ball handler, or most athletic (though he was great at all those things). He was the best leader and, not coincidentally, a winner.

At that point James had already won more games—120—than any player in the history of DeMatha basketball. With four seconds left, Coach Jones called a time-out to calm the troops, strategize, and set up a play for James to take the last shot. It was a play that we had run successively dozens of times in practice. Just as scripted, we successfully inbounded the ball to James:

> 4 seconds left . . . he ripped it across his defender and drove toward the lane.

3 seconds left . . . he got a few feet past the free throw line and elevated to shoot.

2 seconds left . . . he shot the ball on balance and with perfect form.

1 second left . . .

The ball hit the front rim and fell short.

The horn sounded. Game over. We lost by 1. The other team's fans stormed the court in celebration. James instantly collapsed, sobbing. He was inconsolable, and I could only imagine what the young man was feeling. Like he let his teammates down. Like he let his coaches down. Like he let the school down.

After Coach Jones addressed the team for the final time that season, James, all six foot three inches and 210 pounds of him, sat on the court for two hours in tears. Now, I realize there are much bigger losses in life than losing a game. But you have to view the world through James's lens. He was eighteen years old. He had spent his entire life preparing for this moment, and it wasn't the ending he had dreamed about. His heart was heavy. I imagine he had a rough night.

Do you know what James did the next morning? He didn't sulk. He didn't hide. He didn't make excuses. He arrived at the gym two hours before school started—the season is *over*, mind you—and reenacted that same play until he made it a hundred times. He got closure and moved to the Next Play. James made the decision to not let that missed shot define him or cause him further unhappiness. That young man taught me a lesson about resilience that has stayed with me to this day. You will have hard times. You will face adversity, varying levels of challenges, and setbacks. It is inevitable. Your resilience—and by extension your happiness—hinges on your ability to bounce back.

When Winning Is Losing

A loss doesn't magically become a learning opportunity on its own. It only works if you don't attach yourself—and your sense of worth—to winning. Striving for perfection actually keeps us down because it becomes more about the outcome than the experience.

In sports, coaches get nervous around winning streaks. The reason? The pressure builds so high that they're afraid that first loss will crush everyone. When Duke's Coach K is going into the NCAA tournament (which is single elimination), he'd rather *not* be on a long winning streak. A loss allows for a reset, helps you accept fallibility, gives you a chance to examine your holes. At DeMatha, Coach Jones sometimes used to say after losses, "This loss is going to be good for us. It'll teach us a lesson." Sometimes streaks are detrimental because they put forth a feeling of invincibility. Once that gets punctured, you don't have the resilience to withstand this new, unfamiliar feeling. I think of times in baseball when a no-hitter is broken up and then the pitcher implodes and goes on to lose the game. Once the dam gets that first crack in it, the flood rushes in.

Two high-profile examples of this at work are the 2007 New England Patriots and the 2016 Golden State Warriors. The Patriots had the first undefeated season in thirty-five years in the NFL (the first ever to go 16–0) and made it to the Super Bowl only to lose to a far less talented Giants team. The 2016 Warriors won an NBA record seventy-three games in the regular season (they lost a little over once *a month*), were up 3–1 in the NBA Finals, and dropped the final three straight games to LeBron's Cleveland Cavaliers. I'm sure both coaches, Bill Belichick and Steve Kerr, connect their teams' losses with the pressure that built up from being perfect. Of course, both would trade their regular season records for a championship in a second.

Remember to open the valve once in a while so you don't explode. It's win or learn, not win or lose. Failures become what you make of them. Why did I lose? What didn't work? How can

I improve? What did I gain through this experience? What's the feedback telling me? Setbacks can spring you further ahead, but you have to *use* them.

Longtime NBA coach Stan Van Gundy made a habit of getting feedback about his performance. In fact, he told a group of us last year, "After I was let go, I would reach out to players about what they liked and didn't like." The statement blew my mind. I think we all suffer a little wounded pride when we're rejected. Now think about losing a job and then checking in with your colleagues to get some useful feedback you could bring to your next job. It's a vulnerable and beautiful thing, and that's why Stan is such a special coach. You can't ask your players to face criticism and adapt to feedback if you can't do it yourself.

It's been my experience that most people asking for feedback actually want praise. "Can you tell me what you think?" translates into "Can you tell me how great this is?" Next time you ask for feedback, let the person know that **you genuinely want to hear** points of criticism and areas for improvement. They will recalibrate if they understand what you're looking for.

This tendency to avoid or tune out feedback doesn't really make any sense. Think about it: we all start something new seeking feed-back. How else did you learn to shoot a jump shot or swim free-style? You literally can't learn without feedback. But somewhere along the way our pride began to elbow out anything that sounds like criticism. Even though that criticism is simply information to be used for next time.

Turning It Around

My heart goes out to all those whose lives were most affected by the COVID-19 pandemic. Though it's nowhere near the same plane, many of us whose businesses depend on travel and crowds were left in the lurch when the quarantine hit. I could have easily been stagnant or even backward-moving in 2020: after all, a major part of my job is flying around and talking to strangers in crowded rooms, a situation that became untenable. I had to cancel all my speaking gigs, and I was bummed.

Then the competitor in me woke up and turned it around. I decided that *everyone* in my industry was facing the same problem. I just had to adjust—by building up my virtual speaking skills and offerings—so I could continue to be of service and do what I love. The setback was going to be an opportunity because I would make it so.

So I detached myself from the old plan and found a way to turn the loss into the win. (I thought about the slippery gym floor that everyone else had to play on.) The pandemic created a great deal of hardship for many people but it also forced a lot of them to adapt in their business, maybe even shake up a tired formula. The newer iteration may be better. Resilience requires evolution and adaptability. The best coaches, businesses, leaders, and athletes don't let times of change go to waste. They make the most of them.

The Trouble with Laurels

You can't endure over the long term if you're not motivated day in and day out. It's not easy—which is exactly what makes it a separating skill. I asked legendary NBA agent David Falk, most famous for representing Michael Jordan his entire career, how Jordan was able to sustain peak performance for so long. Falk's answer tapped into a truth that anyone who watched Jordan (or had the misfortune of playing against him) undoubtedly believed: "You can't rest on your laurels," Falk said. "You can't say 'hey, here's what I did five years ago.' Because every night you go out, you're going to get tested. No one cares that you won the title. . . . Do you still have it? Are you still motivated?"

Jordan, who would have had more reason to coast than any athlete alive, simply would not let himself do so. (It's worth mentioning that Falk, who could've just watched the Jordan money roll in, didn't either.) MJ played every game like it mattered, because to him, it did. He internalized something that his coach, Phil Jackson, said. "You're only a success at the moment you perform a successful act. You have to do it again." Jordan has also said that he felt a responsibility to everyone in the crowd who had come to see him; he couldn't take a night off, because that's how they would forever remember him.

Baseball's "Iron Man," Cal Ripken Jr., played in 2,632 consecutive baseball games at shortstop and third base for the Baltimore Orioles, breaking Lou Gehrig's record that had stood for almost sixty years. That's every single game, five to six games a week, for seventeen years. It's hard to even wrap your head around. And he didn't just play, he performed at an incredibly high level (two MVP awards and eighteen All-Star Fame appearances). "To me, showing up every day is a matter of principle," Ripken wrote. "Everything you do is a test of how well you do it, not just once or twice, but again and again, after your task has lost its newness and novelty, when it's just the daily repetition of what needs to be done." The resilient show up, simple as that.

Ripken is fond of telling the story of Wally Pipp, who sat out a game in July 1925 for the Yankees, replaced at first base by Lou Gehrig. Gehrig would stay there until 1939 on his way to one of the most legendary careers in sports history. Now, Pipp would not likely have had Gehrig's career, but it took someone sitting down for Gehrig to step in. And he sure made the most of it. "My view is, if you have a job, you go to work," Ripken wrote. "If you don't go to work, don't be surprised if you get replaced by somebody who does."

Action Steps

- Use your struggles as **fuel instead of hindrances**. Go from why is this happening to me to **what is this teaching me**? Try writing the question "What is this teaching me?" on a Post-It and keep it somewhere where you will see it (refrigerator, desktop, bathroom mirror). Next time you get hit with a setback, answer the question.

- Appropriately celebrate your victories and learn from your defeats, but never let either define you. What high and low points in your life have you let define you? Have they become burdens?

- CEO coach Chip Conley suggests that at age fifty we should all mail ourselves a two-sentence letter. It should read: "You may live another fifty years. If you knew you would live to the age of one hundred, what new talent, skill, or interest would you pursue today in order to become a master?" What would your letter say? Write it out, seal it in an envelope, and save it for a milestone birthday in the future.

CHAPTER FOURTEEN
Rest and Play

As a lifetime athlete, I've always valued taking care of my body. Two of the foundational components of a healthy body are nutrition and exercise. While I am a stickler for maximizing and optimizing both, they already get all of the attention. But what are equally important, though less celebrated, are rest, sleep, and play. They are understandably less sexy and—to be honest—harder to make a profit from, so they rarely make the headlines. But without proper rest, adequate sleep, and moments of leisure, your will never become you best self.

Burnout is an emotional as well as a physical experience, but there's a reason we use the word we do to describe it: *Burn out*. As Olympic athlete Carmelita Moscato told me, "Fire can warm or fire can burn." Our fuse is only so long. If we don't step away once in a while, we will have nothing left.

At Rest

I hear too often, "I can't afford to take a break," when the reality is *you can't afford not to*. Maybe you have been getting by, or maybe you don't notice the way your performance has been affected by overdoing it. But I bet the people around you have.

More isn't necessarily better. You don't really get more done the more time you spend at your desk. The "work hard, play hard" crowd promotes excess hours at work, as if that automatically produces better work. But the law of diminishing returns says we reach a point where more yields *less*, and studies show productivity actually decreases after fifty hours of work per week. Going too long without rest can not only lessen the quality of your current work, but it hurts your ability to get back to work later.

Rest is not a nice to have; it is a necessity. I rest my mind (unplug from technology, meditate, embrace silence and stillness) and my body (take days off from strenuous exercise, stretch, massage, cold showers) consistently. I embrace the duality of coupling intense work sessions and decompressed rest sessions. They are my yin and yang.

The Badge of Busy

The term "workaholism" was coined by an American back in 1971, yet today we work two hundred hours more per year than we did then. Overwork is unfortunately treated as a status symbol these days, and I'm sure it's one of the reasons that burnout is on the rise. The self-imposed pressure that we need to be the first in and the last out (and work through the weekends) makes us value the wrong things. Is there a more efficient way to put in the time? Are you doing it to impress your boss? Are you doing it to get ahead? Overwork actually increases our chance of making a mistake, snapping at our coworkers, and hitting the wall.

"Overwork results in lowered performance," writes workplace strategist Rahaf Harfoush. There is a tendency for the twenty-first-century worker to feel like he always has to be "on," because the digital age has gotten rid of conventional office spaces. It's one of the reasons I believe work hours went up during quarantine: the clear lines between home and work were obliterated. Harfoush points out that "the obsession with measuring our productivity has [made us] feel guilty when we're not working." This guilt doesn't allow us to even appreciate our off time, which is so necessary to recharging. There's nothing admirable about skipping vacations, taking a work call during your child's game, or checking office email from bed. It's destructive and a surefire path to burnout.

Even the vacation time we're given—which is far less than that of many European countries—is not something we are taking. A little more than half of US workers don't take all of their paid vacation days, and nearly a quarter don't take them at all! Is it because they don't need them? Of course not! It's because they *feel like they can't*. Even with all these vacation days left on the table, 61 percent of workers still "admitted to feeling pressured to do some work anyway" while on vacation. There's no point to a vacation if you're just doing work in a different location. The time away can't be just physical; it has to be mental and emotional as well.

These breaks are not just deserved, they're necessary. And for those who still stubbornly believe that skipping vacation is how you get ahead, you're working against yourself. It's been shown that "people who take *all* of their vacation time have a 6.5 percent higher chance of getting a promotion or a raise than people who leave eleven or more days of paid time off on the table." If possible, don't schedule your vacation based on *the* calendar; schedule it based on *your* calendar, as in during a natural break in your work cycle. If you have to vacation according to the calendar, then design your deadlines so that you're not spending it working.

Because of the increase of work from home (WFH) culture, the office is now everywhere. And when you can turn the switch "on" whenever you want, a dangerous thing happens: *the off switch disappears*. It is up to you to put an intentional off switch on your job, whether that means a set schedule, a home office that's separate from the living space, or some other resolution. Don't let work overtake your life. Dedication to your job should not sacrifice your basic well-being. If you're in an environment where this is the norm, then it might be worth reconsidering if you can afford to stay there.

Knocking the Hustle

Don't listen to anyone who says the cure for burnout is just to grind it out. Former runner and performance coach Steve Magness told me, "Performers are really good at understanding when to push and then when to pull back to allow them to recover so they can then push hard when they need to." He highlighted both LeBron James and soccer star Lionel Messi for their particular ability to "flip the switch."

LeBron "knows when to recover and save that energy so he can go all in," Magness explained. Part of LeBron's basketball IQ is his efficiency in this manner, recognizing that in his mid-thirties he can't go all out every game. He has to pick his spots. Magness pointed out that those who transition from the athletic world to the business world maintain that one advantage: they already know that rest and recovery is an equal part of the cycle. The body, the soul, the mind, the spirit—they all need you to take a step back before reengaging.

While making it clear that it varies depending on what your work is, Magness (and his writing partner, Brad Stulberg) gives a helpful rule for the way you should weave your work and your rest: "Alternating between blocks of 50 to 90 minutes of intense work and recovery breaks of 7 to 20 minutes enables people to sustain the physical, cognitive, and emotional energy required for peak performance." Again, the rest isn't a reward you give yourself like ice cream (though it can be); it's integral to the productivity of the work itself. This idea that rest is for suckers is not just juvenile and macho, it's scientifically incorrect.

Neuroscientist Lisa Feldman Barrett uses a helpful analogy to explain why we need to step away and rest in order to move forward. There's a direct link between taking these breaks and achieving personal and professional growth.

> Your brain is running a budget for your body. It's not budgeting money, it's budgeting . . . all the nutrients that are necessary to

keep you alive and well. If you are running a deficit because you haven't slept, because you've been on social media too much, because you haven't eaten healthfully, whatever the reason is, then you don't have a lot of extra energy to devote to learning something new or to putting yourself in situations where things are ambiguous or unexpected or novel.

Overdoing it isn't the answer. If you're in charge, keep in mind that you're not serving your workers or your company when you push your employees past the point of productivity. "All it does is increase and reward the behaviors of burnout," writes Jennifer Moss. She suggests those in charge "lead by example and encourage . . . staff to slow down (even when they don't want to) by supporting mental health breaks, taking vacations, and spending time with family."

I got a chance to ask Warriors coach Steve Kerr about beating burnout, and because he's a big picture thinker, Kerr answered by critiquing the culture that creates it. "In our country we celebrate working around the clock. I think that can be really harmful," he said. "The idea that you're just going to grind and grind and grind and sleep in your office. That's a really dangerous way to live and lead." He talked about his own commitments to family time, yoga, and meditation. "Work/life balance is crucial to people being productive. So we got to be careful of this American ideal that we got to just grind all day. . . . It's more about finding the right balance."

The Cycle

Former Yankees performance coach (and World Series champion) Dana Cavalea started as a nineteen-year-old intern for the most storied franchise in sports. At twenty-three, he had already taken over as head strength and conditioning coach and became an integral part of the franchise. We met twenty years ago as hungry newcomers to the performance world. It was fun to check back in on how far we've come, and what lessons we'd learned along the way. Standing in his home office in front of a brick wall spray-painted with an American flag, he still emitted the same youthful energy he had when we first met.

Dana explained that a performance coach can't just be about muscles and tendons; the mind is part of the body, after all. Dana has worked with some of the best athletes in the world on the biggest stages in the world, so he understands what it takes to get there and to stay there. He admitted that when he was a young athlete, he thought he had to put in more hours of work in order to stay on top. But over time, he came to learn that this approach wasn't healthy and came from a "fear-driven, negative" place. Watching players like Derek Jeter and Mariano Rivera be very intentional in their practice taught him a great deal. Over the years he saw plenty of talented athletes burn out because they didn't "develop a routine and a set of habits that work well for them" in the way the veterans had.

Dana now sees these kinds of bad habits in business professionals, only worse. (In sports, you at least have coaches who help you design routines.) He teaches business leaders, accomplished and intelligent men and women, how to set routines, focus on improvement, and monitor their progress. One of the most important lessons he offers is how to create barriers between their work and life. "Most athletes understand recovery," he told me. "Most leaders and executives don't. If you start the company and run the company and set a precedent of answering your phone at 10 p.m., now you're telling everybody, 'Hey, I'm available, I'm accessible, it's okay.' You're conditioning [your people] to facilitate a negative habit that you already have. So it becomes this loop; it becomes so costly."

In interviewing high performers for this book, I was struck by how often rest and recovery came up as *essential* to managing the day-to-day. Entrepreneur and former fitness pro Ryan Lee continues to practice the lessons he learned during his time as a runner.

He told me he "lives life as a bunch of sprints" and naps every day so that he can get back up and "sprint" again. UCLA softball coach Sue Enquist told me that at practice she set up a "zero station" where players would go to . . . do nothing. It was Enquist's way of teaching them that "exhaling was as important as the inhaling." She told me, "We have not learned collectively as a society to value rest and recovery like we do high performance." If we are truly going to implement fruitful rest and recovery into our lives, she recommended that **we schedule it**. That intentional practice will solidify it as something we do every day, just like eating and sleeping.

Office Break

Workplace expert Jennifer Moss notes: "More than 50% of U.S. employees feel like they have to check their email after 11 pm to keep up with work." Now, no matter what your job is, it's rare that something urgent is happening this late at night. So something else must be going on. It's the impression of work. The illusion of work. Not only is this kind of work "performance" unnecessary, but it takes away from our needed recharge time and makes us resent tasks we may otherwise enjoy.

We all want to impress our superiors, but if we are sacrificing our needed downtime, family time, or social time in order to "appear" dedicated, we should take stock of what exactly we're doing at our jobs. Business consultant Julie Morgenstern thinks twenty-first-century workers feel like they have to always be on and available, until you "begin to think your value lies in your accessibility versus your talent." European companies have been at the forefront of building breaks into the workplace. Not necessarily because they're more compassionate than American companies, but because they understand the link between rest and productivity.

It is not selfish to take some time away or to close your door, especially if you are a leader. In *Stillness Is the Key*, Ryan Holiday writes about watching his former boss at American Apparel, Dov

Charney, go through an "epic implosion." Charney completely lost his company because he simply would not take a break. From the beginning, Charney had an open-door policy to his office; but as the company grew, and the employees multiplied, the open-door policy remained, even when it became unmanageable.

In an effort to be everything to everyone all the time, Charney hit full burnout and lost the company. Holiday sees his old boss's experience as a cautionary tale. "The overworked person creates a crisis that they try to solve by working harder," Holiday writes. "Mistakes are piled upon mistakes by the exhausted, delirious mind." Not everything can be solved by going at it harder. Sometimes the answer is the very opposite.

Knowing When Not to Push

As a basketball performance coach, I saw how many coaches took better care of themselves in the off-season than during the season. But during the season is when they needed it! When we're stressed, we start to abandon the very things that can help us tackle that stress. We overstuff our days as if we can catch up, but all we're doing is throwing an inferior version of ourselves out there. If you burn the candle at both ends, don't be shocked when you're completely extinguished.

NBA champion Harrison Barnes said that besides making sure basketball is part of his day, "I also find time throughout the day to decompress, unplug, recalibrate, just to make sure that I'm fresh." He told a group of us coaches and speakers last year, "It doesn't make sense to run myself into the ground every single day. I need to be on when I'm home with the family, I need to be present, I don't need to be dead tired or have my mind on a million different things." There is no "hack" to rest, sleep, and recovery, and don't trust anyone who tells you there is. Your body has the answers; just listen to it.

Load Management

The NBA has finally caught up to the concept that if you are a starter on a team that goes deep into the playoffs, you're looking at nearly four thousand minutes of high-intensity time on the court. It probably took longer than it should have, but teams have gotten wise to the fact that maybe their star doesn't have to play forty-two minutes against a last-place team in February. Spurs head coach Gregg Popovich was the trendsetter here—resting his starters on the second half of back-to-back nights—and the team actually got fined for it. Then Kawhi Leonard and LeBron started to do it before it took off around the league. Now, it has been normalized as "load management." In a few short years it went from fineable offense to common sense.

Both Jordan and LeBron were tactically different in their later years compared with their early years. The thirtysomething version strategically took plays off and spread himself out more so that he'd be at full capacity in the final minutes when others were drained. LeBron has been a pioneer in his dedication to rest and recovery, a step beyond everyone. He spends about $1.5 million on training that falls under the performance umbrella, and almost all of it is for rest and recovery (cold tubs, hyperbaric chamber, etc.), not new workout equipment.

Seasons

Professional and college athletes have three distinct seasons:

1. **In-Season** (several months of practices, games, playoffs)

2. **Off-Season** (several months away from practices/games, focused on improvement/preparation)

3. **Pre-Season** (eight to twelve weeks leading up to the in-season when training is heightened and focused)

I recognize that most folks in the business world work year-round, and don't have an actual off-season, but they can still use these principles. Most NBA players take two to three weeks completely off after their last game of the season. They get away from basketball, go on vacation, sleep in, and relax. Then they slowly start getting back into shape and continue to ramp up until training camp (pre-season). The time away is to help them recover and rejuvenate.

Anyone can adopt a similar framework:

- Every day, take ONE hour completely off from work/devices.

- Every week, take ONE day completely off from work/devices.

- Every month, take ONE weekend completely off from work/devices.

- Every year, take ONE week completely off from work/devices.

Performance Enhancing

When people tell me they'll sleep when they're dead, I tell them, "Well, that's going to be sooner than you think." It's a dark joke, but it comes from a place of basic science. *We need to sleep.* The fact that one missed night of sleep can make us feel so nightmarish, outside-our-bodies terrible, tells us how desperately we need it. Think about it from an evolutionary standpoint. It's wildly inefficient for human beings to be asleep a full *third* of their lives, so obviously our bodies need it.

A few years back, lack of sleep "cost American companies a staggering $411 billion in lost productivity." How could working all these extra hours go so wrong? It's because work on poor sleep is just a lot of hours of unproductive work. Sleep is essential to decision making because your impulse takes over when you haven't rested. Your frontal lobe—which is your decision center—shuts down when you're tired, and your baser instincts take over. So you're putting in more hours on lack of sleep, but what kind of hours are they? You are more likely to set yourself *back* during these hours, messing up in a way that requires time to fix your mistakes later. **More is not always more.**

In the performance space, everyone knows sleep is the secret sauce. (NBA teams now even have sleep specialists on the payroll.) Successful people don't literally work the most; they just know **how to be most effective in the hours they are working**. I speak from a place of experience. I used to subscribe to the less equals more mentality when it came to sleep. I mistakenly believed that if I slept four hours instead of eight, that would give me an extra four hours each day. After a few days, I'd be a whole day in front of the competition! (Yes, a knucklehead thought, but I had it.) I had convinced myself I needed less sleep, but the piper always has to be paid. Sleep science pioneer William Dement coined the term "sleep debt" for the accumulated exhaustion that comes from consistently depriving yourself of sleep. The physiological and emotional effects can be severe.

A 2019 study in *Occupational and Environmental Medicine* determined that sleep-deprived subjects were "as judgment impaired as an intoxicated person." That's right! Rolling into a meeting without enough sleep makes you as productive as a drunk person, so good luck with that! Once I started prioritizing sleep, it shifted my entire day, and my productivity skyrocketed. It began when I started developing an evening routine, or a pre-sleep routine. Morning routines get all the glory, but it's your evening routine that sets you up for the next day.

For my evening routine, I use the **3–2–1 method**, taught to me by my friend and colleague Andrew Cordle:

- Three hours before bedtime: exercise (if you didn't already) and eat your last meal for the night (something healthy of course!)

- Two hours before bedtime: find an activity that helps you relax and unwind, take a warm shower, and put on your sleeping clothes

- One hour before bedtime: avoid electronics and screens, lower the lights

The Alarm

A break is built into our body's needs. In order to achieve at the highest level, you have to bring the stress cycle full circle so the alarm system can turn off. This can be sleep, but it can also include rest and leisure—anything that signals to your body it can pull back from your pressing needs.

Neuroscientist Matt Walker explains that sleep not only recharges us but it helps imprint memories into our brains; it's like "hitting the save button" on our new memories. If we don't sleep enough, we actually lose the ability to recall this information. When we're tired, it's not just our productivity that goes down; our mood plummets as well, making it harder for us to be positive. "The brain interprets a lack of sleep as a threat to the central nervous system," Shawn Achor writes, "then goes on high alert, scanning the world for additional threats—that is, negatives." So the tired are going to notice the negatives because those "threats" are what our ancestors were trained to notice. Our monkey brains take over on lack of sleep, and I don't know about you, but I don't want my monkey brain running the show at work.

Play On

Play promotes creativity, imagination, and sense of freedom. As we get older, we tend to drift away from play and gravitate toward structure, scheduling, and rigidity. We feel a nagging need to always be doing something productive or checking off our to-do list. Many adults impose this belief on their overscheduled children. A benefit of play, as entrepreneur and keynote speaker Josh Linkner explains, is that it is a time where we are more courageous. We are doing it for the sake of doing it, not for the outcome. "The single biggest blocker to creativity is not natural talent. It's fear," Linkner has said. "Fear is a poisonous force that robs us of our most creative thinking." I'm reminded of how in Iceland, the adults are encouraged to make art just like the kids, even if they have no skill for it. It carries over from childhood because the process, not the product, is what matters.

As a parent, I allow plenty of space for my children to play. No electronics, nothing scheduled, and minimal direction.

"What should we do?" one of them asked when we first started.

The answer: "Whatever you want!"

In his book *Shift Your Mind*, Brian Levenson tells an illuminating story about the 2018 Washington Capitals and their coach Barry Trotz. Before they took the ice for game 1 in the second championship series in their history (and their first in twenty years), the last thing he said was "Have some fun."

Fun?! Wait, what?

Didn't he care about the win? Of course he did. He just knew that telling his team to tap into what made the game fun was what they needed to hear. Doc Rivers has said that in his playing days, he never even used the word practice. He'd always just say, "I'm going to play basketball."

Give yourself permission to play around once in a while. Tap into that younger self, the one who found joy just in the doing. It just might be what you need.

Action Steps

- Katrina Onstad, author of *The Weekend Effect*, suggests that we shouldn't leave our chores for the weekend. **Do them during the week**, even if you're wiped out after work, in order to give yourself a true weekend.

- Coach Sue Enquist recommended that we regularly **schedule an empty gap** in our calendars. If we keep doing this, we can make "rest a standard." Try it for a week: schedule a break into your schedule. Learn the best place to put it. Stick to it. Note how it feels compared with breaking when you "have a chance."

- Give yourself a block of **time without screens**—you'll be surprised how refreshed you feel. "The average time an American adult spends staring at a screen is seventy-four hours a week," a recent study showed. Tiffany Shlain, whose book *24/6* is a guide to giving one day a week to nonscreen activities, notes: "That's more than we spend sleeping, eating, and having sex combined."

- Social lives need breaks too! Your friends will understand. **Set boundaries** and get okay with saying no. Accept that FOMO (fear of missing out) is a childish mindset that social media has just exacerbated.

- Work from homers: separate your worlds! Create a new system and process. Put on work clothes, designate an area of your house that is your work station, set clear timetables and a schedule. **Your body, your space, your time.**

CHAPTER FIFTEEN
Fulfillment

Western society encourages us to always want more. The messages tell us that no matter what we have, it isn't enough. We are told we should want nicer cars, nicer houses, and nicer clothes. We are pressured to want better bodies, better vacations, and better job titles. We are pushed to want more money, more gadgets, and more social media followers. But you never get to a point where you're satisfied, because there's always more to want.

Instead of WANTING more, shift your focus to BECOMING more. Work to develop new skills, better habits, and an improved mindset. If you become the best version of yourself, you will attract the stuff that matters most. Fulfillment isn't about playing the game better; it's about rejecting the game entirely and focusing on what matters to you. The drive for fulfillment is a process that will ebb and flow. It is not a finish line to reach because you're always striving for it. It's an *evolution*, an active process of becoming.

I've not been immune to materialistic pursuits, but I've learned to change my approach. Currently, I'm working toward becoming a minimalist. Over the past five years I've donated or thrown out about 60 percent of my belongings and only keep the things I truly need. When I was having some work done in my apartment, the repairman asked if I had just moved in (because of how barren my place is). I took it as a compliment that he was shocked I'd lived there for three years! The only exception I have regarding objects is my office, where I've proudly accumulated decades of knick-knacks, memorabilia, and books. I consider these mementoes from life experiences.

Every few months I go through each room of my apartment and get rid of anything I haven't used or worn for the past sixty days and/or don't plan on using for the next sixty days. The best part about these purges? Donating to those less fortunate is very fulfilling, and throwing stuff out is incredibly liberating. I realize how little I need the things that I once thought of as part of who I am. I'm not suggesting you do things as I did, but think about actions you can take to reject the material mindset and spend time and energy on what truly matters to you.

Quality over Quantity

Steve Magness told me that "when the work you're doing has purpose and meaning behind it—to you—you see lower levels of burnout even given the same amount of work." This is an essential point: It's not the amount of work that burns you out. It's the feeling (or lack thereof) of purpose around it. As a former competitive runner, Steve used an example from his world. Runners' times are remarkably consistent, "but there's wiggle room between that performance based on how much it means. How far you can dip into that well of fatigue isn't limited based on necessarily your physical capacity."

It's our brains that tell our body whether or not something is worth doing, so even runners can find a little more when the motivation is there. Putting in heavy hours on what you think is a meaningless project is draining; doing it for something creative or purposeful is an invigorating experience. It's not the work itself; it's how much of yourself you put into it.

Magness also pointed out that this kind of motivation increases based on the kind of feedback people get. For instance, when janitors at a hospital are told that their job "is vital to this hospital," their performance level actually goes up. Their literal job is the same, but they are putting meaning behind it, which adds motivation and purpose. Our interview was during the 2020 lockdown, and I thought of the push across America to recognize "essential workers"—from grocery store clerks to delivery drivers—in a new, appreciative way. I imagine being told that they were keeping the country running during a crisis helped to motivate and inspire them during a truly difficult time.

"Finding meaning is the source of renewal and nourishment," *Burnout* authors Amelia and Emily Nagoski explain. "Meaning has the potential to make your life much easier." Why? Because it helps you push when you just don't have it in you. You're connecting to something deeper inside yourself, which works as an engine on days where the drive isn't there. We are human and bound to get distracted, lazy, and shortsighted. These are waves that are going to come in and crash on us. Meaning acts as an anchor that keeps us in place. We can blame no one else for a lack of fulfillment in our lives and look to no one else to give it to us. It is within our power.

Plateauing

Similar to my own experience with college basketball, Division I swimmer Cory Camp went through a phase where his sport stopped giving him that feeling of excitement and satisfaction. During our interview, we spoke about our shared experiences with burnout. Cory talked about how burnout is a feedback loop that powers itself: as you lose interest, your effort wanes, and then you're not improving, which makes it harder to stay interested. The term that is often used to describe this state is **plateauing**. It's the perfect word because you have neither the motivation that comes with the uphill nor the momentum that comes with the downhill. You and the experience itself are flat. You are showing up, but that's all you're doing.

After leaving swimming, Cory spent time at a sales job but felt disconnected working toward other people's definition of success (salary, bonuses, and promotions). He wanted to do something he could put his whole self into, as he once did in the water. That led him to embark on an inner journey and a process of "reframing around the idea of success." Our culture bandies about the word *success* as though we all were working off the same idea. But everyone draws an individual picture of success; knowing the image of yours is a key part in the search for fulfillment. Cory left sales and explored performance coaching because it had meaning for him. It got him thinking: "How can I pass forward what swimming brought to me to the next generation [and] be that coach that inspired others?" He saw himself as part of a **long line of give and take, a community that stretched over generations,** and that mattered to him.

Now Cory works with former athletes on taking that athletic mindset into the next chapter of their lives. Athletes lose their identity when they stop competing—as Cory and I both know—and finding a new one is difficult. Cory works to show former athletes that there are plenty of "soft skills" they can bring to their new career. He shared with me the example of a client, an ex-NFL player who was trying to get into online coaching. The player found himself stuck with writing and creating content. The player was just sitting down at the computer and trying to come up with ideas. Cory challenged him on this (lack of) process. "Well, did you just show up on the football field?" Cory asked. *Of course not.* You need *discipline and routines.* Cory helped the player see the bridge between the old commitment and the new one. He's doing it for others while he continues to do it for himself.

The Balance Myth

There is no such thing as work/life balance, because those two areas will never be perfectly equal. It's mathematically impossible. We all need to strive for work/life flow, work/life harmony, and work/life integration. As Stewart D. Friedman writes, we should drop the image of the scale because it "forces you to think in terms of trade-offs instead of the possibilities for harmony."

Yale professor Dr. Amy Wrzesniewski explains that there are three "orientations" or approaches one can take to work. Those who see it as a **job** see it as "a means to end"; those who see it as a **career** are focused on the "success or prestige"; those who view it as a **calling** see their work as part of their identity. Which word best captures how you view your work? Are you interested in changing it? What could you do to make that shift?

Best-selling author and performance coach Dave Meltzer told me he grew up poor, which once acted as a motivating force in his life. He hit the books hard, and nine months out of law school, he was already a millionaire. Soon enough, he was a millionaire many times over. Everything he touched turned to gold. He founded Sports 1 Marketing (with former NFL quarterback Warren Moon), worked at Samsung as CEO of its first smartphone, ran Leigh Steinberg's sports agency (Steinberg was the basis for *Jerry Maguire*), ran $2 billion in management, partied with celebrities, stayed out all night, and lived what some people would consider the dream.

But that was the old Dave Meltzer. When I interviewed him, his Zoom background included a giant printout of a hundred–dollar bill with a smiley face over Ben Franklin's, along with the scrawled words *Money Doesn't Buy Happiness.*

But it took time for him to get there.

Dave's path to fulfillment is fascinating and instructive. At thirty-six, Dave opened his eyes and realized he wasn't someone he liked. Driven by money and status, neglecting his family duties, he saw he'd been "living in the wrong light . . . believing my own b.s., buying things I don't need to impress people I don't like."

It was a combination of factors that brought him to this conclusion—from his wife's and friends' admonishments, to a realization about his father, to his own maturity. When it all converged, Dave decided it was time to change. So he "re-engineered" his life to become a motivational coach and mentor. He is still measuring his life based on the numbers, but it's no longer dollars: it's *impact*. Meltzer's goal? To make one billion people happy. He knows how it sounds, but he's committed, passionate, and willing to put in the work. Dave wants to empower and inspire others to feel what he feels: *abundance*.

If anyone can impact a billion people, it's Dave. It's hard to describe the experience of a conversation with him because he's so vibrant and infectiously enthusiastic. He's a gracious and generous person, a true giver, and a man fully dedicated to his purpose. He talks fast, *real* fast, and I got this sense that it's because all this wisdom and desire to contribute are just flowing out of him.

He recommends practices of gratitude and humility to stay grounded, and one thing above all: **take an inventory of your values**—every day—so you always know what you want. That way, you won't wake up years from now realizing you've been working hard toward a goal that doesn't matter to you.

Toxic Choices

Because we are bombarded by distractions and opportunities, we all have this nagging feeling of: *What else is there?* This is not to say the knights and farmers of earlier centuries didn't ask this question, but it wasn't as central to their lives. They were who they were and that was that. They didn't know much about what else there was, so they didn't think much about it. To put it mildly, this is no longer the case. On one hand, there are more opportunities for everyone, which is fantastic. But on the other hand, we are surrounded by this question: what else?

Look at the online dating world. Even if you find someone with whom you are a good match, there will be this magnetic pull to see who else is out there. Even if you're happy with your choice, most people will be nagged by this sense that there might be someone better. Of course, it's *designed* that way, so you keep using the product. If everyone was encouraged to stay with a match they liked, the sites would go out of business. YouTube, Facebook, Amazon—they are all designed this way. *What else is there?* This feeling has spilled into all areas of life: work, vacation, shopping, extracurricular activities, colleges, restaurants, media—you name it. There is always so much more than we could ever get to. It takes concerted effort to block it all out.

When you combine the culture of unlimited opportunities with the demand for instant gratification, it's easy to see why our fuse is that much shorter. Burnout is almost inevitable. If you're pursuing fulfillment instead of pleasure, then you are grounded in something sustaining and enduring. When you are pursuing fulfillment, much of the unnecessary noise of "what else?" fades into the background.

Growing Up

When we're younger we're often chasing a more immediate kind of pleasure, which is expected: that's part of being young! However, as we mature, if we don't switch our ideas of happiness into something more permanent, something that requires work and commitment, we will struggle. If we don't adapt to the long game, we are going to be lost.

I was in a seminar with Marquette University basketball coach Shaka Smart, who deals with this challenge each season, as young people are naturally not long-term thinkers. A good coach encourages them to be. Smart told us that "the best teams have to commit to something larger than themselves which is challenging for young people with individual goals." It's a challenge for adults as well. If you haven't developed a more multidimensional version of happiness that includes serving others, contributing, contentment, and an understanding of your place in the world, then you will fail to feel fulfilled. You will run on empty calories until you burn out.

Round Up

I love being a professional keynote speaker. The "high" I get onstage—sharing my passion in front of a live audience of engaged attendees—is almost intoxicating. However, speaking is simply my platform for expression. The real fulfillment comes from filling others' buckets. Speaking is what I do, but it's not who I am. At my core I am a performance coach, and I gain fulfillment from helping, inspiring, and empowering people to raise their game. Being motivated to improve is one of the great gifts anyone can receive.

One of my earliest memories of this was as at my first sleepaway camp, the Mason-Dixon Basketball Camp, run by the legendary Morgan Wootten of DeMatha Catholic High School. At the end of the week, each camper was given a report card that noted what areas of his game were strongest and which had "opportunities of growth." We were also given a printed and stapled packet of drills— essentially homework—we could do by ourselves for the rest of the summer. It was the kind of thing that you could take or leave. I'm sure players came home and never looked at it again.

But to me, this kind of feedback was gold. That packet became my blueprint. I would spend hours and hours every single day on the blacktop, under the scorching hot sun with my boom box blasting, doing those drills. And nothing felt better than making progress. Whether it was wrapping the ball around my waist as fast as possible for one minute or seeing how many consecutive free throws I could make (my record was 119), I got so much joy out of making progress. I was bit by the self-improvement bug, and I don't think I ever looked back.

As a father, I feel equal joy in watching my children do things that they find fulfilling. Whether it's Lyla taking hip-hop dance class, Luke taking boxing lessons, or Jack playing hoops—seeing them have fun provides me a sense of fulfillment, bonds us together, and connects me to my previous, younger self.

You can't be fulfilled until you know what it looks like. Figure out what fulfillment is for you: visualize it, write it down, talk to someone you trust. Write out your perfect day. How close is it to the life you're living right now? Is there any transfer? Overlap? How much of it is in your hands?

Fulfillment is not something you feel at the end of your career or your life, looking back. It's something you should strive for day in and day out. It's something you should be working toward *now*. The constant pursuit of it keeps you level and motivated, though never complete.

Life is not an *-ed* thing; it's an *-ing* thing. It is about going, building, growing and becoming, not completed and reached. As long as we keep the wheels turning, we know we're on the right path.

Action Steps

- Keep a weekly journal that checks in on how fulfilled you are at work. Questions can include:

  » How did I invest my time/attention this past week?

  » What do I regret? What wasn't the best use of my time/attention?

  » What did I enjoy most? What was the best use of my time/attention?

  » Where do I get my value?

  » What is my best opportunity for growth?

  » If I visualize the concept of fulfillment, what does it look like?

- Spend some time reflecting on the activities that give you the deepest fulfillment. Is it watching your children play a sport they enjoy? Is it preparing for a 10K? Is it a simple morning ritual of quiet meditation and a warm cup of coffee? Whatever this list consists of, how can you do these things more often? How can you make them a consistent part of your day?

- Find someone who represents fulfillment to you; spend time with them, ask them questions, just listen. What do they care about? How do their actions express that?

FINAL THOUGHTS

I gave up on perfectionism a long time ago. What I'm focused on is continual progress. Are the wheels still moving? Which direction am I headed? These are the things I look for. It's bigger than the day-to-day, though each day brings an opportunity to refine and contribute to it.

Sustain Your Game is built upon a simple premise: each of us will always be under construction, a work in progress, and constantly evolving. The goal is to be moving toward our highest potential, toward making a meaningful contribution, and toward becoming the best version of ourselves. In essence, *live the life you love and love the life you live* (a mantra I had tattooed on my arm several years ago).

Your relationship with fulfillment will ebb and flow. Some days you'll be motivated, while other days it will feel elusive. So please give yourself some grace. Part of living a fulfilled life is to be inspired by progress, not stifled by perfection.

Recognize that the circumstances of your life simply *reveal* stress, stagnation, and burnout—they don't *create* them. Only you can do that. And I hope this book has given you the tools you need to handle whatever comes along.

Good luck out there.

ALAN STEIN JR.
Gaithersburg, Maryland
2021

NOTES

Introduction

xiv **Jerry Seinfeld, one of the all-time:** *The Tim Ferriss Show*, December 8, 2020.

Part I: Perform

1 **Stress is a reality:** Emma Pattee, "The Difference Between Worry, Stress and Anxiety," *New York Times*, February 26, 2020.

1 **"An office used to be a thing":** Amanda Mull, "How Your Laptop Ruined Your Life," *The Atlantic*, February 10, 2020.

1 **"spend 10 percent more time working":** Derek Thompson, "Why White-Collar Workers Spend All Day at the Office," *The Atlantic*, December 4, 2019.

2 **Two out of three of American workers:** Rebecca Zucker, "How to Stop Thinking About Work at 3 am," *Harvard Business Review*, December 20, 2019.

2 **"We're simply not designed":** Jon Spayde, "The Science of Stress," *Experience Life*, May 21, 2019.

2 **"Stress is defined as a reaction":** Pattee, "The Difference between Worry."

Chapter 1: Focus

5 **"a golf ball–size portion":** Bill Donahue, "Fixing Diane's Brain," *Runner's World*, June 22, 2018.

5 **However, it came with a strange:** "Epileptic Ultra-Runner Diane Van Deren Runs for Good Health on The Buzz," *Outside TV*, November 9, 2011.

5 **"keep track of where"**: Alex Hutchinson, *Endure: Mind, Body, and the Curiously Elastic Limits of Human Performance* (New York: William Morrow, 2018), 43.

6 **"The less you hold on"**: Benjamin Hardy, *Personality Isn't Permanent: Break Free from Self-Limiting Beliefs and Rewrite Your Story* (New York: Portfolio, 2020), 122.

8 **"I'd like to go out"**: Christian D'Andrea, "Bill Belichick says the only thing he still wants to accomplish in his career is a 'good practice today,'" *SBNation*, June 7, 2017.

8 **"You got 24 hours"**: *The Playbook*, Netflix, Episode 5.

9 **Tolle realized that if one**: "How Eckhart Tolle Came Back from His Lowest Point," Oprah Winfrey Network.

10 **"When you're really in the body"**: "Eckhart Tolle Reveals How to Silence Voices in Your Head," *Oprah's Super Soul Sunday*.

10 **"The pain that you create"**: Eckhart Tolle, *The Power of Now* (New York: New World Library, 1999), 33.

10 **"always say 'yes'"**: Tolle, *Power of Now*, 28.

11 **"The traffic was real"**: Brian King, *The Art of Taking It Easy* (New York: Apollo Publishers, 2019), 23.

11 **"The vast majority of the stress"**: King, *Art of Taking*, 39.

13 **"It kind of got me into this"**: Julie Kliegman, "Paddy Steinfort and the Craft of Mental Performance Coaching," *Sports Illustrated*, October 2, 2020.

14 **Michael Jordan had twenty-five**: Jackie MacMullan, "Rise above it or drown: How elite NBA athletes handle pressure," Espn.com, May 29, 2019.

15 **"We're on an island"**: Michael Lewis, "The Kick Is Up and It's . . . A Career Killer," *New York Times Magazine*, October 28, 2007.

16 **"a chemical that elevates"**: Elizabeth Millard, "5 Tips to Stay Cool Under Pressure," *Experience Life*, February 22, 2018.

16 **"the Eagle's instruments showed"**: Taylor Clark, *Nerve: Poise Under Pressure, Serenity Under Stress, and the Brave New Science of Fear and Cool* (New York: Little, Brown, 2011), 12.

16 **Studies have shown that actors**: Clark, *Nerve*, 172.

16 **Meanwhile, competitive ballroom dancers**: Po Bronson and Ashley Merryman, *Top Dog: The Science of Winning and Losing* (New York: Twelve, 2013), 7.

17 **"everything just stops"**: ESPN, "30 for 30," *Vick: Part One* (director: Stanley Nelson).

17 **"extract more information"**: Matthew Syed, *Bounce: The Myth of Talent and the Power of Practice* (London: Fourth Estate, 2010), 31.

19 **"much better control"**: Vox, *Mindfulness Explained*.

19 **"one of the NBA's premier"**: Scott Davis, "A 38-year-old mental coach has become one of the NBA's premier resources," *Business Insider*, April 17, 2017.

20   **"the faster you can get back":** Chris Bailey, *Hyperfocus: How to Be More Productive in a World of Distraction* (New York: Viking, 2018), 30.

21   **"a productivity black hole":** Bailey, *Hyperfocus*, 8.

21   **the average person checks his phone:** Johann Hari, *Lost Connections: Why You're Depressed and How to Find Hope* (New York: Bloomsbury, 2018), 87.

21   **Jeremy Dean's book:** Jeremy Dean, *Making Habits, Breaking Habits: Why We Do Things, Why We Don't, and How to Make Any Change Stick* (Cambridge, MA: Da Capo Lifelong Books, 2013), 112–113.

21   **whether it's being used or not:** Tiffany Shlain, *24/6: The Power of Unplugging One Day a Week* (New York: Gallery, 2019), 45.

21   **affects the connection:** Mo Perry, "How to Break Free of Tech Addiction" *Experience Life*, April 2018.

21   **researchers found that it's the constant looking:** Emily Reynolds, "Looking at Your Phone at Work Might Make You Even More Bored," *Research Digest*, March 16, 2020.

21   **"it can take over a minute":** Dean, *Making Habits*, 112–113.

22   **"was a persistent nausea":** MacMullan, "Rise above it or drown."

22   **"[the creative person] doesn't":** Mihaly Csikszentmihalyi, "Flow, the Secret to Happiness," TED Talk, February 2004.

23   **"students who wrote out":** Jason Selk and Tom Bartow with Matthew Rudy, *Organize Tomorrow Today: 8 Ways to Retrain Your Mind to Optimize Performance at Work and in Life* (New York: Da Capo Lifelong Books, 2015), 4.

Chapter 2: Time and Energy Management

25   **The ancient Greeks:** I first read this in *The School of Life: An Emotional Education* (London: School of Life Books, 2019).

26   **"that relate to my life goals":** Laura Vanderkam, *168 Hours: You Have More Time Than You Think* (New York: Portfolio, 2010), 3.

27   **"The majority of people":** Vanderkam, *168 Hours*, 5.

27   **"There is easily time to sleep":** Vanderkam, *168 Hours*, 21.

27   **"being busy is a form of laziness":** Tim Ferriss, *Tools of Titans: The Tactics, Routines, and Habits of Billionaires, Icons, and World-Class Performers* (New York: HMH, 2016), 201.

27   **"Your problem is not that":** Rory Vaden, *Procrastinate on Purpose: 5 Permissions to Multiply Your Time* (New York: Tarcher Perigee, 2015), 8.

28   **"business professionals now spend":** Carl Honoré, *The Slow Fix: Solve Problems, Work Smarter, and Live Better in a World Addicted to Speed* (New York: Harper One, 2013), 24.

28   **"structured procrastination":** *The Jordan Harbinger Podcast*, "Dan Ariely: The Hidden Logic That Shapes Our Motivations," October 15, 2020.

28 **high performers across all disciplines:** Laura Vanderkam, *What the Most Successful People Do Before Breakfast: And Two Other Short Guides to Achieving More at Work and at Home* (New York: Portfolio, 2013), 7.

30 **"Only once you give yourself":** Greg McKeown, *Essentialism: The Disciplined Pursuit of Less* (New York: Currency, 2014), 4.

31 **"If we don't plan our days":** Nir Eyal, *Indistractable: How to Control Your Attention and Choose Your Life* (Dallas: BenBella, 2019), 54.

32 **"the consequences of not deciding":** Dan Ariely, *Predictably Irrational: The Hidden Forces That Shape Our Decisions* (New York: Harper, 2009), 150–151.

32 **He recommends making a list:** Justin Bariso, "I Just Discovered Warren Buffet's 25/5 Rule and It's Completely Brilliant," Inc.com.

32 **"High achievers aren't completing":** Jason Selk and Tom Bartow with Matthew Rudy, *Organize Tomorrow Today: 8 Ways to Retrain Your Mind to Optimize Performance at Work and in Life* (New York: Da Capo Lifelong Books, 2015), 5.

33 **"people were the *least* creative":** Honoré, *Slow Fix*, 43, quoting Teresa Amabile at Harvard Business School.

33 **time-pressure hangover:** Henri Weisinger and J. P. Pawliw-Fry, *Performance Under Pressure: The Science of Doing Your Best When It Matters Most* (New York: Currency, 2015), 28.

33 **Procrastination actually has more:** Christian Jarrett, "Why procrastination is about managing emotions, not time," BBC, May 14, 2020.

35 **Most people follow a circadian:** Christopher Barnes, "The Ideal Work Schedule, as Determined by Circadian Rhythms," HBR.org, January 28, 2015.

35 **"the Bermuda Triangles of our days":** Daniel Pink, *When: The Scientific Secrets of Perfect Timing* (New York: Riverhead, 2019), 3.

36 **Judges' rulings:** Francesca Cormack and Rosa Backx, "How your 'body clock' may affect cognition," Cambridge Cognition, October 28, 2016.

36 **"a twenty-minute period":** Pink, *When*, 10.

37 **"I would rather optimize":** Cory Stieg, "Twitter CEO Jack Dorsey: People think 'success means I work 20 hours a day' like Elon Musk—'which is BS,'" CNBC, *Make It*, August 26, 2020.

39 **Slowing down can be tough:** Mo Perry, "5 Ways to Slow Down," *Experience Life*, November 2017.

Chapter 3: Prepare

43 **"No top performer":** Matthew Syed, *Bounce: The Myth of Talent and the Power of Practice* (London: Fourth Estate, 2010), 169.

43 **"it's because you haven't practiced enough":** Jackie MacMullan, "Rise above it or drown: How elite NBA athletes handle pressure," ESPN.com, May 29, 2019.

45 **a locus of control:** Maria Konnikova, *The Biggest Bluff: How I Learned to Pay Attention, Master Myself, and Win* (New York: Penguin Press, 2020), 110.

46 **"People who think they control":** Konnikova, *Biggest Bluff*, 110.

48 **Hall of Famer Scottie Pippen:** *The Last Dance*, Episode 2 (director: Jason Hehr).

50 **he tells a story about drilling:** Kevin Eastman, *Why the Best Are the Best: 25 Powerful Words that Impact, Inspire, and Define Champions* (Charleston, SC: Advantage, 2018), 45

50 **"The main thing about teaching":** Rob McClanaghan, *Net Work: Training the NBA's Best and Finding the Keys to Greatness* (New York: Scribner, 2019), 6, 10.

51 **"Rebounding isn't brain surgery":** Chris Ballard, *The Art of a Beautiful Game: The Thinking Fan's Tour of the NBA* (New York: Simon & Schuster, 2009), 52.

51 **"I used to have my friends":** *The Last Dance*, Episode 3 (director: Jason Hehr).

51 **Rodman would watch his teammates:** Nick Greene, *How to Watch Basketball Like a Genius* (New York: Abrams, 2021), 239.

52 **Anytime you leave your ATM:** Annie Duke, *Thinking in Bets: Making Smarter Decisions When You Don't Have All the Facts* (New York: Portfolio, 2018), 200–203.

53 **"The game happens up":** *The Brian Cain Mental Performance Master Podcast*, "NFL Star Courtland Sutton's Elite Mindset," October 13, 2020.

54 **Remarkably, this third group:** Roy Skillen, "The Power of Positive Visualization," Player Development Project.

54 **A similar study:** Skillen, "Power of Positive."

54 **"muscle memory just kicked into work":** Kobe Bryant, *The Mamba Mentality: How I Play* (New York: MCD, 2018), 187.

54 **"When I was walking down":** MacMullan, "Rise above it."

54 **L.A. Clipper Reggie Jackson:** Matt Coates, "NBA Superstar Reggie Jackson on Visualization: The 6 Phase Meditation, and How to Master Your 'Inner Game,'" *Mindvalley*, May 18, 2020.

55 **"Players get confidence":** *Finding Mastery Podcast* with Michael Gervais, "Jill Ellis on the Pressure of Coaching the U.S. Women's National Soccer Team," Episode 245, October 7, 2020.

56 **Roth needed to perform:** Jacob Ganz, "The Truth About Van Halen and Those Brown M&Ms," NPR, *The Record*, February 14, 2012.

56 **"When we engage":** Daryl Chen, "One effective way to manage stage fright: Make it a habit," Ted.com, February 12, 2020.

57 **"most of the difference":** Jason Selk and Tom Bartow with Matthew Rudy, *Organize Tomorrow Today: 8 Ways to Retrain Your Mind to Optimize Performance at Work and in Life* (New York: Da Capo Lifelong Books, 2015), xx.

57   **he had visualized this exact thing:** Julie Kliegman, "Paddy Steinfort and the Craft of Mental Performance Coaching," *Sports Illustrated*, October 2, 2020, and Childs Walker, "A grown-up Michael Phelps looks back on the Beijing Olympics, 10 years later," *Baltimore Sun*, August 10, 2018.

57   **future Hall of Famer Adam:** Michael Lewis, "The Kick Is Up and It's . . . A Career Killer," *New York Times Magazine*, October 28, 2007.

58   **"[He] has always insisted":** Kevin Loria, "What the brain of a guy who climbs massive cliffs without ropes can teach us about fear," *Insider*, August 26, 2016.

58   **"There is no adrenaline":** "The Ascent of Alex Honnold," *60 Minutes*, December 27, 2011, on CBS.

58   **He preps his climbs for:** Katherine Laidlaw, "This Will End Well," *The Walrus*, April 21, 2016.

59   **"There's something about being":** Bryant, *Mamba Mentality*, 36–37.

59   **"You build things from practice":** "Handling the Pressure: 4 Greats Reveal How to Handle Finals Pressure," *Chicago Tribune*, June 7, 1998.

60   **"We need to be humble":** Brian Levenson, *Shift Your Mind: 9 Mental Shifts to Thrive in Preparation and Performance* (New York: Disruption Books, 2000), 14.

Chapter 4: Poise

69   **coined the term "objective optimism":** Jonathan Fader, *Life as Sport: What Top Athletes Can Teach You About How to Win in Life* (Boston: Da Capo Lifelong Books, 2016), 9.

70   **This led to his noticing:** Fader, *Life as Sport*, 153–154.

70   **"Being mentally tough":** Jonathan Fader, "Revisiting Life as Sport," *Leadership Under Fire*, August 27, 2020.

70   **"They just know how":** Fader, *Life as Sport*, 94.

70   **"our posture and the way":** Thomas Gilovich and Lee Ross, *The Wisest One in the Room: How You Can Benefit from Social Psychology's Most Powerful Insights* (New York: Free Press, 2015), 102.

71   **smiling before you feel:** Nicole Spector, "Smiling can trick your brain into happiness—and boost your health," NBC.com, November 28, 2018.

71   **Your mind processes the smile:** Helen Thomson, *Unthinkable: An Extraordinary Journey Through the World's Strangest Brains* (New York: Ecco, 2018), 183.

72   **"we elevate the past":** Trevor Moawad and Andy Staples, *It Takes What It Takes: How to Think Neutrally and Gain Control of Your Life* (New York: Harper, 2020), 25.

74   **Scientists once measured:** Sian Beilock, *Choke: What the Secrets of the Brain Reveal About Getting It Right When You Have To* (New York: Free Press, 2010), 35.

75   **"in response to a highly stressful situation":** Beilock, *Choke*, 6.

75   **"choking off *access*":** *The Rich Roll Podcast*, "Dr. Michael Gervais: The Sensei of Human Performance," Episode 550.

75   **"When the coach reviews":** Daniel Goleman, *Focus: The Hidden Driver of Excellence* (New York: Bloomsbury, 2013), 30

76   **"When athletes think about":** Beilock, *Choke*, 183–184.

78   **"How am I gonna sit?"** Clay Skipper, "Jalen Rose Says He Has 'Irrational Confidence'," *GQ*, January 14, 2020.

78   **"Confidence comes from one place":** Clay Skipper, "Why Mindfulness is the Next Frontier in Sports Performance," *GQ*, February 26, 2020.

78   **"we internally talk to":** Ethan Kross, *Chatter: The Voice in Our Head, Why it Matters, and How to Harness It* (New York: Crown, 2021), xxii.

79   **"faster is always better":** Carl Honoré, *In Praise of Slowness: How a Worldwide Movement Is Challenging the Cult of Speed* (New York: HarperOne, 2004), 14.

79   **Honoré offers a strategy:** Mo Perry, "What's the Rush," *Experience Life*.

Chapter 5: Using Stress

83   **77 percent according to one:** Lisa Fritscher, "Glossophobia or the Fear of Public Speaking," Verywellmind, October 6, 2020.

84   **Manu Ginobli:** Chris Ballard, *The Art of a Beautiful Game: The Thinking Fan's Tour of the NBA* (New York: Simon & Schuster, 2009), 16.

84   **Kyrie Irving:** Jackie MacMullan, "Rise above it or drown: How elite NBA athletes handle pressure," Espn.com, May 29, 2019.

84   **"Recent research is showing":** Amy Gallo, "Turning Stress into an Asset," HBR.org, June 28, 2011.

84   **"slamming on the brakes":** Adam Grant, *Originals: How Non-Conformists Move the World* (New York: Viking, 2016), 216.

84   **"the ability to view stress":** Shawn Achor, *Before Happiness: The 5 Hidden Keys to Achieving Success, Spreading Happiness, and Sustaining Positive Change* (New York: Currency, 2013), 97.

86   **"how you frame something":** Clark and Sternfeld, *Hack Your Anxiety*, 122.

86   **"had 23% fewer stress-related":** Clark and Sternfeld, *Hack Your Anxiety*, 122.

87   **The decision to tell themselves:** Olga Khazan, "Can Three Words Turn Anxiety into Success?" *The Atlantic*, March 23, 2016.

87　**"If you aren't nervous":** MacMullan, "Rise above it or drown."

89　**Next time you find yourself:** Ama Marston and Stephanie Marston, "To Handle Increased Stress, Build Your Resilience," HBR.org, February 19, 2018.

Part II: Pivot

91　**The word *career*:** Bruce Feiler, *Life Is in the Transitions: Mastering Change at Any Age* (New York: Penguin Press, 2020), 32.

93　**Self-evaluation boxes:** Created by psychologists Joseph Luft and Harrington Ingham in 1955.

93　**"numbs our interest":** Daniel Pink, *When: The Scientific Secrets of Perfect Timing* (New York: Riverhead, 2019), 115.

94　**However, if it alerts us:** Pink, *When*, 133.

94　**"If you're bored":** George Mumford, *The Mindful Athlete: Secrets to Pure Performance* (Berkeley, CA: Parallax Press, 2015), 168.

Chapter 6: Take Control

95　**"the most in-demand basketball influencer":** Justin Tinsley, "A day in the life of Chris Brickley, the NBA's most sought-after 'influencer,'" *The Undefeated*, September 27, 2017.

95　**"one of the most renowned":** Zion Olojede, "Star Basketball Trainer Chris Brickley Talks His Journey, Training J. Cole, and More," *Complex*, September 23, 2019.

97　**Data suggests that a staggering:** Joe Mechlinski, *Shift the Work: The Revolutionary Science of Moving from Apathetic to All in Using Your Head, Heart and Gut* (New York: Morgan James, 2019), 85.

97　**"How are you complicit":** Jerry Colonna, *Reboot: Leadership and the Art of Growing Up* (New York: Harper Business, 2019), 30.

97　**Studies have found that nearly half:** Kristi DePaul, "What Does It Really Take to Build a New Habit," HBR.org, February 2, 2021.

98　**Goals are fine, but:** My friend James Clear has opened up a lot of my thinking on goals, including this idea.

99　**"It's one thing to say":** James Clear, *Atomic Habits: An Easy & Proven Way to Build Good Habits & Break Bad Ones* (New York: Avery, 2018), 33–34.

102　**"quit fast and often":** David Epstein, *Range: Why Generalists Triumph in a Specialized World* (New York: Riverhead, 2019), 136.

102　**"we would rather stand by":** Carl Honoré, *The Slow Fix: Solve Problems, Work Smarter, and Live Better in a World Addicted to Speed* (New York: HarperOne, 2013), 20.

102　**"aversion to change":** Honoré, *The Slow Fix*, 20.

103 **Evan Williams never let:** Nick Bilton, *Hatching Twitter: A True Story of Money, Power, Friendship, and Betrayal* (New York: Portfolio, 2013).

103 **Williams eventually made his:** Bilton, *Hatching Twitter.*

104 **"People don't find their":** Marcus Buckingham, *Standout 2.0: Assess Your Strengths, Find Your Edge, Win at Work* (Cambridge: Harvard Business Review Press, 2015), 5.

105 **"I wanted something hard":** Hrishikesh Hirway, *Partners* (podcast), "Kevin Systrom & Mike Krieger," February 19, 2020.

105 **"The thing that mattered the most":** Hirway, "Kevin Systrom."

106 **"I had to experience the pain":** Amy Morin, *13 Things Mentally Strong People Don't Do* (New York: William Morrow, 2014), 4.

107 **"suppressing our emotions":** Morin, *13 Things*, 12.

108 **"That required evolving as":** Marcus Thompson, *KD: Kevin Durant's Relentless Pursuit to Be the Greatest* (New York: Atria, 2019), xxii.

108 **"I realized that, like, my view":** "Brooklyn Nets star Kevin Durant says development, not titles, is what drives him now," ESPN.com, April 10, 2021.

112 **The physical world also plays:** Ethan Kross, *Chatter: The Voice in Our Head, Why it Matters, and How to Harness It* (New York: Crown, 2021), 111.

112 **"Environment is the invisible":** Clear, *Atomic Habits*, 82.

112 **leave a Post-It:** James Clear suggested this during our interview.

113 **"If you can find a physical":** Stewart D. Friedman, *Leading the Life You Want: Skills for Integrating Work and Life* (Boston: Harvard Business Review, 2014), 160.

113 **"a third of your brain is":** Leonard Mlodinow, *Subliminal: How Your Unconscious Mind Rules Your Behavior* (New York: Pantheon, 2012), 35.

113 **which can lead to procrastination:** Libby Sander, "The Case for Finally Cleaning Your Desk," *Harvard Business Review*, March 25, 2019.

113 **"removing every object of attention":** Chris Bailey, *Hyperfocus: How to Manage Your Attention in a World of Distraction* (New York, Viking, 2018), 82–83.

114 **"your environment opposes your":** Benjamin Hardy, *Willpower Doesn't Work: Discover the Hidden Keys to Success* (New York: Hachette, 2018), xii.

Chapter 7: Reinvent

118 **"Identities seem permanent":** Steve Magness, "Separating My Identity from Running," ScienceofRunning.com, March 19, 2019.

120 **"younger workers who sample":** Anne Kreamer, *Risk/Reward: Why Intelligent Leaps and Daring Choices Are the Best Career Moves You Can Make* (New York: Random House, 2015), xvii.

120 **"the linear life is dead":** Bruce Feiler, *Life Is in the Transitions: Mastering Change at Any Age* (New York: Penguin Press, 2020), 15.

120 **The average person will move:** Feiler, *Life*, 52–53, 58.

120 **Before he's fifty:** Feiler, *Life*, 58, 62.

120 **staying in a single job:** Kreamer, *Risk/Reward*, xiv.

120 **A pre-pandemic survey found:** Tim Vaughan, "How to Engage Millennials in the Workforce," *Poppulo*, August 12, 2020.

121 **"cultivate our native curiosity":** Feiler, *Life*, 89–90.

122 **"some combination of a bird":** John P. Kotter, "Leading Change: Why Transformation Efforts Fail," *Harvard Business Review*, May–June 1995.

122 **"to succeed financially we must":** Adam Davidson, *The Passion Economy: The New Rules for Thriving in the Twenty-First Century* (New York: Knopf, 2020), xix.

123 **I read a an analogy that compares:** Feiler, *Life*, 144.

125 **Daymond John was a waiter . . . Phil Knight was a CPA:** Guy Raz, *How I Built This: The Unexpected Paths to Success from the World's Most Inspiring Entrepreneurs* (Boston: HMH, 2020), 24–27.

128 **As a teenager, Steph Curry:** Ben Cohen, *The Hot Hand: The Mystery and Science of Streaks* (New York: Custom House, 2020), 18.

129 **"There are no tools that":** David Epstein, *Range: Why Generalists Triumph in a Specialized World* (New York: Riverhead, 2019), 250, referencing Weick.

129 **"I knew that this desire":** Bob Rotella, "What sets LeBron James truly apart? His mind," *Fortune*, May 12, 2015.

130 **"not be imprisoned by the":** *Choose Yourself: The James Altucher Story*, Episode 1 (director: Nick Nanton).

130 **Twitch, a video gaming app:** Raz, *How I Built*, 185–189.

131 **They offer a feeling:** Ethan Kross, *Chatter: The Voice in Our Head, Why it Matters, and How to Harness It* (New York: Crown, 2021), 124.

133 **"You can't connect the dots":** Steve Jobs, Stanford Commencement Speech, https://news.stanford.edu/2005/06/14/jobs-061505/.

133 **"Before we adjust anything":** Eastman, *Why the Best Are the Best*, 110.

133 **"The intersection of personal":** Raz, *How I Built*, 8.

Chapter 8: Reach Out

136 **"a place where the weight of":** Nick Greene, *How to Watch Basketball Like a Genius* (New York: Abrams, 2021), 116.

137 **Sociologists found that we:** Sherry Turkle, *Alone Together: Why We Expect More from Technology and Less from Each Other* (New York: Basic, 2011), 168.

137 **so-called functional inconveniences:** Amanda Mull, "A Cubicle Never Looked So Good," *The Atlantic*, October 2020.

137 **"arbitrary collisions of people":** Andrew Wallace, "The real reason open offices won't go away any time soon," *Fast Company*, June 23, 2020.

137 **There's also evidence:** "Employee Job Satisfaction and Engagement," Society for Human Resource Management.

137 **keep us engaged in our work:** "The Truth About Job Satisfaction and Friendships at Work," National Business Research Institute.

138 **"Social connection is such a basic":** Leonard Mlodinow, *Subliminal: How Your Unconscious Mind Rules Your Behavior* (New York: Pantheon, 2012), 82–83.

138 **"the effects of cigarette smoking":** Mlodinow, *Subliminal*, 84.

138 **Those who reported:** Johann Hari, *Lost Connections: Why You're Depressed and How to Find Hope* (New York: Bloomsbury, 2018), 77.

138 **sickness and weakened immune systems:** Hari, *Lost Connections*, 75.

138 **The health improvement:** Frank Martela, "Helping Others Is Good for Your Health," *Psychology Today*, September 4, 2020.

138 **giving money away improves:** Thomas Gilovich and Lee Ross, *The Wisest One in the Room: How You Can Benefit from Social Psychology's Most Powerful Insights* (New York: Free Press, 2015), 188.

138 **those who spend time doing:** Gilovich and Ross, *Wisest One*, 81.

139 **"Start by making a plan":** Scott Gerber, "Why Your Inner Circle Should Stay Small and How to Shrink It," HBR.org, March 7, 2018.

140 **"attracting your allies":** Vishen Lakhiani, *The Buddha and The Badass: The Secret Spiritual Art of Succeeding at Work* (New York: Rodale, 2020), 18.

140 **"Join a group or tribe":** James Clear, *Atomic Habits: An Easy & Proven Way to Build Good Habits & Break Bad Ones* (New York: Avery, 2018), 118.

141 **"Every billionaire suffers":** Tim Ferriss, *Tools of Titans: The Tactics, Routines, and Habits of Billionaires, Icons, and World-Class Performers* (New York: HMH, 2016), 175.

141 **"ask a lot of questions":** Tim Kight, *Focus 3 Podcast*, Episode 66.

142 **If you're trying to develop:** Sonja Lyubomirsky, *The Myths of Happiness: What Should Make You Happy, but Doesn't, What Shouldn't Make You Happy, but Does* (New York: Penguin Press, 2013), 140.

142 **"if you became happier":** Shawn Achor, "The Ecosystem of Potential," *Thrive Global*, May 21, 2018.

142 **This principle especially holds:** Amrisha Vaish, Tobias Grossmann, and Amanda Woodward, "Not all emotions are created equal: The negativity bias in social-emotional development," *Psychological Bulletin*, May 2008.

142 **Stressed-out people release:** Shawn Achor, *Big Potential: How Transforming the Pursuit of Success Raises Our Achievement, Happiness, and Well-Being* (New York: Currency, 2018), 149.

142 **"We can also pick up":** Achor, *Big Potential*, 149.

143 **Emotional contagion theory:** Carlin Flora, "Protect Yourself from Emotional Contagion," *Psychology Today*, June 21, 2019.

143 **"Quite apart from the ups":** Daniel Goleman, Richard E. Boyatzis, and Annie McKee, *Primal Leadership: Unleashing the Power of Emotional Intelligence* (Brighton, MA: Harvard Business Review Press, 2016), 8.

144 **"Surround yourself with people":** Benjamin Hardy, *Willpower Doesn't Work: Discover the Hidden Keys to Success* (New York: Hachette, 2018), 109.

Chapter 9: Expand (Your Circle and Your World)

146 **"When we're in trouble":** Tanya Menon, *The Secret to Great Opportunities? The Person You Haven't Met*, TED Talk, February 2018.

146 **"We keep our social networks":** Tim Harford, *Messy: The Power of Disorder to Transform Our Lives* (New York: Riverhead, 2016), 53.

146 **One example of a tangible:** Marc Miller, "To Get a Job, Use Your Weak Ties," Forbes.com, August 17, 2016, and Everett Harper, "Weak Ties Matter," *TechCrunch*, April 26, 2016; both articles citing "The Strength of Weak Ties," by Mark S. Granovetter, Johns Hopkins University, *American Journal of Sociology*, Vol. 78, No. 6 (May 1973), University of Chicago Press.

148 **"group members unknowingly end":** Thomas Gilovich and Lee Ross, *The Wisest One in the Room: How You Can Benefit from Social Psychology's Most Powerful Insights* (New York: Free Press, 2015), 156.

148 **dissent and debate yield:** Matthew Syed, *Bounce: The Myth of Talent and the Power of Practice* (London: Fourth Estate, 2010), 197.

148 **This is why before the military:** Annie Duke, *Thinking in Bets: Making Smarter Decisions When You Don't Have All the Facts* (New York: Portfolio, 2018), 140.

149 **"We already know why":** Duke, *Thinking in Bets*, 138.

149 **"the highest percentage of these":** Syed, *Bounce*, 200, citing Kevin Dunbar's work at McGill University.

149 **It is why science moves:** This idea is discussed in Duke, *Thinking in Bets*, 72.

149 **"filter bubble":** Term coined by internet activist Eli Pariser.

150 **Josh Linkner says:** Mindshift Labs, "Creating Big Little Breakthroughs," Episode 8.

150 **"experts can become so narrow-minded":** David Epstein, *Range: Why Generalists Triumph in a Specialized World* (New York: Riverhead, 2019), 11.

150 **The same thing happened to experienced:** *Stay Tuned with Preet Bharara*, "Thinking 2.0" (with Adam Grant).

152 **Teaching forces you to think:** Sian Beilock, *Choke: What the Secrets of the Brain Reveal About Getting It Right When You Have To* (New York: Free Press, 2010), 8.

152 **"I think the jump shot":** Nick Greene, *How to Watch Basketball Like a Genius* (New York: Abrams, 2021), 125.

152 **They couldn't see what the attraction:** Greene, *How to Watch*, 124–125.

152 **"The first jump shooters":** Greene, *How to Watch*, 126.

152 **bringing an outsider:** David Rock, Heidi Grant, and Jacqui Gray, "Diverse Teams Feel Less Comfortable—and That's Why They Perform Better," HBR.org, September 22, 2016.

153 **This happened not in spite:** Shawn Achor, *Big Potential: How Transforming the Pursuit of Success Raises Our Achievement, Happiness, and Well-Being* (New York: Currency, 2018), 76.

153 **"were ineffective and complacent":** Harford, *Messy*, 50.

154 **Competition can be motivating:** Adam Grant, *Work Life* (podcast), "Become Friends with Your Rivals," March 14, 2019.

154 **"Endurance athletes can tolerate":** Alex Hutchinson, "Why Do You Race Faster Than You Train?" *Runner's World*, August 9, 2016.

154 **there was a positive correlation:** Grant, "Become Friends."

154 **Though the giver:** Grant, "Become Friends."

156 **"a mentor is a mirror":** Chip Conley, *Wisdom at Work: The Making of a Modern Elder* (New York: Currency, 2018), 33–34.

156 **"I try to find the top":** Conley, *Wisdom at Work*, x.

156 **"The mentorship casts you":** Brendon Burchard, *The Charge: Activating the 10 Human Drives That Make You Feel Alive* (New York: Free Press, 2012), 214.

156 **Studies have shown that racial and gender diversity:** Allana Akhtar, "Increasing diversity in management is good for productivity, a study suggests," *Insider*, June 15, 2020; Stephen Turban, Dan Wu, and Letian (LT) Zhang, "Research: When Gender Diversity Makes Firms More Productive," HBR.org, February 11, 2019.

157 **Kobe cornered Michael Jordan:** *The Last Dance*, Episode 5.

157 **"I asked a ton of questions":** Kobe Bryant, *The Mamba Mentality: How I Play* (New York: MCD, 2018), 40.

Chapter 10: Positivity

168 **"Resentment is like taking":** The origin of this saying is unclear, but it most likely began with Alcoholics Anonymous in the 1930s.

170 **You choose to feel:** This is based on "No one can make you feel inferior without your consent," a quote by Eleanor Roosevelt from *This Is My Story*, 1937.

173 **"Grateful living is possible":** A. J. Jacobs, *Thanks a Thousand: A Gratitude Journey* (New York: Simon & Schuster/TED, 2018), 11.

173 **"a person who experiences":** Robert A. Emmons, *Thanks!: How Practicing Gratitude Can Make You Happier* (New York: Mariner Books, 2008), 11–12.

173 **"gratitude does not depend":** Emmons, *Thanks!*, 16.

174 **"Writing a thank-you note":** Marshall Goldsmith with Mark Reiter, *What Got You Here Won't Get You There: How Successful People Become Even More Successful* (New York: Hachette, 2007), 159.

175 **"40 percent more likely":** Vishen Lakhiani, *The Buddha and The Badass: The Secret Spiritual Art of Succeeding at Work* (New York: Rodale, 2020), 123.

177 **known as the availability heuristic:** Daniel Kahneman, *Thinking, Fast and Slow* (New York: Farrar, Straus, & Giroux, 2011), 7.

177 **We see ourselves:** Laurie Santos, *The Happiness Lab* (podcast), "A Silver Lining," Episode 3, Oct 1, 2019.

177 **They chose to make less:** Thomas Gilovich, Amit Kumar, Lily Jampol, "A wonderful life: experiential consumption and the pursuit of happiness," *Journal of Consumer Psychology*, August 25, 2014.

177 **This tendency pops up:** Santos, "A Silver Lining."

178 **"Nothing great was ever achieved":** Samuel Taylor Coleridge, *The Statesman's Manual* (1816).

179 **positive projection:** Brendon Burchard, *The Charge: Activating the 10 Human Drives That Make You Feel Alive* (New York: Free Press, 2012), 122.

179 **compares it to falling asleep:** Interview with Seth Godin on *The Tim Ferriss Show*, episode 476.

180 **"Recruiting enthusiastic kids":** Pete Grathoff, "UConn coach Geno Auriemma's 2016 talk about how selfish athletes are these days goes viral," *Kansas City Star*, March 21, 2017.

180 **"Kevin Garnett plays the game":** Sean Grande, "In an Age of Apathy, Garnett Brings Energy, Enthusiasm," Celtics.com, August 1, 2007.

180 **"I'm going to roll":** "Kevin Garnett, Glen Davis Recall Time Big Baby Lived Up To Name On Celtics Bench," NESN.com, December 23, 2016.

181 **It is now held:** Mara Leighton, "Over 2.2 million students enrolled in this free Yale class on how to be happier—here's what it's actually like to take," *Insider*, March 5, 2021.

182 **"We often can get in":** *Today Explained* (podcast), "How to Be Happy," Vox.com, May 2020.

182 **The happier are healthier:** *Today Explained* (podcast), "How to Be Happy."

182 **"employees who started the day":** Heidi Reeder, *Commit to Win: How to Harness the Four Elements of Commitment to Reach Your Goals* (New York: Avery, 2014), 97–98.

182 **"upbeat moods boost cooperation":** Daniel Goleman, Richard E. Boyatzis, and Annie McKee, *Primal Leadership: Unleashing the Power of Emotional Intelligence* (Brighton, MA: Harvard Business Review Press, 2016), 10.

183 **"were always looking for causes":** Angela Duckworth and Stephen Dubner, *No Stupid Questions* (podcast), "Is Optimism a Luxury Good?" January 3, 2020.

183 **"optimists aren't just dreamers":** Brendon Burchard, *The Charge: Activating the 10 Human Drives That Make You Feel Alive* (New York: Free Press, 2012), 42.

183 **Optimism actually conserves:** Shawn Achor, *Before Happiness: The 5 Hidden Keys to Achieving Success, Spreading Happiness, and Sustaining Positive Change* (New York: Currency, 2013), 98.

183 **also been connected to longevity:** Duckworth and Dubner, "Is Optimism a Luxury Good?"

183 **One large study published:** Boston University School of Medicine, "New evidence that optimists live longer," *Science Daily*, August 26, 2019.

184 **"Your brain constructs":** Achor, *Before Happiness*, 99.

184 **"Negative people literally":** Achor, *Before Happiness*, 99.

184 **"might actually use failure":** Derrick Carpenter, "5 Unbelievable Facts About Optimists," Verywellmind, June 28, 2020.

184 **"insurance agents":** Goleman et al., *Primal Leadership*, 14.

185 **"Because optimists expect their efforts":** Jonathan Haidt, *The Happiness Hypothesis: Finding Modern Truth in Ancient Wisdom* (New York: Basic Books, 2005), 146.

185 **Marshall Goldsmith suggests making:** Marshall Goldsmith with Mark Reiter, *What Got You Here Won't Get You There: How Successful People Become Even More Successful* (New York: Hachette, 2007), 159.

185 **"25% happier":** Dacher Keltner and Jason Marsh, "How Gratitude Beats Materialism," *Greater Good Magazine*, January 8, 2015.

185 **Ethan Kross calls "distanced self-talk":** Ethan Kross, *Chatter: The Voice in Our Head, Why it Matters, and How to Harness It* (New York: Crown, 2021), 73.

Part III: Prevail

187 **burnout was rising:** Alex Janin, "How to Prevent and Recover from Job Burnout," *Wall Street Journal*, March 6, 2021, citing Gallup poll.

187 **despite being home more:** Michelle Davis and Jeff Green, "Three hours longer, the pandemic workday has obliterated work-life balance," Bloomberg, April 27, 2020.

187 **"a special type of work"**: Mayo Clinic, "Job Burnout: How to Spot It and Take Action," November 20, 2020.

188 **"weakened immune systems"**: Adam Grant, "Burnout Isn't Just in Your Head. It's in Your Circumstances," *New York Times*, March 19, 2020.

188 **the official description of burnout:** Christina Maslach and Michael P. Leiter, "Understanding the burnout experience: recent research and its implications for psychiatry," *World Psychiatry*, June 2016.

188 **Inefficacy means your productivity:** Alex Janin, "How to Prevent and Recover from Job Burnout," *Wall Street Journal*, March 6, 2021, citing Gallup poll.

188 **Only one in three takes:** Brad Stulberg and Steve Magness, *Peak Performance: Elevate Your Game, Avoid Burnout, and Thrive with the New Science of Success* (Emmaus, PA: Rodale, 2017), 18.

188 **The average US worker:** Stulberg and Magness, *Peak Performance*, 19, citing Daniel Hamermesh and Elena Stancanelli, "Americans Work Too Long (and Too Often at Strange Times)," Voxeu.org, September 29, 2014.

188 **In the past three years:** Rahaf Harfoush, *Hustle and Float: Reclaim Your Creativity and Thrive in a World Obsessed with Work* (New York: Diversion, 2019), 236–237.

188 **an estimated 70 percent:** Jim Harter, "Employee Engagement on the Rise in the U.S.," Gallup, August 26, 2018.

190 **"a signal, not a long-term sentence":** Monique Valcour, "Beating Burnout," HBR.org, November 2016.

Chapter 11: Engage the Process

191 **"The problem of judging":** Michael Lewis, "Against the Rules: The Coach in Your Head," Season 2, Episode 3.

192 **"shift from doing the whole":** Steve Chandler, *Shift Your Mind, Shift the World* (Anna Maria, FL: Maurice Basset, 2018), 4.

192 **Kobe would get tapes:** Chris Ballard, *The Art of a Beautiful Game: The Thinking Fan's Tour of the NBA* (New York: Simon & Schuster, 2009), 10.

192 **As a player, he didn't skip:** Kobe Bryant tribute video, www.youtube .com/watch?v=7mFGeA5YDzw.

192 **"Those times when you don't":** Kobe Bryant, 2017 retirement speech.

192 **"if the players were making":** Jason Selk and Tom Bartow with Matthew Rudy, *Organize Tomorrow Today: 8 Ways to Retrain Your Mind to Optimize Performance at Work and in Life* (New York: Da Capo Lifelong Books, 2015), 103.

193 **"It's not that I don't know":** Tim Gallwey, *The Inner Game of Tennis: The Classic Guide to the Mental Side of Peak Performance* (New York: Random House, Revised, 1997), 3.

193 **the students were correcting:** Gallwey, *Inner Game of Tennis*, 5.

194 **"The first skill to learn":** Gallwey, *Inner Game of Tennis*, 17.

195 **"Even a dramatic career":** Mitchell Lee Marks, Philip Mirvis, and Ron Ashkenas, "Rebounding from Career Setbacks," HBR.org, October 2014.

195 **Luck can and will fall:** Annie Duke, *Thinking in Bets: Making Smarter Decisions When You Don't Have All the Facts* (New York: Portfolio, 2018), 7.

195 **use the example of the batter:** Selk and Bartow with Rudy, *Organize Tomorrow*, 93.

196 **Larry Bird used this knowledge:** The story is told by Jack McCallum, but I read it in Taylor Clark's *Nerve*, 204.

196 **Right before Bird walked:** Bird told this story on Dan Patrick's show, to guest host Reggie Miller, www.danpatrick.com/2016/08/09/larry-bird -yup-said-whos-coming-second/show.

197 **"Film is deceptive":** Jerry Colonna, *Reboot: Leadership and the Art of Growing Up* (New York: Harper Business, 2019), 25.

197 **"Slowing down the movie":** Colonna, *Reboot*, 26.

198 **"I went out to Long Island":** David Itzkoff, "Jerry Seinfeld on Louis C.K., Roseanne and Tense Times in Comedy," *New York Times*, October 26, 2018.

198 **He talked to his friend Chris:** Jerry Seinfeld, *Is this Anything?* (New York: Simon & Schuster, 2020), 256.

199 **"You either learn to do it":** *The Tim Ferriss Show*, "A Comedy Legend's Systems," December 8, 2020.

199 **"My writing technique":** David Itzkoff, "Jerry Seinfeld Is Making Peace with Nothing: He's 'Post-Show Business,'" *New York Times*, May 4, 2020.

201 **Stephon Marbury grew up:** *A Kid from Coney Island* (director: Chike Ozah and Coodie Simmons).

201 **"could be part of your Plan B":** Reid Hoffman and Ben Casnocha, *The Start-up of You: Adapt to the Future, Invest in Yourself, and Transform Your Career* (New York: Currency, 2012), 76.

Chapter 12: Growth

205 **"They walk into the gym":** Rob McClanaghan, *Net Work: Training the NBA's Best and Finding the Keys to Greatness* (New York: Scribner, 2019), 39.

205 **"is always looking to add":** McClanaghan, *Net Work*, 127.

205 **"if they don't keep improving":** McClanaghan, *Net Work*, 126.

205 **The average person:** Annie Duke, *Thinking in Bets: Making Smarter Decisions When You Don't Have All the Facts* (New York: Portfolio, 2018), 89, referencing Ariely, *Predictably Irrational*.

205 **"the self-serving bias that":** Duke, *Thinking in Bets*, 108.

206 **"Lying to oneself destroys":** Matthew Syed, *Black Box Thinking* (New York: Penguin, 2015), 87.

206 **"error denial increases":** Syed, *Black Box*, 111.

206 **"One of the differentiators":** Henri Weisinger and J. P. Pawliw-Fry, *Performance Under Pressure: The Science of Doing Your Best When It Matters Most* (New York: Currency, 2015), 31.

210 **"I don't think you should run":** *The Playbook*, Netflix, Episode 1.

210 **He took the term:** Noel King, "When a Psychologist Succumbed to Stress, He Coined the Term 'Burnout,'" NPR.org, December 8, 2016.

214 **growth mindset:** This term is based on Carol Dweck's work in *Mindset: The New Psychology of Success* (New York: Random House, 2006).

215 **At the end of 2017:** Emily Winter, "I Got Rejected 101 Times," *New York Times*, December 14, 2018.

215 **"If you've never experienced rejection":** *WorkLife with Adam Grant*, "Bouncing Back from Rejection," TED, April 17, 2019.

216 **led to the most prolific:** *WorkLife with Adam Grant*, "Bouncing Back."

216 **"One result of this freewheeling attitude":** Eric Weiner, *The Geography of Bliss: One Grump's Search for the Happiest Places in the World* (New York: Twelve, 2008), 163.

217 **Conducting a "truth audit":** Eastman, *Why the Best Are the Best*, 35.

Chapter 13: Endurance and Resilience

224 **"as a coach you always try to get better":** *Basketball Telegraph*, November 29, 2010.

235 **"You're only a success":** *The Last Dance*, Episode 6.

235 **"To me, showing up every day":** Cal Ripken Jr., and James Dale, *Just Show Up: And Other Enduring Values from Baseball's Iron Man* (New York: Harper, 2019), 2.

235 **"Everything you do is a test":** Ripken Jr. and Dale, *Just Show Up*, 13.

236 **CEO coach Chip Conley:** Conley, *Wisdom at Work*, 13.

Chapter 14: Rest and Play

238 **productivity actually decreases:** Tiffany Shlain, *24/6: The Power of Unplugging One Day a Week* (New York: Gallery, 2019), 24.

238 **The term "workaholism":** Conley, *Wisdom at Work*, 100.

238 **"Overwork results in lowered performance":** Rahaf Harfoush, *Hustle and Float: Reclaim Your Creativity and Thrive in a World Obsessed with Work* (New York: Diversion, 2019), 247.

238 **"the obsession with measuring":** Harfoush, *Hustle and Float*, 243.

239 **A little more than half:** Quinton Skinner, "7 Self-Care Strategies at Work," *Experience Life*, March 4, 2019.

239 **61 percent of workers:** Harfoush, *Hustle and Float*, 7.

239 **"people who take *all* of their vacation":** Shawn Achor, *Big Potential: How Transforming the Pursuit of Success Raises Our Achievement, Happiness, and Well-Being* (New York: Currency, 2018), 173.

240 **"Alternating between blocks of 50":** Brad Stulberg and Steve Magness, *Peak Performance: Elevate Your Game, Avoid Burnout, and Thrive with the New Science of Success* (Emmaus, PA: Rodale, 2017), 66.

240 **"Your brain is running a budget":** *The Jordan Harbinger Show*, episode 479: "Lisa Feldman Barrett, Seven and a Half Lessons About the Brain."

241 **"All it does is increase":** Jennifer Moss, "Helping Remote Workers Avoid Loneliness and Burnout," HBR.org, November 30, 2018.

243 **"More than 50% of U.S. employees":** Jennifer Moss, "When Passion Leads to Burnout," HBR.org, July 1, 2019.

243 **"begin to think your value":** Karen Olson, "Reclaim Your Weekends," *Experience Life*, July 4, 2018.

243 **European companies have:** Jerry Useem, "Bring Back the Nervous Breakdown," *The Atlantic*, March 2021.

244 **"The overworked person creates":** Ryan Holiday, *Stillness Is the Key* (New York: Penguin, 2019), 230.

246 **Lack of sleep "cost American companies":** Harfoush, *Hustle and Float*, 7.

247 **Your frontal lobe:** Meditation teacher Bob Roth discussed this at the Jesse Itzler retreat I mention in chapter 1.

247 **Sleep science pioneer William Dement:** Rosanne Specter, "William Dement, giant in sleep medicine, dies at 91," Stanford Medicine News Center, June 18, 2020.

247 **"as judgment impaired as an intoxicated person":** Quinton Skinner, "The effects of workplace burnout are real and widespread. But there is hope for recovery," *Experience Life*, February 28, 2020.

248 **In order to achieve at the highest:** Claudia Canavan, "How to De-Stress: Why You Need to Learn How to Complete the 'Stress Cycle,'" *Women's Health*, February 11, 2020.

248 **If we don't sleep enough:** Matt Walker, "Sleep Is Your Superpower," TED Talk, Ted.com, May 10, 2019.

248 **When we're tired, it's not just our productivity:** Shawn Achor, *Before Happiness: The 5 Hidden Keys to Achieving Success, Spreading Happiness, and Sustaining Positive Change* (New York: Currency, 2013), 43.

248 **"the brain interprets":** Achor, *Before Happiness*, 44.

249 **"The single biggest blocker":** *Mindshift Labs*, "Creating Big Little Breakthroughs," Episode 8.

249 **Before they took the ice:** Brian Levenson, *Shift Your Mind: 9 Mental Shifts to Thrive in Preparation and Performance* (New York: Disruption Books, 2000), 51.

249 **Doc Rivers has said that:** *The Playbook*, Netflix, Episode 1.

250 **The average time an American:** Shlain, *24/6*, 41.

250 **"That's more than we spend":** Shlain, *24/6*, 41.

Chapter 15: Fulfillment

253 **"Finding meaning is the source":** Quinton Skinner, "The effects of workplace burnout are real and widespread. But there is hope for recovery," *Experience Life*, February 28, 2020.

255 **we should drop the image:** Stewart D. Friedman, *Leading the Life You Want: Skills for Integrating Work and Life* (Boston: Harvard Business Review, 2014), 4.

255 **there are three "orientations":** Katharine Brooks, "Job, Career, Calling: Key to Happiness and Meaning at Work?," *Psychology Today*, June 29, 2012.

ACKNOWLEDGMENTS

As I mentioned at the end of my previous book, *Raise Your Game*, showing gratitude is one of my core values. I strive to consistently let as many people as I can know how much I appreciate them.

I try to share a sincere "thank you" or "I appreciate you" with the same ferocity that Steve Nash used to dish out assists, high fives, and fist bumps.

That's because I have an overwhelming abundance of things to be thankful for, and I aim to never take them for granted.

There are so many impactful people that deserve to be thanked, recognized, and acknowledged, not only for their direct contributions to this book, but for loving me, supporting me, and rooting for me as I navigate life.

People who have poured into me, encouraged me, and empowered me to evolve.

People who have challenged me, held me accountable, and pushed me to grow.

People who have helped me sustain *my* game.

That list is so extensive, I won't even attempt to list the names.

I only hope I've already told you how much you mean to me.

I appreciate you more than you know.

Dear reader:

One of my most sacred core values is the belief that *a candle loses nothing by lighting another candle.* I believe in championing, promoting, and endorsing messages that add value, messages that make the world a better place, and messages worth sharing.

When I hear a message that I believe is helpful, practical, and significant, I immediately start asking myself questions like:

"How can I help amplify this?"

"Who do I need to share this with?"

If you're like me in that way, here are seven ways you can spread the **Sustain Your Game** message and even contact me to continue the conversation:

1. **Leave an honest rating/review wherever you purchased this book.**

2. **Share a picture of this book on Instagram, Twitter, Facebook, and/or LinkedIn (please tag me at @AlanSteinJr).**

3. **Gift a copy to a friend/colleague.**

4. **Organize a formal group book read with your organization.**

5. **Hire me to deliver this book's core principles to your organization or at your next event (fill out the contact form at AlanSteinJr.com or email me directly).**

6. **If you haven't already, read** *Raise Your Game: High Performance Secrets from the Best of the Best* **(it was the precursor to this book).**

7. **Regularly visit SustainYourGameBook.com for additional bonuses, supplements, and constantly updated content.**

Please know the time/money investment you made into this book is not lost on me. I appreciate you more than you know and would be honored to serve you.

Feel free to email me directly at Alan@AlanSteinJr.com to have me deliver this message in person, or if I can do anything else to help you Sustain Your Game!